Recruiting and Training Genocidal Soldiers

Human Resource Development Perspectives on Genocide and Crimes against Humanity

Greg Procknow, MHRD

Francis & Bernard

Copyright © 2014 by Greg Procknow

All rights reserved. No part of this book may be reproduced in any manner whatsoever without written permission except in the case of brief quotations embodied in critical articles and reviews.

Published By Francis & Bernard Publishing
906-371 Gilmour St
Ottawa, Ontario
Canada
K2P 0R3

ISBN 978-0-9868374-0-1

Trade paperback edition 2014
Printed and Bound in the United States of America.

Original Credits - 2011
R. Mcleod – Cover Photography
J.Monkman - Cover Layout and Design
Revised Credits - 2014
R. Mcleod – Cover Photography
J.Monkman - Cover Layout and Design
G. Procknow – Text Overlay

CONTENTS

Preface

Chapter One
Human Resource Development in Democratic Kampuchea, 1975-1979
1

Chapter Two
Serbian Volunteer Guard (SDG) and the Critical Events Model
23

Chapter Three
Differentiating Rwanda's perpetrators through the training lens
71

Chapter Four
Genocidal youth movements: A comparative analysis of political learning curriculums
119

Chapter Five
Literature review: Sudan's Janjaweed as a performance system
155

Bibliography
175

Index
201

Acknowledgements
213

Preface
The field of human resource development is in dire need of new breakthroughs. The work presented herein I believe results in five *sui generis* breakthroughs. No other author has attempted to use the HRD lens to make better sense of genocidal events that occurred in foregone times. Nor has any author produced scholarship on any monolithic political party's prescription of political indoctrination to its citizens to ready them for murder. Furthermore, HRD theory has never been used by history educationists, historians, social scientists, or comparative genocide researchers to rearrange educational events amid a genocidal context, to make better sense of regimes responsible for crimes of genocide. HRD has contributed nothing to the historical archaeology of genocide. The chapters of this book contribute something ground-breaking that no other HRD work has attempted to undertake: the use of an HRD lens to make better sense of genocide history. The work here is presented as a cross-fertilization of history, adult education, and human resource development. Alagaraja and Dooley (2003) hold that "in the field of HRD, there is a great need for high-level collaboration with other disciplines" (p. 84). A seachange of new developments in HRD thought is much needed to usher in a new era of scholarship in this stagnant discipline, thus my research indelibly marks an epoch in the history of human resource development.

In Chapter One, Procknow's (2014) work on human resource development in Democratic Kampuchea, 1975-1979, deconstructs the dearth of literature and research that has framed education and learning in Democratic Kampuchea (DK). The past is deconstructed to challenge the historical record as evidenced by historians, relating to how the Khmer Rouge learned during the Cambodian Genocide, 1975-1979. To summarize, the following work is an HRD deconstruction of the historical subject matter of learning during the Democratic Kampuchean period. Historical analysis of Democratic Kampuchea asserted that education under the Khmer Rouge was unorganized, inconsistent, and without planning. The deconstruction of the historical record called these views into question. Historians and educationalists have called into question the strategies and consistencies of education in the Pol Pot regime. Such a historicization of the Communist Party of Kampuchea's (CPK) educative practices impugns the achievements of DK. My counter-argument is that when an HRD lens is utilized to make sense of the madness, the strategies undertaken by the Khmer Rouge were conducive to learning and consistently structured, astutely planned, and implemented throughout DK. The application of an HRD lens helps us to perceive the situation differently, as this chapter demonstrates.

In Chapter Two, Nadler and Nadler's (1994) critical events model (CEM) is applied to the Serbian Volunteer Guard (SDG), otherwise known as Arkan's Tigers. The model will be utilized to thematize the historical record pertaining to learning of the SDG under each step of the CEM. Aspects covered in this research include, *inter alia*, the length of training, training locations, physical and mental development with ample examples provided, a detailed list of instructors used, and a comprehensive organizational needs-analysis of both the Government of Republika Srpska and the SDG. This chapter is useful, as it demonstrates how HRD can once again contribute to fields other than business or education. The chapter shows how HRD or adult educational models can be used to thematize or reorganize data. Better sense of history from the viewpoint of learning, training, education, or development can prove useful in suggesting historical patterns and delving most accurately into the lives of the learners during genocidal times.

In Chapter Three, a comparative analysis is undertaken of two perpetrators of Rwanda's 1994 genocide: Interahamwe and civilian defense (CD). The historical record confuses these two genocidal perpetrators and likens the actions of civilian defense to Interahamwe. The nature of their differentiation is seldom explicitly discerned. Through the HRD lens and through a reorganization of the historical record, it becomes apparent, by comparing and contrasting their learning curriculums, how the two can be differentiated. More so, the research suggests that one of the major differentiators between the two is that curriculums organized for civilian defense resembled a national human resource development (NHRD) program, whereas learning for the Interahamwe did not. This chapter sufficiently demonstrates how HRD as a field can work to hold perpetrators of crimes against humanity and genocide culpable for their actions through proper identification.

In Chapter Four, a different approach is considered to the previous three chapters. This chapter applies the HRD lens to pedagogical political curriculums contrived for the youth of the Khmer Rouge and the Hitler Youth. A comparative analysis of their political indoctrination curriculums are contrasted in this chapter. Although the Hitler Youth curriculum was Fascist and racist and the Khmer Rouge zealously Communist and classist, my review of the historical record had shown both political curriculums replete with similarities. It is imperative to include a chapter that looks at the evil in curriculums contrived for children audiences amid these two genocidal moments in history, because from infancy to adulthood their respective Parties committed these learners to a life-long scheme of ideological indoctrination and hate-themed education.

Chapter Five characterizes the relationship between the Janjaweed and the Government of Sudan (GOS). This chapter pursued a three-fold approach. First, to provide a comprehensive literature review on the learning interventions contrived by the GOS for augmenting the performance vis-à-vis the Janjaweed. Next, the misconceptions of the performance paradigm of HRD levied by learning paradigm advocates are related to the relationship between these two entities. With this in mind, performance systems theory is then applied to the relationship, considering the Government of Sudan as the host performance system and Janjaweed as a symbiotically dependent or sponsored performance system, created to serve the mission of the host system. This chapter posited that the mission of the host-performance system is to create a genocidal group distinct from the nation's army to carry out the wholesale slaughter of Tutsis. Moreover, HRD is offered by the host to the dependent performance system to improve their performance in murder of Tutsi.

I hope and expect that you, the readership of this work, will learn that even if you are confounded by a field of academia, despite the field, you can still contribute to ancillary fields of research, as I have.

Greg Procknow, MHRD

Recruiting and Training Genocidal Soldiers

Human Resource Development Perspectives on Genocide and Crimes against Humanity

Greg Procknow, MHRD

CHAPTER ONE
Human Resource Development in Democratic Kampuchea, 1975-1979

Introduction

My aim is to "deconstruct" (Callahan, 2010) the body of literature that frames education and learning in Democratic Kampuchea (DK). Callahan (2010) holds that historically oriented deconstructive manuscripts "challenge dominant paradigms" (p. 312). I deconstruct the past by challenging "the nature of truth on which historical evidence [has been] created" (Callahan, 2010, p. 311). Historical analysis of DK asserts that education under the Khmer Rouge (KR) was unorganized, inconsistent, and without planning. My deconstruction of the historical record will call these views into question. Moreover, when reviewing the historical record through a human resource development (HRD) lens, the educative initiatives of the KR within the madness they perpetrated made sense. Historians and educationalists have called into question the strategies and consistencies of education in the Pol Pot regime. Such a historicization of the Communist Party of Kampuchea's (CPK's) educative practices impugns the achievements of DK.

My counter argument is that when an HRD lens is used to make sense of the madness, the strategies undertaken by the KR were consistently implemented through DK, structured, and astutely planned. The application of an HRD lens helps us to perceive the situation differently. To reiterate, the following work is an HRD deconstruction of the historical subject matter on learning during the Democratic Kampuchean period.

In a sense, I deconstruct primary and secondary sources. I construct new meaning from the limited primary documents of historical provenance that survived the DK period. Consultation of primary sources was threefold: Party documents that survived DK; *Revolutionary Flags*, one of three magazines published by the KR; and textually rich accounts of few who survived the KR. The Party documents I speak of were derived from Chandler, Kiernan, and Boua's (1988) work. The authors authenticated and translated (from Khmer to English) eight Party documents and published their translation accordingly in Pol Pot Plans the Future (Confidential Leadership Documents from DK, 1976- 1977). Two of the documents translated were consulted for use in this present research as they pertained to education or reeducation of Khmer citizens: the Party's 4-year plan to build socialism in all fields, 1977-1980 and preliminary explanation before reading the plan, by the Party secretary. The generation of research data relied on a close reading of these primary sources. These primary sources were analyzed by first extracting the language where the Party indicates its current provision or future provisions for training or education. Scholars may find an insignificant amount of information in these documents as it pertains to education, but when an HRD lens is used, greater currency can be derived from these sources. When analyses are drawn from a wider variety of sources, more confidence can be reposed in the results. At the same time, this paper draws on comparative genocide research and HRD literature. The works of Hinton (2005), Ayres (1999, 2000), and Clayton (1998) are particularly deconstructed more than the other authors' contribution to the historical record on DK. Additional secondary sources consulted were foreign broadcasts, academic journals, text-books, and few online sources.

My research has been a long work in progress; therefore, limitations and shortcomings can be expected. Because the assessment of the literature and DK policies germane to learning were conducted by me, a certain degree of subjectivity is to be found in my analysis. Furthermore, this article only uses an HRD lens to analyze genocidal curriculums of DK, not learning under other genocidal groups, for example, Serbia's Arkan's Tigers, Nazi Germany's Hitler Youth, or Sudan's Janjaweed. In addition, this chapter references only education or training of political consciousness, farm-work, and violence; other learning programs also existed including construction of dams, removal of forests, and technical subjects such as radar operation. This research was conducted using sources that consider learning policies in the DK as education (or reeducation) rather than HRD (or training and development), which complicates finding congruence of opinions and support for my arguments. Furthermore, the results are highly unlikely to be confirmed, as the known sources to survive only provide limited verification. Moreover, an HRD lens has all but once been applied to a genocide event (Nabb & Armstrong, 2005) on HRD of training in German-occupied Europe. However, Nabb and Armstrong identify themselves as adult educators, and their work was presented as a diatribe against HRD, and its potential implications were ruminated on training soldiers for atrocities in the Holocaust. KR literature pertaining to education has what Maxwell (2009) calls an ideological "hegemonic advantage," which makes it troubling to perceive "phenomenon in ways that are different from those that are prevalent in the literature" (p. 227). By the same token, Becker (1986) asserts that serious scholars should "routinely inspect competing ways of talking about the same subject matter" and warns, "Use the literature, don't let it use you" (p. 139). However, the content for analysis was limited, so I regretfully could only make inferences and meaning of the nature of learning through the documents that survived the DK period.

DK: The Cambodian Genocide

On April 17, 1975, Pol Pot and his coterie of French educated elite commanded a sizable faction of Communists, the Red Khmers, or better known as the Khmer Rouge, to infiltrate Phnom Penh, Cambodia's capital city and economic hub. Pot's aspirations were to drive the city's citizenry into the small pockets of villages that scattered Cambodia's countryside. Pol Pot accomplished this aim unrivaled with ease. The KR instituted manifold swift reforms including renaming Cambodia, Democratic Kampuchea. Democratic Kampuchean policies converted the bourgeoning capitalist economy into a communistic, rural-centric, independent, self-sustainable nation, with an emphasis on self-mastery. Money was abolished, foreign trade collapsed, traditional schooling predicated on western models became moribund, and most notable was the inestimable death toll wrought on the Khmer people. As with any grandiose genocidal event, it is difficult to approximate the number of casualties, but conjectural estimates place the toll at 1.7 million to 3 million (Kiernan, 2008). Death came swiftly for the fortunate, slow and punctuated by violence and cruelty for others. Urbanites were transferred to the countryside to learn and work agrarian techniques. Intellectuals and students, middle-class bourgeoisie, and city folk, unaccustomed to farming conditions, suffered overexertion, accentuated by a rationed low-caloric diet, inadequate living conditions, and arduous work hours. The KR flipped access to privilege in Cambodia society. Khmer peasants, farmers, and low-income workers were bestowed unmitigated privilege as a form of reparation for years of oppression the KR believed peasants workers incurred. Rural families, Party members, and KR supporters, before April 17, were proclaimed the "old" or "Base People" on whose backs the Khmer revolution was carried. All others were known as "New People": new to the revolution, liberated from cities, and new to the work Pol Pot had in store for them. Urbanites noticeably begrimed their image to blend in with peasants and rustics. New People, only through political education or training, would break their chains of servitude and free themselves of the stigma of being an oppressor. Political education was proffered to "Base" members to inculcate political consciousness and hatred toward the state's designated enemies: capitalists, Vietnamese, and republican soldiers. Political reeducation was given to "New" members and the middle-class of the old regime (Postiglione & Tan, 2007).

Genocide is defined by Article II of the Convention on the Prevention and Punishment of the Crime of Genocide as:

> Acts committed with intent to destroy, in whole or in part, a national, ethnical, racial or religious group, as such: Killing members of the group; Causing serious bodily or mental harm to members of the group; Deliberately inflicting on the group conditions of life calculated to bring about its physical destruction in whole or in part; Imposing measures intended to prevent births within the group; Forcibly transferring children of the group to another group.

DK atrocities involved perpetrating many variations of genocide and murder that don't fall under article II. However, this paper details political demonization of enemy groups (e.g., class-enemies) through political education (or political training) and propaganda; hence, I employ the terms *politicide* and *autogenocide*. Rummel's (1997) definition of politicide suggests any systematic attempt to facilitate the annihilation of an independent social or political group. He continues to describe it as "the murder of any person or people by a government because of their politics or for political purposes" (Rummel, 1997, p. 31). Counterfeit CPK members or known republicans (Lon Nol administration) or imperialists were targeted by Khmer Communists. Autogenocide, a term first applied to the acts perpetrated by the KR, is mentioned here as Martin (2006) posits autogenocide, specifically within the KR context involved massacring "believers in a banned ideology" or members of a particularly differing socioeconomic group (p. 141). Autogenocide, the extermination of a nation's citizens by its own government or people, DK pitted members of lower socioeconomic status (peasant workers; "Base People") against the middle-and-high-income earners common to cities ("New People"). Makino (2001) claims that of those deemed as "New People" or "enemies of the revolution," 29% were killed. According to one commentator, Makino (2001) holds policies contrived by the CPK on social engineering culminated in the moments of genocide. The Party's experimentation with social engineering, "the radical and total transformation of a society" (p. 59), fostered an atmosphere of persecution intended on a permanent polarization of society. Makino opined that it was through the experiment that crimes against humanity and extreme cases of genocide transpired.

Political training and education being used interchangeably in DK historical record

Through the lens of HRD, ambiguities surface in the DK historical record pertaining to the scholarly use of political education and training interchangeably to denote a political learning event in DK. Development will not be discussed in this context, as the historical record of learning in DK to my knowledge has not used development interchangeably with training or education. Discussing these inconsistencies, and learning discourses and their potential misuse are an excellent starting point for my analysis of learning in DK through the lens of HRD. When education is used by an HRD scholar or practitioner, it invokes different connotations, as does training. Gold and Smith (2003; as cited in Jorgensen & McGuire, 2010) suggested that "the terms training, development, education, and HRD seem to have been incorporated into the generic term learning" (p. 65). McLagan and Suhadolnik (1989) proffer a plausible definition on HRD: "HRD is the integrated use of training and development, career development and organizational development to improve individual and organizational effectiveness" (p. 7).

Training is invariably defined as "referring to the process of imparting specific skills" (Aswathappa, 2007, p. 194), "usually tak[ing] place at working places" (European Center for the Development of Vocational Training, 1996, p. 52), and "usually consist[ing] of a short-term focus on acquiring skills to perform one's job" (Saks & Haccoun, 2008, p. 6). Whereas education "is considerably broader in scope . . . has a less immediate and less specific application than training and is often perceived as being delivered in educational institutions" (Wilson, 2012, p. 6), and encompasses theoretical and structured learning in a controlled environment such as a classroom (Aswathappa, 2007). The KR connected all learning of general and technical subjects with state production and work. Given the definition of HRD and training, through the HRD lens, we can alternatively perceive the Party's educational model resemblances as a national HRD program for its forced labor. Despite these similarities, a discussion of political training and political education is warranted as all KR curriculums as noted by the historical record were centered on "political education and agricultural skills rather than academic subjects" (Walque, 2007, p. 229).

After reviewing the literature through an HRD lens, it becomes evident that no author makes a clear-cut contradistinguished analysis of how or whether political training and education in DK were approached differently by Pol Pot. Ambiguities abound when scholars discuss "political education" or "political training" under the CPK, making no clear differentiation between the two terms, treating the two mutually alike. First, political learning will be defined in the KR context, and second, a brief comparison of how political education is made synonymous with political training in the KR literature is provided.

Hinton's (2005) sociological work into the KR discusses learning in numerous contexts. However, he does not distinguish education from training. Nonetheless, Hinton gives us an idea of what political learning generally encompassed: It intentioned to "instill ideological conceptions that would generate class ardor and fury" (p. 59). Political learning embraced Marxist-Leninist doctrine, especially the idea that "the suffering of the poor was due to the exploitation of the oppressor classes" (Hinton, 2005, p. 59). Clayton (1998) provided some distinction between political training and education. He opined that "there existed programs of political education for the general population, [and political] training for Khmer Rouge cadres and party members" (p. 12). In any event, Clayton does not ascertain how political-themed curriculums differed between political education for the general populace and political training for cadres and Party members. Clayton's work here was referenced by Postiglione and Tan (2007) who further postulated, "The Khmer Rouge provided political education for the general population, [and] training for Khmer Rouge cadres" (p. 48). After reflecting on Clayton's claim, I consoled the literature to see whether political training was only mentioned in a cadre and Party-member learning context, and whether political education was mentioned only when referring to the learning of the general masses. There was no consensus in this opinion, nor was anything of the like confirmed by primary sources. Hinton (2005) opined that children and poor peasants received political instruction through political training. Cadres and Party members were derived from impecunious villages pre-April 17, which does suggest some support by Hinton for Clayton's distinction. Another incompatible point of view is given by Valentino (2004). Valentino maintained political learning centers established in communes for the masses as instructing political education.

The cultivation of political consciousness was a hallmark of the DK educational infrastructure and espoused by all political learning curriculums. When looking at the record through the HRD lens, further incongruencies emerge. Ayres (2000), Clayton (1998, 2005), Kiernan (2002), and Walque (2007) refer to learning political consciousness as a political education event. In contrast, few authors refer to learning political consciousness as political training (Hinton, 2005).

The pursuance of an HRD perspective here required the reorganization of the record by the language used to denote a learning event. By emphasizing the differences between training and education, and its use in the fostering of Khmer political consciousness, we start to place a greater importance on the length of the learning event. Training, as implied earlier, is intended for short-term learning. Kiernan (2002) presents various fluctuating durations of what he considers "political education" courses. In one version, the author claimed that political education for returnees, Lon Nol republican politicians and soldiers, students, and few peasants was as short as 3 days. In another account, Kiernan notes "twenty-day political education courses" (p. 147). Given the length of each learning session suggested by Kiernan, through the lens of HRD, it is possible to think that Kiernan's representation of what is political training or political education is questionable. CPK policies for the learning of technical subjects (e.g., aviation repair and flight) used similar short-term, expedient learning language as provided by Kiernan: "be learned rapidly" and "swiftly" so long as it is "stated clearly," presumably meaning for easy dissemination, and ease of transferability—"We can learn anything at all, and we can learn it swiftly. Things only need to be stated clearly, and then we can move rapidly" (Chandler et al., 1988, p. 160). In view of the subject matter examined through the HRD lens, we see that the Party used short-term learning language to denote events of a training nature. However, Kiernan's interpretation associates short-term expeditious learning programs with education.

In a December 20, 1976, Party Center meeting, the Party discussed strengthening and expanding the working peoples' and peasants' political consciousness. The Party's directive suggested that "there are also tasks concerned with training in political matters. . . political consciousness is a part of this" (Chandler et al., 1988, p. 204). The contrast between political training and political education becomes markedly clearer in the following excerpt, as it pertains to strengthening Party members, progressives, and the core organization:

> We must pay attention to political consciousness. This means that education must be firm. Educate as we have been doing. If we do no educational work, we will not be able to produce leadership strength because they will not know the enemy from the revolutionary comrades and from the non-revolutionaries. They will not yet be clear. What the oppressing class and the base class means will not yet be clear. Understanding will come after having been through schooling. (Jackson, 1989, p. 295)

When reviewing the aforementioned two primary sources of the DK period through an HRD lens, three new perspectives emerge. Clayton (1998), Valentino (2004), and Postiglione and Tan's (2007) combined assertion that political education was offered to develop the political consciousness of the "Base-working-peasant" population is incongruous with the true historical record. Conversely, by looking at the December 20, 1976, Party document, political training was proffered to "Base members" and political education was given to Party members, progressives, and members of the core organization. Hinton tends to use the correct form of political training more than other authors. On the other hand, when Party members speak of cultivating political consciousness of potential Party leaders, or members of the core organization, they were afforded access to political education through a state-sanctioned school. This new HRD perspective is supported by the document (E3/1094) dated August 4, 1978, sent from the West Zone to the Party Central, explicating the following primary objective of political education: "The main factor here [is] to build leadership forces" (as cited in Chen, 2012, para. 38). The document (E3/1094) further maintained that only "Party members from all sectors in the zone, including members of the sectors, district secretaries, cooperative committees, and Party members" would receive political education (as cited in Chen, 2012, para. 39). The HRD perspective suggests that learning programs for political consciousness were organized and planned, as the KR were studious enough to acknowledge the differences between training and education in addition to differentiating which group would receive training or education when cultivating political consciousness. While still in an inchoate phase, primary and secondary education was offered to all children and youth. Whereas with adults, the Party had to decide which "Base People" would receive political education or training, or which "New People" would receive political reeducation or training.

KR employees

Vickery (1984) commented that "education in Democratic Kampuchea was at a virtual standstill" (p. 173). I recommend that the analysis of education or learning in DK be revived from where it stopped, through an HRD lens. In using an HRD lens, we can see the relationship between forced labor and CPK differently. Through the lens, we can alternatively perceive training programs, or HRD interventions replaced education in DK for those engrossed in forced labor. The CPK viewed citizens as employees of the revolution. The Party placed instant servitude on the Khmer population, relegating them from civilian to employee status; hence the emphasis the CPK placed was on training, not education. Kiernan (2008) explained "Cambodians . . . become an unpaid rural plantation workforce, tending vast fields of irrigated rice land" (p. 547). When analyzing the historical account through an HRD lens, the linkages become clear that the Party connected all aspects of learning with work and production. The Party remarked on October 4, 1977, that "theory should be learned at the same time it is being applied to actual work. Our people study and at the same time directly serve the production movement" (Jackson, 1989, p. 96).

Whereas education typically tends to serve the self, HRD "encompasses activities and processes which are intended to have impact on organizational and individual learning" (McGoldrick & Stewart, 1996, p. 1). Education, in general, does not connote a learning-work relationship, whereas training and development do. HRD integrates the use of training and development (McLagan & Suhadolnik, 1989). Assuming through the HRD lens that training and development programs were contrived by DK, such programs served primarily organizational development; individual development was peripheral:

> Our goal is to keep schooling close to production work...we learn technological skills and implement them while working (as cited in Jackson, 1989, 76). . . . You should learn while working. The more you work, the more you learn and the more competent you become. (as cited in Jackson, 1989, p. 76)

All citizens, including children, were considered employees. The Party brought primary-and middle-school students into the sphere of workplace learning. Children, as early as the age of five, played an integral role in DK obtaining its politico-socioeconomic and cultural objectives. Learning interventions for children and young people espoused agricultural themes, field-work practice, and hands-on experience. Clayton (1998) surmised that children attended class (an amalgam of political education and field-work practice) up to half a day, and then would perform work. In Part II of the document, preliminary explanation before reading the plan, Pot decreed that "our students aren't merely students. They are productive workers come to study subjects to serve production" (Chandler et al., 1988, p. 160). The aforementioned Party statements when reviewed through an HRD lens are indicative of HRD policy contrived for augmenting worker-peasant performance.

In a vein similar to the KR regime, Arkan's Tigers otherwise known as the Serbian Volunteer Guard (SDG) employed forced labor during the Yugoslav wars of 1991-1999. SDG with its figurehead Željko Ražnatović, aka Arkan, served as a paramilitary group providing tactical support to the armies of Republika Srpska Krajina and Republika Srpska within the Croatian and Bosnian wars. The Tigers are most notable for their campaigns of ethnic cleansing of non-Serbs. Arkan was granted license to capture and imprison Croatian-Bosnian Serb men guilty of disserting front-line combat. Nonetheless, Arkan saw the opportunity to expand the efficiency of his organization by forcing these men to join the Tigers in primarily ancillary supportive roles. In August 1995, units comprising "scum," as Arkan bluntly remarked, arrived by the busloads of five to six hundred at Arkan's 101st Training Center (also known as Erdut's training center) in Croatia. Reminiscent of the manner in which "New People" in DK were forcibly assimilated and trained, Arkan's "scum" underwent a similarly shocking transformation through Erdut. According to Radović (2006), as Serbian-Croats exited the bus, Arkan shouted,

> Get out! You Serbian traitors, motherfuckers! We will kill you; we will cut your throats! Run into line! Clubs fall onto heads from all directions . . . You are Serbian volunteers now. I'll fuck you for having betrayed Krajina. (Radović, 2006, p. 32)

Men were strapped to dog kennels positioned face-to-face with cantankerous dogs intentionally starved for days. Others were strong-armed into inflicting pain on fellow forced conscripts helplessly strapped to a chair bolted to the floor. Arkan conditioned his conscripts to accept their roles. Arkan's forced labor assisted in ancillary roles being "dispatched to walk through minefields or to dig frontline trenches as mortars rained down around them" (Stewart, 2008, p. 154). To effectuate this conditioning, Arkan ordered these men to stand under the blistering sun for invariably long hours, deprived of food and water, inciting dehydration. On occasion, trainees would stand immersed in a near-frozen barrel of water for a guttural 24-hr period. The objective was to subject forced labor to physical torture and psychic humiliation with the intent to improve the labor pools performance in foreign domains such as the battlefields of Bosnia. Regular SDG went through an extensive ideological and military education program typically 3 months in length, in a similar vein as "Base People," and Party leaders in DK were also accorded access to a comprehensive political education. Whereas Arkan's forced labor underwent less than a week's learning prior to being ordered to the frontlines, KR's "New People" and class-enemies were afforded less training and placed in a role underprepared, culminating in the deaths of hundreds of thousands of Khmers from overexertion. In both cases, through the HRD lens, we conclusively suggest that a lack of learning furnished to forced labor (accustoming them to work conditions) culminated in death and destruction of members of their own groups, that is, in autogenocide. Totten, Bartrop, and Markusen (2008) assert that forced labor is an economic factor within the context of genocide, thereby calling it "economically motivated genocide" (p. 125). The authors referenced the forced Jewish labor between 1939 and 1945 in Nazi Germany. Totten and his colleagues mention that the Jews constructed roads, "worked in ghetto factories, dug anti-tank ditches, and engaged in other forms of slave labor . . . Indeed, their forced contribution to the German war economy was significant" (p. 126). The authors concluded that the working conditions were "so stringent that labor frequently led to their death" (p. 126).

Using an HRD lens to assess the quality of learning in DK
The quality of learning in DK should be a discussion, or a question, at least addressed holding an HRD view-point. The quality of learning under the KR is questionable no matter what lens is employed: What should we make of the supposed squalid conditions in which learners acquired new knowledge? Can learning transpire when facilitated by inexperienced, noncertified or nonlettered educators or trainers? Genocides are, without a doubt, well-oiled machines, or else, how do they carry on as they do for so long—Education or training and development would ensure the longevity of the regime. Learning

under any genocidal regime could be construed as oppressive from an outsider, when banality is viewed from a distance. However, when attempting to assess the quality of learning in DK, it is best to, in my view, to do so from the genocidist's purview and through an HRD lens. The following examples demonstrate how we can view learning in DK differently through an HRD lens, as opposed through educationist spectacles.

Rurality space and place, and the effects on learning
HRD suggests that learning environments be conducive to learning. The consensus of HRD literature suggested that learning sites should complement learning. Saks and Haccoun (2008) contend training locations be "set up in a manner that is appropriate for the training program" (p. 243). Ayres (1999) opined that within DK, "educational facilities undermined the quality of education" (p. 214). The learning facilities remarked by Ayres constituted stables, or under trees in close proximity to cultivated farm-land, typically outside traditional symbolic educational structures such as school buildings. The Party commented on October 4, 1977, "To implement [learning programs], schools [would be] located mainly in the cooperatives and factories" (Jackson, 1989, p. 96). When reviewing DK's chosen learning sites through an HRD lens and the effect it had on learning, the selection of location makes greater sense than what Ayres' argument suggested. Learning close to and on farmland provisioned readily available land for learners to develop agrarian skills (practice followed instruction); the workable farm-land was close, thereby complementing learning and transferability of skills. Reasons abound why Pol Pot mandated that learning be conducted in farming facilities and on farmland; however, the two prevalent reasons were identity construction (mainly for urban, intellectuals, bourgeoisie, and students) and conditions of practice.

Pol Pot provided the vehicle by which rural identities would be fashioned out of his employees. The HRD lens posits that Pot cultivated a place-based identity by training the nation's future workers on farming techniques in the countryside, first, to reinforce learning through practice and second, to improve the likelihood of training transfer. Woodward (2000) opined that human identities can be created through place. Her study examines soldiers, military training, and the role of the countryside and rurality in the construction of a soldier's military masculinity. Woodward argues that the "role of the countryside and rurality" shape the military masculinity produced in the training programs for soldiers (p. 641).

As Woodward's work relates to the rural learning locations of urban Khmers in DK, Woodward suggests that learners adopting "a new way of being [in] the countryside requires a new way of seeing that countryside" (p. 648). Urban Khmers floundered, not quite knowing what to do. They performed poorly in this domain. Similarly, Woodward noted that "by dominating this landscape through meeting the physical and emotional challenges it poses, the recruit passes the selection process and the soldier is made" (p. 653). "New People," through hard-work and determination, transcended the work environment. Pot's forced rurality is indelibly constructed in "New" and urban Khmer rural identities. The rural as location and the rural as social construction were necessary for Pot to accomplish a state-wide transition of urbanites to rustics. Through the HRD lens, it's understandable why the KR chose farms and fields as domains of learning, which on the contrary did not undermine or hinder learning. The significance Pot accorded to place and space in the forging of rural identities was emphasized similarly for all learners in DK, which suggests, through the HRD lens, that learning was organized and planned.

Standard Total View (STV), instructor credibility, and the quality of learning

Ayres (1999) opined that DK instructors lacked credibility that affected learning: "The nature of the teaching corps further exacerbated problems . . . the teaching staff . . .were drawn from the old people who lived in rural communities before the revolution, despite the fact that they had no formal teaching qualification" (p. 214). Other authors describe these "often illiterate teachers" (Ayres, 1999; Clymer, 2004) as being chosen from the worker-peasant population on the basis of their "revolutionary attitude" (Clayton, 1998; Vickery, 1984) and possessing "minimal education" and "no real teaching experience" (Ayres, 1999; Burgler, 1990). Such claims, combined together, diminish the credibility of many DK instructors. Through an HRD lens, these authors' claims can be called into question for two specific reasons: (a) Evidence exists that discredits the assertion that DK instructors were of no real teaching experience and were illiterate, and (b) the forenamed authors neglect due consideration of subject matter expertise in favor of certified teaching credentials.

Vickery (1984) enumerated of Damban 3: "One woman, a prewar schoolteacher…had been put to work teaching primary classes" (p. 52), and in other Dambans, primary school teachers "were mostly real schoolteachers who had joined the revolution before 1975" (p. 171). Vickery's assertion is in stark contrast to Ayres (1999) remark that "teaching staff . . . had no formal teaching qualifications" (p. 214) or minimal education. Vickery believes that this and similar inconsistencies, as they pertain to education in DK, constitute a standard total view (STV). He holds incomplete and often selective evidence from refugees culminated in this view, which has "permeated most of the writing on Cambodia since 1975" (p. 28). Vickery opined that nearly all refugees were diametrically biased against the KR, namely bourgeois refugees, who Vickery claims to have been the majority population composing the camps. More to the point, Vickery cautions researchers and historians of DK to be wary of taking all refugees accounts on the quality of education as definitive truth. Through the application of an HRD lens here, it is suggestible that the KR offered structured, consistent, and organized learning to children. "Base" Khmers experienced in instructable subjects were employed as teachers; therefore, we can argue that instructors did have the credibility, and more so, a lack thereof was not responsible for reducing the quality of learning the primary and secondary students received.

When reviewed through HRD spectacles, we see that the historical record has undermined instructors' practical experience in a subject (e.g., rice cultivation), thereby giving little currency to prior and practical knowledge. Training regiments are dependent on the knowledge, skills, and experience of the trainer. If trainers are selected because they are knowledgeable about the course material, they would be construed as a subject matter expert (SME), "a person who is familiar with the knowledge, skills, and abilities required to perform a task or job" (Saks & Haccoun, 2008, p. 238). So, if CPK chose instructors because they were experienced in agricultural work (for agrarian training or education) or possessed a well-developed revolutionary attitude (for political training or education), through the HRD lens, their choice in instructors makes sense. Saks and Haccoun (2008) contend that not only will trainees learn more under a SME, but also, "the trainer will be perceived as more credible" (p. 238). In fact, the new perspective as posited by the HRD lens is that the new interpretation is consonant with (or confirms) elements of Vickery's STV, as it relates to instructor credibility and the subsequent impact on learning. Furthermore, Williams (2001) posits that no study exists that indicates a causal link between a trainer's effectiveness and a trainer's experience in training and development, having a degree in education, or a certificate in training and development.

Analyzing KR learning methods through an HRD lens

The purpose of this section is to derive and underscore new interpretations, through an HRD lens, of how learning transpired from DK training or educational programs. Issue 3 of the March 1978 publication *Revolutionary Flags* proffers a detailed list of educative methods by which political consciousness could be inculcated in potential Party members through political education: "meetings, listening to radio broadcasts, studying short documents, by word of mouth itself" (Jackson, 1989, p. 295). The lens can really be applied to any learning event within DK to make better sense of a training or educational situation. In recognition of this fact, four learning methods were identified through the HRD lens and explicated in greater detail: over learning, simulation, behavior modelling, and demonstrations through what Sihanouk (1980) refers to as the school for cruelty.

Revolutionary Flags proffered ideal durations of political consciousness education follow-up. The issue stipulates that when building on Party members' political consciousness, there should be an ensuing steady learning regimen designed for fostering over learning: "for example, a meeting once a month. [Learning] on some type of problem every ten days. If possible one education session per month, or attending class once every three months; or attending a two-day class every six months" (Jackson, 1989, p. 296). The publication concluded that learning should be continuous and should be done "over and over and yet again" (Jackson, 1989, p. 295), until political consciousness was firm. Through an HRD lens, it becomes evident that the Party Center called on members to over learn political content. Over learning as defined by Saks and Haccoun (2008) suggests that trainees be provided with practice as to learn something "until the behavior becomes automatic . . . in other words, trainees are provided with continued opportunities for practice even after they have mastered the task" (p. 135).

Political indoctrination instilled hatred and desensitized children and young adults for violence. In the July 1977 issue of *Revolutionary Flags*, students were encouraged to envelop "a constantly burning rage for the enemy" (Hinton, 2005, p. 82). Contrastingly, as what war games are to military simulations, Pol Pot and Ieng Sary were purported to have rigorously advocated training students in torture games. Torture games were noted as being a cadre's principal training tool (Teng, 1997). Learners received ample violent practice on dogs, cats, and other animals ravaging their targets with bayonets and clubs. Torture games were contrived to obdurate learners' minds and hearts (Sihanouk, 1980; Teng, 1997). Through an HRD lens, we see, first, the use of simulation as a learning method, and second, the curriculum simulated the killing of humans with the killing of animals. Through the lens, we see how simulation was used successfully to desensitize learners for violence against human subjects.

Swanson and Holton (2001) asserted that "social learning focuses on how people learn by interacting with and observing other people" (p. 156). Bandura, Ross, and Ross (1963) theorized that individuals, particularly children and youth, learn to behave aggressively by observing and imitating aggressive models. Furthermore, Bandura developed the concept of vicarious learning. The author demonstrated that children would likely imitate models that have been rewarded for exhibiting aggressiveness. Imitation is central to social learning theory: "social learning also occupies a central place in HRD" (Swanson & Holton, 2001, p. 156). Moreover, the authors claim that "central to social learning theory is that people learn from models" (Swanson & Holton, 2001, p. 156).

"Base" and "New" Khmers astutely observed demonstrations of torture and murder of perceived Party enemies. Khmer learners were instructed to smash any enemy of the revolution. Partaking in violence conveyed a learner's political progress to KR upper-echelons. Failing to violently expel the enemy exhibited a regression of political aptitude and was punished by the Party accordingly. Sihanouk (1980) described such indoctrination for violence as the "school for cruelty" (p. 27). Sihanouk remarked that "Pol Pot and Ieng Sary quite rightly thought that if they trained their young recruits on cruel games, they would end up as soldiers with a love of killing and consequently war" (p. 30). When reviewing the evidence through an HRD lens, behavior modeling and demonstrations surface as prevalent inculcation methods used within this school. Saks and Haccoun (2008) describe behavior modeling as "a training method in which trainees observe a model performing a task and then attempt to imitate the observed behavior" (p. 158). Learners bore witness to planned executions. An experienced executioner was often the model. However, few children took the stage to perform the demonstration. Victims were positioned adjacently to the children so that they could closely experience the bloodletting of the accused (Teng, 1997). Teng (1997) recollects an experience she had in the school for cruelty. She recalled that in the center of the gathering spot was one woman, targeted as a traitor, had both hands fastened behind her back. She was pregnant, her stomach noticeably bulged out. Standing to her side was a little adolescent boy aged six, holding an axe. In the child's shrilled voice, he yelled for all other children to watch the ravishing spectacle. Teng remarked "the boy wielded the axe in the air, sending it hard into the pregnant woman's body until she dropped to the ground and did so continuously until he was too tired to continue" (p. 157). The boy was rewarded by a resounding applause and a cacophony of cheers. When such history is reviewed through an HRD lens, we can discern the use and implications of behavior modeling and demonstrations as learning tools when used to incite violence and murder. Because the behavior modeled was congruent with curriculum content, for example, "smashing" the enemy, we can make better sense of the educational aspirations of the government. Through the lens, we can perceive the similarities between how social learning theory is reminiscent within the school for cruelty, and how a common HRD strategy such as behavior modeling can culminate in genocidal outcomes. Removing the cruelty and inhumanness from the learning event, we are undoubtedly presented with behavior modeling.

Classical conditioning in DK through an HRD lens
Swanson and Holton (2001) suggest that behaviorism, a meta-theory of learning, "has played a central role in human resource development" (p. 151). The authors posit that an underlying assumption shared by all behaviorists is that "learning process can be studied most objectively when the focus of the study is on stimulus and response" (Swanson & Holton, 2001, p. 150). This learning process could alternatively be construed as classical conditioning. Nevid (2012) advances classical conditioning as "the process of learning by which a previously neutral stimulus comes to elicit a response identical or similar to one that was originally elicited by another stimulus as the result of the pairing or association of the two stimuli" (p. 181).

Viewing DK history through an HRD lens, we can identify some resemblances between KR programs for learning and political propaganda, and classical conditioning. Halpern (2002) is of the opinion that "clever propagandists" have been using classical conditioning to influence the way people think, primarily through the perpetration of hateful political-themed propaganda. Halpern referred to Nazi German movies that paired repulsive scenes of rats spewing from sewers, running over waste and garbage. She remarked that "exaggerated pictures of Jews were flashed on to the screen," the long noses of rats were "superimposed over the . . .facial features of Jews" (Halpern, 2002, p. 48). The author opined that "it does not take long before the facial features evoke feelings of disgust, which were learned through the repeated pairing of the repulsive rat scenes and the faces" (Halpern, 2002, p. 49). As a result, Halpern credits Hitler Youth and other audiences as then associating certain facial features of Jews with repulsive bugs and rodents, "You will recognize this technique as classical conditioning" (p. 208). She also acknowledges that similar conditioning techniques, although she has not specified which, were used in the promotion and justification of genocide in "the slaughter of Cambodians in Asia" (Halpern, 2002, p. 208).

Makino (2001) asserts that "the Pol Pot era was . . . about conditioning people, especially children, to commit atrocities" (p. 57). In a similar manner to that of Halpern (2002), historical examples surface of classical conditioning in DK when reviewed through an HRD lens. Chalk (1990) recounts that the KR characterized enemies of the revolution as "sub-people." CPK documents, propaganda, and speeches referred to political enemies as threats of contamination through "agricultural metaphors" or "biological metaphors" (Kiernan, 2008, p. 549). Corrupted Party members were referred to as infections that "must be cut out" or "what is rotten must be removed" (Smith, 2009, pp. 209-210). "New People" were contrasted to animals to justify inhumane treatment (Bellamy, 2012). Kiernan maintained that further Party documents and propaganda reviled enemies as "diseased elements," "microbes," "pests buried within," and traitors "boring in," just as the Nazis had talked of Jews as "vermin" and "lice" (Kiernan, 2008, p. 549). Bellamy (2012) postulated that those not matching the desired stereotype (the Khmer peasant) were labeled "carriers of foreign influence" in need of a good "smashing" (p. 267). Agricultural metaphors referred to enemies as burrowing within DK, and to eviscerate the enemy, "pull up the grass, dig up the roots. . . the bodies of city people . . . would be used for fertilizer" (Kiernan, 2008, p. 547). Tyner (2008) believes that the idea of removing weeds by pulling them out by the root referred to "to kill one's enemy, you must also kill his/her relatives" (p. 153). The application of an HRD lens here assisted in deriving new perspectives on the potentiality of learning theories being used by the KR to organize learning in the DK. If classical conditioning (behaviorism) and social learning theory were used in educational policy formation, it is plausible to accept that learning programs contrived by the Party were structured and well-planned.

Political development emerges from analysis with an HRD lens
Through an HRD lens, we can derive a new interpretation of political learning in DK, political development. As shown earlier, historical

accounts of political learning in DK constructed by Hinton (2005), Clayton (1998), and Ayres (1999; 2000) use political training and education interchangeably. The idea of political development and its different methods for cultivating political consciousness are nowhere mentioned. By and large, when using an HRD lens to analyze CPK's practice of criticism sessions, they make sense as a political development initiative. Development refers to "learning opportunities designed to help employees grow" (Aswathappa, 2007, p. 195), and "usually includ[ing] elements of planned study and experience" (Wilson, 2012, p. 6). In an article from the April 1976 edition of *Revolutionary Flags*, the Party explicated the ongoing need for "self-criticism" to cultivate "pure revolutionary consciousnesses" as well to continuously maintain it. The CPK required all Khmers' participation in criticism sessions, either as the sole participant (self-criticizer), or as an onlooker (criticizer) being mindful of a participant's weaknesses and incongruence with Party policies. The KR tested learners on their retention of knowledge and expertise of political subject matter during criticism sessions (Picq, 1989). After onerous review of Party documents pertaining to class struggle and revolutionary hate, learners were gauged on "their state of morale and feelings" (Hinton, 2005, p. 73). Khmers who criticized themselves had to admit their shortcomings, own their mistakes, and promise to keep improving themselves.

Through the HRD lens, we see the meaning of criticism sessions as intended to grow a learner's political consciousness. Moreover, the lens makes sense of criticism sessions as an avenue for conditioning an individual's political development as it combined "elements of planned study and experience" (Wilson, 2012, p. 6). On another note, self-criticism sessions have been illustrated as a learning priority to be complemented by a "training" or "education" event: "criticism-sessions and political seminars" (Hinton, 2005, p. 231); cadres "were required to attend frequent political meetings and self-criticism sessions" (Hinton, 2005, p. 237). Sarin's (1973) testimony affirms that criticism sessions were distinct from political education sessions. He distinguished political education "[as] supplemented by criticism and self-criticism sessions" (Hinton, 2005, p. 73). Sheared and Sissel (2001) argue that self-criticism is "not unfamiliar in the field of [HRD]" (p. 147). The authors contend that platforms for self-criticism are being used to assist employees to unburden themselves of "self-imposed restraints" (Sheared & Sissel, 2001, p. 174). Furthermore, few authors have noted a lack thereof of self-criticism's use in today's workplace learning schema. Garrick (1998) claims that modern workplace learning strategies ever rarely employ paradox, doubt, irony, or self-criticism; however, the author continues "yet it is precisely these qualities that give substance to learning" (p. 79). Through the HRD lens, considering all other political learning (particularly for "New People" and few "Base People") as political training or political education (for Party members or cadres), it becomes evident that the learning of revolutionary language, political theory, and Party documents would be tested during political development. The HRD lens perceives political training or political education and political development to be existing hand-in-hand. Thereupon, the HRD lens holds that a political development event was complemented by and complementary to a political education or training event.

Implications for research and practice
By using an HRD lens, incongruences in the historical record surfaced over the proper use of learning terms such as training, development, or education. HRD can be used to organize and explicate historical educative or learning events differently from a perspective that's not education specific. As shown through an HRD lens, startling comparisons can be made between past and present genocidal curriculums of tyrannical regimes. The primary implication of this work is to highlight how HRD could, and perhaps has been used to train and develop citizens into stalwart killing machines able to perpetrate crimes against humanity. Few readers may egregiously mistake the purpose of this article and view the subject matter as proffering potential strategies for augmenting performance of genocidal agents or governments; or, some may perhaps alternatively view the usefulness of HRD processes to inculcate citizens for violence to do harm, not good. Through the HRD lens, the comparison between DK learning interventions and common HRD strategies is uncanny, and I expect will disturb few in the field of HRD. The application of an HRD lens is instead intended to assist interventionists and policy makers to interrupt educational policy formation and or destabilize the educative aspirations of incipient tyrannical governments.

Furthermore, through an HRD lens, new interpretations of genocidal curriculums are expected to conflict or contend with "dominant paradigms" (Callahan, 2010), and knowledge history has bestowed a "hegemonic advantage" (Maxwell, 2009).

Recommendations for future research

The primary recommendation for future research is to, first, consider the distinctions (as done in the present work) of the three learning terms, "training," "development," and "education," and, second, partition historical learning events into a "training," "education," or "development" grouping. Thematizing each learning event under analysis into its respective heading whether "training," "education," or "development" should assist HRD researchers to not only organize historical information as history intended it, but also organize pertinent information as it relates to each grouping more fully. For instance, reviewing the length of a learning event can often indicate whether history intended it as training or education, despite the event being reconstructed by an author as "training" or "education." Moreover, I am of the same opinion as Lee (2002): "HRD has learnt from other disciplines, so, I suggest, other disciplines can learn from HRD" (p. 18.). With hope, the current research encourages cross-fertilization or collaboration of other academic disciplines such as education and business to see the merits in relating their expertise to genocide research as I have done for HRD. The application of an HRD lens to other known genocidal events such as the Armenian Genocide or East Timor is highly recommended. In addition to using an HRD lens to make a better sense of genocidal curriculums, the lens should be applied to erstwhile genocidal groups (e.g., paramilitaries) such as Serbia's Arkan's Tigers, Nazi Germany's Schutzstaffel (SS), or Sudan's Janjaweed.

Conclusion

Through the use of an HRD lens, primary and secondary sources were reviewed and deconstructed as they pertained to learning in DK. The historical record of DK posits that education under the KR was unorganized, inconsistent, and without planning. Through an HRD lens, these claims have been called into question. We can make more sense of the madness in the context of the time through an HRD lens. Through the lens, it appears that the KR replaced traditional education in place of calculated HRD interventions to connect the nation's populace with agrarian work through carefully contrived learning programs to serve the Party's politico-socioeconomic objectives.

Learning interventions, as the review through an HRD lens suggests, were consistently implemented, organized in accord with the Party's goals, and well-planned to maximize their forced labor performance. In the final analysis, through the application of an HRD lens, we can make more sense of how learning transpired in DK. It is comprehendible that the KR identified appropriate learning theories (social learning and behavioral theories) to improve their educational output. The review of the historical record through the lens demonstrates that the CPK were mindful in their selection of instructional strategies (behavior modeling, demonstrations, and simulations) and sites of learning (fields and farms).

CHAPTER TWO
The Serbian Volunteer Guard (SDG) and Nadler's (1994) Critical Events Model (CEM)

Introduction

My objective is to demonstrate Nadler's (1994) critical events model (CEM) usefulness as a tool for revisiting curricula of foregone times. The CEM program design model, as will be shown, is useful for reorganizing historical record as it pertains to the learning of the Serbian Volunteer Guard (SDG). I argue that educational historians, by rearranging relevant sources around Nadler's eight-stage critical events model, can draw factive conclusions on how the SDG, otherwise known as Arkan's Tigers, trained. Although my research bears considerable formal resemblance to the work of Nabb and Armstrong (2005), my work is different for two reasons: Firstly, Nabb and Armstrong self-identify as adult educators, whereas I am a practitioner of human resource development; secondly, "their work is presented as a diatribe against HRD and its potential implications were ruminated on training soldiers for atrocities in the holocaust" (Procknow, 2014, p. 371). Comparatively the authors and I use the CEM to organize history. A purpose of the present research is to show how the critical events model contains the requisite components to reorganize and reinterpret historical sources to make clearer academic sense of historical curricula.

The research questions guiding this present work are two-fold: Can HRD-based insights and inferences be derived from reorganizing the historical educational record of the Serbian Volunteer Guard around a program design model e.g., Nadler's (1994) CEM; and, how can the CEM be used to identify the training interventions prepared for the SDG to enact ethnic cleansing and crimes against humanity against Croatians and Bosniaks?

The desire to answer these two questions led me on a relentless pursuit of archival evidence that documented this gruesome period in history. As demonstrated by Procknow (2014), new interpretations can be drawn from historical records when an HRD lens is applied. The author contested and challenged that the historical record which advanced that learning in Democratic Kampuchea was unorganized, inconsistent, and unplanned. Moreover, Procknow's review of the record through an HRD lens, conveyed a contrary viewpoint that learning under the Khmer Rouge was in fact organized and planned. The curricula contrived for the Khmer Rouge were grounded in social learning theory. They also encompassed numerous instructional strategies including; demonstrations, simulations, and behaviour modelling, all similarly used by Arkan's Tigers. The present research will build upon Procknow's (2014) work and proffer detailed explanations on how the CEM is beneficial to HRD historians for retrospectively analyzing historical curricula.

In the present analysis, the researcher depended on the avalanche of written testimonies produced by the *International Criminal Tribunal for Former Yugoslavia* (ICTY). On the whole, it is in my opinion that the ICTY evidence denies absolute validity, as testimony is limitedly predicated upon authenticated documents of the Serbian Volunteer Guard. An entire corpus of testimonies exists. However, the researcher has found very few that relate to the training and development of SDG. The conclusions drawn from the historical record may appear anecdotal as evidentiary materials were principally narrative and restricted to personal accounts. For this reason I am compelled to explain briefly the absence of primary documents created by the Serbian Volunteer Guard. According to witness B-129 (2003, April 17), SDG personnel destroyed all orders relating to daily work undertaken in Erdut's 101st Training Centre. All documents were destroyed in the evenings: "papers and documents relating to day-to-day obligations, either of the staff or members of the Serbian Volunteer Guard, after the work was done, would be destroyed" (p. 19058). Procknow (2014) commented: "when analyses are drawn from a wider variety of sources, more confidence can be reposed in the results" (p. 370). Nonetheless, the vast number of testimonies navigated in this research clearly evidence the existence of an extermination policy.

Manifold sources of testimony were consulted. Testimonies from erstwhile SDG members include those from military, administrative, and instructor positions in the SDG, plus external observers of the SDG training program, totalling over 25 ICTY court summaries, convictions, and documents. These sources involved a multiplicity of witness and prosecutorial evidence. Protracted ICTY hearings presented some insight into the organization of training for the SDG. The cases against Stanišić and Simatović, and Slobodan Milošević culminated in the greatest currency of data for this present work. Stanišić and Simatović trial documents (ten in total, spanning three years) were useful in implicating the SDG's involvement in mass atrocities. Testimonies adduced at Milošević's trial inextricably linked the ethnic cleansing perpetrated by Arkan's SDG to Milošević's puppet governments in Serbian Krajina and Republika

Srpska. For the purpose of this paper, verbatim quotes will be used extensively throughout to ease transferability of research findings.

Secondary academic sources were of limited assistance. Observational reports were derived from Balkaninsight.com, Australian refugee review tribunals, U.S State department findings (including tape-recorded video presentations depicting SDG training in Erdut), and a few newspaper and print media accounts of the situation in former Yugoslavia. Notwithstanding the lack of primary documents surviving the SDG, ample evidence was obtained through the CEM lens to advance new conclusions and interpretations of the learning contrived for them.

Shortcomings and limitations are to be expected in any pioneering work within an emerging field such as HRD. As avowed by Swanson and Holton (2001), HRD is still in its infancy. This paper only utilizes a combined HRD and CEM lens to revisit genocidal curricula of the Serbian Volunteer Guard. Moreover, only one version of the affair is precipitated in the present work. This research does not describe genocidal actions of competing Bosnian and Croatian paramilitaries, but rather a myopic overview of Arkan's SDG (Klip & Sluiter, 2001). This paper references the training namely of two learner groups. Firstly, Arkan's core group, composed of convicts, street thugs, and criminals; secondly, transferees from the former Yugoslavian People's Army (JNA). A third group of trainees were also known to have circulated through Arkan's Erdut: conscripted Slovenian-Serbs, Croatian-Serbs, and Bosnian-Serbs arrested for abandoning their homes and circumventing conflict with the enemy (Stewart, 2007; Radović, 2006). This research is limited to those who desired and sought training. Regardless, I know of no model in existence that is designed specifically for reviewing historical curricula, which makes it difficult to contrast opinions and approaches.

A Nation Divided
The Socialist Federal Republic of Yugoslavia (SFRY) was conceived shortly before the end of World War II. The SFRY was partitioned into six regional Republics: Slovenia, Bosnia and Herzegovina, Croatia, the Republic of Macedonia, Montenegro, and Serbia. Within Serbia were two autonomous regions, Vojvodina and Kosovo. The boundary of each republic corresponded with territory and ethnicity, with each republic claiming religious and cultural specificity. After the dissolution of the Soviet Union in 1989-1990, preparations for the disintegration of the SFRY were well underway until January 1990,

when the Yugoslavian League of Communists disbanded as a national entity. Furthermore, secessionist and non-communist states were established in the republics of Bosnia-Herzegovina, Slovenia, Macedonia, and Croatia. In March 1991, General Veljko Kadijević, SFRY Minister of Defence, organized a meeting of the six presidents of the republics, presidents of the autonomous republics, and the SFRY president. Kadijević acknowledged the formation of illegal paramilitary groups within each republic and emphatically declared martial law. Slovenia and Croatia proclaimed independence from Yugoslavia on June 25, 1991. Slovenia's and Croatia's simultaneous declarations of independence culminated in two wars: the Slovenian Independence War, lasting ten days; and the protracted Croatian War of Independence, fought for four years. The Bosnian War began shortly thereafter.

By exercising their right of self-determination, Serbian-Croats formed the Republic of Serbian Krajina (RSK) that absorbed a land area totalling more than a quarter of Croatia. Serb-Croats organized the Serbian National Council (SNC) in July 1990, primarily to coordinate an opposition to Croatian independence. The council decreed: "if Croatia could secede from Yugoslavia, then the Serbs could secede from Croatia" (Thompson, 2013, p. 417). The following month, in August 1990, the council held a referendum in Krajina to settle the matter of bestowing sovereignty and autonomy to Serbs in Croatia. The results, unsurprisingly, came out in Serbian favour. On December 21, 1990, President Milan Babić carved out the *Serbian Autonomous Oblast of Krajina* (SAO Krajina). Babić's administration held a plebiscite on March 16, 1991, asking the SAO Krajina population to constitutively annex to the united territories of the Serbian Republic; the majority obliged. Consequentially, on March 31, 1991, the Croatian War pitted Croatian paramilitaries against the Serbian controlled Yugoslav Army (JNA) and the Serbian Krajina (SRK). On April 1, 1991, SAO Krajina withdrew formally from Croatia; the SNC further conferred autonomy to SAO Eastern Slavonia, Baranja and Western Syrmia (SAO SB WS) from Croatia on June 25, 1991. On August 12, 1991, by right of self-determination the Serbian Autonomous Oblast of Western Slavonia (SAO Western Slavonia) broke from Croatia, allowing easier absorption by the RSK. In February 1992, Goran Hadžić, elected first president of SAO SB WS, oversaw his territory's annexation to the RSK. The official army of the Republic of Serbian Krajina formed on March 19, 1992. Goran Hadžić replaced Babić as president, a position he maintained until 1994.

Nearby Bosnia and Herzegovina held a referendum on February 29, 1992, seeking independence from Yugoslavia. Slobodan Milošević, with Serb interests in mind, attempted to suppress the move for independence, launching military action on March 1, 1992. Belligerents involved the joint participation of Bosnian-Muslims, also known as Bosniaks and Bosnian-Croats, under the Republic of Bosnia and Herzegovina (ARBiH) banner against the JNA backed Bosnian-Serbs of the SAO Bosanska Krajina and the army of Republika Srpska (VRS). Bosnian-Serbs seceded from Bosnia on January 9, 1992, creating the Bosnian-Serb Republic, better known as the Republika Srpska, under the presidency of Radovan Karadžić. Karadžić embarked on unilateral initiatives to unite Bosnian-Serbs with a putative Serb population in Croatia and Bosnia of 1.8 million. SAO Bosanska Krajina later merged with Republika Srpska on April 6, 1992, solidifying a geographically indissoluble compact of Bosnian-Serbs. On May 12, 1992, the JNA ceased military operations in Croatia, abandoning equipment and armaments to the VRS commanded by Ratko Mladić.

Slobodan Milošević served as president for the SFRY from 1989 to 1997, renaming it the Republic of Serbia in 1990. Momir Bulatović became the first president of the Republic of Montenegro in 1990, serving until 1998. Shortly after the SFRY's dissolution in 1992, the combined Republics of Serbia and Montenegro together formed the Federal Republic of Yugoslavia (FRY). Bulatović and Milošević continued to serve their republics respectively. A single president was needed to govern the two republics, to work hand-in-glove with Bulatović and Milošević. On June 15, 1992, FRY appointed Dobrica Ćosić as President. Milošević, however, exerted political sway and influence over both Ćosić and Bulatović. On June 1, 1993, Ćosić was forced out of his presidency after a spat with Milošević. Disputes with FRY presidents were customary with Milošević, until he himself ascended to the presidency in 1997, maintaining it until 2000.

Serbian nationalism

Milošević's coming of power signalled a massive militaristic change in Serbia. At the outset of 1990, Milošević commissioned preparations for war with Croatia at a time when the latter was transitioning from communism to democracy. Letica (1996) opined that in the inchoate phase that ushered in the Croatian War of 1991: "Serbia was completing a process of psychological, institutional, economic, propagandistic, and military preparation for war" (p. 101).

Letica explicated that Milošević was making in-roads into intellectual, ideological, political, psychological, and military preparations well before 1991.

Intellectual and ideological preparations began in 1986 (Letica, 1996). State-sponsored propaganda contrived for Serbian audiences peddled nationalistic and anti-Muslim sentiments. Documents such as the highly debated *Memorandum of Serbian Science and Art* echoed these sentiments. The 'Memorandum', drafted by a 16-member apparatus employed by the Serbian Academy of Arts and Sciences, rendered Serbians as victims. Commingled feelings of oppression and victimization, that were moribund in many parts of the Serbian Republic, were part and parcel of revitalized Serbian nationalism. The memorandum itself proffered no military strategy. Moreover, Letica suggests that the memorandum manifested "[a] clear purpose of reviving the slumbering Greater Serbian consciousness and to put it into active, political practice" (p. 102). In 1989, Milošević ushered in the ideological phenomenon, the *Anti-Bureaucratic Revolution*, an amalgam of National Socialism, Titoist Populism, and Bolshevism. The revolution was commonly regarded as a series of rallies held by disillusioned Serbs, within autonomous Vojvodina, Kosovo, and Montenegro, who were still bitter after the shortcomings of Tito Communism. They demanded a new leader evincing pro-Serbian interests with outward authoritarian qualities. Letica claimed that Serbs little desired democratic reform, but rather sought a satisfying ideological equipoise. Mass denunciations and public protests by Milošević supporters proved instrumental in replacing oppositional government leaders with Milošević's marionette governments. Milošević's proverbial slogans e.g., "it happens with the people", his Serb-centric policies, and charisma converged the sympathy of Serbs in want of ethnic homogeneity.

It is imperative at this juncture to comment on Serbian nationalism before broaching Letica's (1996) further two preparations. In 1986, the Serbian Academy of Arts and Sciences published *The Serbian Memorandum*. The memorandum propositioned a unified Serbia, endorsed territorial unity of all Serbian peoples, and called for: "the establishment of the full national integrity of the Serbian people, regardless of which republic or province it inhabits is its historic and democratic right" (Cigar, 1996, p. 55). Given the dissolution of Yugoslavia into a patchwork of culturally-unified lands, the memorandum preempted Serbians to adopt Milošević's plan for Serbian wholeness. The memorandum is considered by many as the progenitor of the then-contemporary Serbian nationalist agenda. At first, a few communist politicians hastily denounced the provisions. At the same time, Milošević and his Serbian League of Communists rallied communist and nationalist support around the memorandum's platform. The platform was successfully inaugurated in the ensuing years. Milošević encouraged his people to aspire toward Serbian homogeneity. He entrusted celebrities, intellectuals, and media agencies carefully selected for their scintillating wit, to draft plans to allure undecided Serbs to adopt an 'us' against 'them' mentality.

Cigar (1996) propounded that "Serbia's state controlled media, as well as many intellectuals, began a sustained campaign in support of the Serbs, and the alleged present-day danger of renewed genocide, and accusing virtually every other ethnic and religious community of threatening the Serbs" (p. 56). Serbian media invoked prejudicial violence against Bosniaks and Croatians. At rallies in Serbia and Montenegro in 1988 and 1989, Serbs parroted the following catch-cries: "Slobo, send us lettuce, there will be meat, we will be slaughtering Croats" (Irwin, 2012, para. 8); "oh Muslims, you black crows, Tito is not around to protect you" (Cigar, p. 34); "we love you Slobodan because you hate the Muslims" (Cigar, p. 34); "I'll be first, who'll be second to drink some Turkish blood?" (Cigar, p. 34).

Over a five-year period from 1985 to 1990, psychological preparations dominated public engagement, dialogue, and discourse. Public meetings "continued without interruption from 1986 until the famous Vidovdanski meeting on Kosovo Field 28 June 1989" (Letica, 1996, p. 104). From 1987-88, Milosevic began replacing disobliging media personalities, editors, and directors with willing producers of war propaganda. At the same time, Milošević sought support from Serbia's two most venerated psychiatrists, Dr. Jovan Raskovic and Dr. Radovan Karadžić, who had the farthest-reaching influence in Serbia and who courted mass psychological support during this period. Raskovic specialized in group therapy; Karadžić was experienced in diagnosing and treating paranoid states. Raskovic and Karadžić's influence, Letica opined, "provided the impetus of assimilating Serbs into forthcoming perpetrators of violence", allowing Milošević "to have at [his] disposal a wide-ranging state of mass-psychological preparedness on the part of the population, rendering it willing to approve, support, and participate in aggression" (p. 104).

Initially, Milošević encountered resistance to his early campaigns for military preparedness. At first, he was unable to muster enough military mobilization on part of the Yugoslav People's Army. His coterie vigorously solicited JNA officer support by inundating them with a plethora of pamphlets teeming with nationalist propaganda advocating Serbian solidarity (Cigar, 1996).

Milošević grew confident that, with time, the appeal of a 'Greater Serbia' would bring the majority of JNA membership under Serbian employ. To this end, many officers did identify as either Serbian and/or Montenegrin. JNA officers who commanded the respect of their troops accompanied their officers to Serbia. Officers imbibed the ideological ferment of nationalism and were callously indifferent to the pluralist, separatist thought encapsulated by Croatian and Slovene JNA officers. The expanding influence of Serbian propaganda stretched the credulity of Serbian JNA members beyond the threshold of absolute hatred for Bosniaks and Croats, making "the rapid Serbinization of the Yugoslav army all the more easier" (Letica, 1996, p. 105). However, JNA participation was not without its problems. Not long after the beginning of the wars in Croatia and Bosnia, multitudes of JNA soldiers either mutinied, deserted, or draft-dodged. Mueller (2000) suspects that 150,000 men quickly emigrated or went underground during the incipient stages of both wars. Burg and Shoup (1999) contend: "only 50 percent of Serbian reservists and only 15 percent in Belgrade obeyed orders to report for duty" (p. 84). Suffice it to say that many recalcitrant Serbs refused outright to fight. Belgrade had little option but to rethink their enlistment strategy; relief was found in the Greek Volunteer Guard (GVG).

Greece and Serbia were united in their condemnation of Muslims. During the Bosnian War, the Serb propaganda machine continued to play on the populace's prejudices and heightened anxiety of a Turk and Muslim threat to Serbian communities. Together with Serbia, Greek media promulgated stories of Serb bravery and spoke of a similar Turkish threat. Serbian dignitaries relished meeting Greek politicos and media personalities. One dignitary remarked: "Greece [was] facing a Turkish-Muslim threat; a Muslim arc [was] encircling Greece" (Michas, 2002, p. 32). During the Bosnian conflict, a few dignitaries confided to Greek statesmen that Serbia was fighting Bosniaks to protect Greece. Moreover, in December 1993, Dusan Kanazir, representative of the Serbian Academy of Science, heralded to Greek audiences that they shared genetic inheritance and traceable consanguinity with Serbs. The Greek Ministry of Foreign Affairs and the Academy of Athens venerated Kanazir's conclusions.

Milošević curried massive Greek support militarily. Serbia advanced an answer to the Muslim question. Greece assisted in its solution. Greek media "conjure[d] up a powerful picture of a bloodstained Mujahedeen of preferably Turkish descent ready to swarm into Greece" (Michas, 2002, p. 32). Greek publications chock full of anti-Muslim messages were placed into mass circulation. A greatly perturbed Greek contingent of 100 soldiers was organized at the request of General Mladić in March 1995 to support Bosnian-Serbs' quelling of the Muslim problem. The Greek Volunteer Guard sported a two-headed white eagle insignia displayed over a black background. The Army of Republika Srpska also assimilated GVG under their military command (Eleftherotypia, 1995). Greek volunteers were provided no monetary compensation for their service. Similarly, GVG motives and SDG motives were intrinsically one and the same: to dispel Muslims from Europe. Religion was cited by many GVG recruits as their principal motivation for entering the fray. Koutakos, a Greek volunteer commented: "I am an Orthodox and I must help my Serb brethren against the Muslims". Another recruit named Vasiliadis mentioned: "I gave my blood to fight the Muslim arc" (Eleftherotypia, 1993). GVG successes in Bosnia were met with praise in Greece. Their stories inspired Greek newspapers to dedicate two-page spreads memorializing GVG heroism. Michas (2002) opined that the "Greek public seemed mesmerized by their stories of the hardships of military life, the danger involved in fighting the insidious Muslims, and the bravery of their Serbian brethren" (Michas, 2002, p. 18). The Greek Volunteer Guard, according to Michas, "by the open and proud admission of its own members, took part in the events that led up to the murder of eight thousand innocent civilians in Srebrenica" (p. 40). The fall of Srebrenica and the ignominious defeat of Muslims was a joint Greek-Serbian achievement. In September 1995, for rendering selfless service to Serbia, Karadžić awarded four GVG members with the medal of the White Eagle (Michas, 2002).

Ethnic cleansing in Bosnia

The U.N enumerated that in 1994, 83 active paramilitary groups existed in the now defunct Yugoslavia: 56 Serbian, 13 Croatian, and 14 Bosnian-Muslim (Judah, 1997). By and large, warlords and mafia figures fathered independent and semi-independent paramilitaries. Block (1993) dutifully noted that criminals, gangsters, and outlaws held "a special place in the war in the Former Yugoslavia" (p. 9). Block continued: "Their skills in organizing people and their ruthlessness made them natural choices for Balkan rabble-rousers looking for men to defend their cities or serve as nationalistic shock troops" (p. 9). The interior minister and Milošević knowingly recruited "thousands of prison inmates" (Brown, 2001, p. 104) for their capacity to rape and slaughter innocents. Out of sheer necessity, Serbia furnished weaponry to able-bodied volunteers in Serb communities within Croatia and Bosnia; their fighting proved despicable. Notwithstanding waning JNA support, Milošević employed stolid paramilitary groups e.g., SDG, Yellow Wasps, and the Scorpions to operate in toto with the VRS, primarily as the purveyors of genocide and ethnic cleansing. Cigar and Williams (1997) posited: "Invariably after [paramilitary] deployment, these forces engaged in acts of ethnic cleansing and plunder" (p. 18). It should be duly acknowledged that Croatian and Bosniak paramilitaries reciprocated violence, though to a lesser degree and in smaller proportions, towards Serbs. In Srebrenica in July 1995, on orders from Karadžić and Mladić, the VRS and other Serbian groups massacred more than 8000 men and boys and forcefully displaced 30,000 Bosnian-Muslims. To this end, 2,700,000 people in the Balkan regions have been displaced since 1991 as a result of Yugoslavia's dissolution (Erlanger, 1996).

As remarked in the 1996 findings of the Commission on Security and Cooperation in Europe, parliament deputy and part-time paramilitary leader Paroski recollected to General Tomislav: "My goal is not only to defend Serbianness but to cleanse territory, to have an ethnically clean state. You can have progress [only] within such a state" (Cigar & Williams, 1997, p. 17). Maass (1996) holds that a majority of the genocidal participants responsible for atrocities possessed an "odd enthusiasm...laughed, sang, and got drunk while inflicting their crimes. They weren't just doing a job, they were doing something they enjoyed" (p. 100). In a similar vein, Judah (1997) contended: "plenty of Serbs...enjoyed killing civilians and eagerly sought the opportunity to do so...these killers never had so much fun" (p. 233). In executing directives to this effect, most Serbian paramilitaries "behaved in a wholly unsoldierly way, wearing all sorts of chauvinist insignia...were often drunk, looted, and killed or harassed civilians...Officers rarely disciplined them" (Vasic, 1996, p. 128). The Serbian Volunteer Guard stood apart from the others; they were more disciplined, organized, and far better trained.

The Serbian Volunteer Guard (SDG)

Arkan's Tigers (*Arkanovci*), with its celebrity figurehead Željko Ražnatović, undoubtedly better known by his nom de guerre 'Arkan', formed the vanguard of Milošević's ethnic cleansing plan. Milošević regarded Arkan's energy and yearning for Serbian homogeneity with admiration. LeBor (2012) commented on their relationship: "Milosevic needed Arkan to help channel the nationalism that he was unleashing" (p. 21). In October 1990, Arkan became the eminent ringleader of the Red Star Belgrade football fan-club, otherwise known as the Delije (literal translation, Rebels). He formed the Serbian Volunteer Guard at the same time that he gained control of Delije's hooligan operations. Hooligans were Arkan's overriding first choice for enrolment in the SDG. Stewart (2007) referred to Delije as "weapons of mass destruction" (p. 119). They clashed with fans of opposing football teams "with fists, bayonets, iron bars, and Louisville sluggers, a kind of warfare modeled after English soccer thugs" (Stewart, 2007, p. 119). They violently intimidated team players and coaches squarely blamed for game losses. Delije chants turned out to be a premonitory indicator of the genocidal violence they'd be capable of in Bosnia: "axes in hand…and a knife in the teeth/there'll be blood tonight" (Stewart, p. 119). Conjectural estimates place Arkan's initial contingent at 200 men; some appraisals submit substantially higher figures in the 500-1000 range. Arkan dispensed a small fraction of the Delije to recruit teens from the gritty city neighbourhoods of Serbia. His enlistment strategy targeted young criminals looking for employment "that would elevate them" (Stewart, p. 129). The Delije targeted hardened street thugs identifiable by scars on their legs, stomachs, and arms. Gang members of the day sported hairstyles with a mishmash of straight and jagged lines which Stewart claimed were created by "their own hands using store bought razor blades" (Stewart, 2007, p. 129). Ramet (2005) affirmed that one out of every five Delije volunteers had previously been in trouble with the law. In recognition of this, Alvarez (2009) posited: "one reason why many young men are attracted to sports fan clubs is that these organizations provide meaning, status, and a sense of belonging and identity from membership" (p. 63). Alvarez believes that the energy young men channel into sports clubs "can easily be transferred to more violent outlets, ones that are possibly political and/or genocidal" (p. 90). Arkan convoked daily morning meetings at his sweatshop with Red Star thugs and local crime elements. With a dozen or so men in attendance, Arkan galvanized meetings with a customary caustic warning: "hard times are coming, boys! Our enemies are upon us" (Stewart, 2007, p. 129). Arkan explained he was recruiting a private militia to protect and serve Serbia.

Serbia's netherworld was emblematic of Arkan's recruitment pool. He selectively recruited from the innards of Serbian prisons. He toured penitentiaries, given permission to do so by the then Interior Minister, Pavle Bulatović. Stewart (2007) contends: "like a quick-eyed scout, he personally selected murderers and bank robbers, and when the day came they would be released to him" (Stewart, 2007, p. 129). Criminals relocated from a prison to the paramilitary were promised that for every one month spent in the SDG, three months would be deducted from their sentences (Stewart, 2007). The SDG comprised an average of 80% criminals and 20% zealous nationalists (Vasic, 1996). The author continued: "The latter did not usually last long" (p. 134). Convicts were also enticed by the proposition of retaining booty from the war effort (Mueller, 2000).

In its incipient stage, the Serbian Volunteer Guard swore fidelity to Arkan on October 11, 1990. On this day, novices were transported to Pokajnica, "the Church of Regret", to sign a written affidavit asseverating their loyalty to the Orthodox Church. Arkan believed this further differentiated his soldiers from Catholic Croats and Bosniaks. Recruits were subject to drug-testing and fiercely reminded that if they "fucked up...acting like drunk Chetnik army guys" there would be serious repercussions (Mueller, 2000, p. 131). Thereafter, fledglings were officially sworn in as Tigers and baptized by an Orthodox priest. Their first order was to discard personal identification e.g., licenses, certificates or anything that could signal SDG involvement in the conflict (Mueller, 2000). The Commission on Security and Cooperation in Europe (1996) found that the SDG in the Bosnian and Croatian conflicts "in fact, served the domestic interests of Slobodan Milošević, while enabling him to avoid giving the appearance that the government [as well himself] was involved [in ethnic cleansing]" (p. 17).

As early as January 1992, Arkan offered SDG enlistees the option to serve three, six, or 12-month contracts (Witness B-1738, 2003). Recruiters insisted serving as a volunteer would fulfil the same requirements as serving in the JNA (Witness B-1738). While the evidence is not overwhelming, it is believed that Arkan also attempted recruitment of Greek nationals. Arkan circularized to Greek audiences: "in Bosnia, 10,000 Turks are fighting on the side of the Bosnian Muslims...we must bring about the union of all the orthodox peoples...It is not only Serbia that is threatened by Turkey but also Greece" (Antischolio, 1999, p. 198).

Critical Events Model

Nadler and Nadler (1989) explicated human resource development (HRD) as: "organized learning experiences provided by employers...within a specified period of time...to bring about the possibility of performance improvement and/or personal growth" (p. 6). The model was first pioneered in 1965, then named the *Process of Training*. The authors introduced a model they believed could cultivate the personal and professional growth of adult learners. The *critical events model* (CEM) is a model with which to primarily design training programs (Nadler, 1989), although Nabb and Armstrong (2005) remark that the model is "intended to facilitate HRD" (p. 30). As the model is intended for training use, it begins by looking at the issues the training is prescribed to remedy. Nabb and Armstrong describe the CEM as a sequential guideline for meeting the needs of program design, tailored or modified to meet the needs of the program's stakeholders. Nadler (1994), as noted by Nabb and Armstrong, discerned that "the program design process can move to another event as appropriate, repeat the current event, or return to the previous event as needed" (p. 38). The following sections will thoroughly explicate each of Nadler's eight critical events.

Evaluation and Feedback

Nadler (1994) stated: "job performance cannot be evaluated until the participant returns to the job and is asked to perform" (p. 220). Cookson (1998) argued that evaluation and feedback is not really an event, but rather an activity that needs to be incorporated into the end of each event prior to proceeding to a new event in the model. Evaluation can be two-fold in this event: summative and formative. Formative evaluation is continuous throughout the training or education program, whereas summative evaluation is for assessing learning post-training. However, Nadler (1994) claimed that summative evaluation "cannot at this stage predict actual performance" (as cited in Nabb & Armstrong, 2005, p. 38). Valid summative evaluation is determined when the learner is observed performing on the job. The researcher has yet to come across any source speaking to the summative evaluation of the SDG. Possibly, testimonies of those who endured or witnessed ethnic cleansing first-hand in its totality could serve as sources for summative evaluation. Summative feedback was derived from the dearth of commentary relaying SDG performance in the field, including the unimpeded demand by which Serb citizens wanted access to Erdut to join the notorious Serbian Volunteer Guard. The researcher found no objective evidence of SDG performance measurement. SDG training is perhaps one such domain that does not lend itself well to performance evaluation. Arkan avowed that the self-mastery of the SDG was "fifty times better than the regular army" (NIN, 1991, p. 12). Arkan, and indeed others, believed the Tigers had produced a higher output of disciplined leaders than the JNA. The SDG were trained to be unsurpassed in force and fitness, committing members to undergo daunting endurance development. Another source of summative evaluation is the commentary from former Tigers, who had entered Erdut with antecedent military experience, that elucidated on the program's level of difficulty. Stewart's (2007) interviews with former JNA then turned SDG who had such previous experience, characterized the SDG training regimen as "gruelling" to say the least (Stewart, 2007, p. 153).

Incontrovertible evidence of formative evaluation was procured through the many stories of Arkan's physical maiming of trainees. If they failed to meet his predefined performance standards amid participation in the training program: "disrespect of the rules of this stoic school of humanity can bring the old Serbian measure: 25 strokes on the buttocks, in front of the entire ranks" (Radović, 1995, p. 13). Some received fifty to one hundred lashes with a heavy electrical cord on both their legs and back.

Moreover, Arkan imposed a forced alcohol-cessation program. Trainees caught drinking were excoriated, as one Tiger remarked: "the offender was hoisted up a flagpole in the training yard, lashed upside down, and then forced to run off the buzz, a trek that could take place in the middle of a freezing winter night" (Spiric, Knezevic, Jovic, & Opacic, 2004, p. 155). Witness C-047 concurred with Spiric et al., (2004) that discipline in Arkan's centre was "maximum discipline, highly disciplined. No alcohol, you had to follow orders, hygiene, top-level hygiene" (Testimony of Witness C-047, 2003, June 4, p. 21717). If their insolence persisted they were permanently ostracized from the group.

Identify the Needs of the Organization
The need of Arkan's SDG was to ethnically cleanse Serbian Republics of non-Serb populations by intimidation, forced expulsion, or extirpation, to the avail of an Orthodox and Greater Serbia. Specific to Nadler's (1994) model, the first step to identifying the needs of the organization is to see whether agreement is reached on the identification of the problem, before training is identified as the proper response (Cookson, 1998; Nabb & Armstrong, 2005). Nabb

and Armstrong (2005) reiterated Nadler's suggestion that training is not to be pursued unless an organizational need exists, and only once that need is diagnosed, should a learning program then be created. The needs of the SDG arose from outside the organization. Milošević's needs were made the needs of the SDG. Through the HRD lens, utilizing the CEM to reorganize the historical record, my objective here is to determine the needs of the SDG and thus evidence training as a viable option for the Tigers to accomplish such needs. Cookson (1998) claimed that identifying the needs of the organization "is probably the most important event in the entire model" (p. 58). It became evident after rearranging the sources through the CEM lens that an agreement within Milošević's Serbia was reached as to what the problem was: the threat from Croats and Muslims on Serbian hegemony. Milošević avoided outright declaration of war on either Croatia or Bosnia and Herzegovina. Instead, he elicited the help of Serbian paramilitaries. Using the SDG and other paramilitaries, instead of committing the Army of the Republic of Serbia, provided Milošević with what Cigar and Williams (1997) noted: "An effective, instrument to…carry out some of the more odious acts in support of his broader strategic goals…the evacuation, disappearance, or neutralization of entire non-Serb communities as territorial control was established and expanded" (p. 25).

Stewart (2007) queried: "Was Arkan perpetrating genocide for Milošević? Was the intention of this man and his soldiers not only to move bodies out of the Serb-targeted villages and towns, but also to wipe out non-Serbs altogether" (p. 148)? The needs of the organization trickled from top to bottom, thus suggesting that the organizational needs were hierarchical. At the top was the puppeteer Milošević, controlling the movements of his two puppet governments of Karadžić and Hadžić. All in all, these three governments colluded with Arkan to institute the genocidal plan, thus bestowing the need for ethnic cleansing upon the SDG. Arkan required a well-trained contingent to oversee the ethnic cleansing of a newly-carved-out Serbia. Arkan ultimately served Milošević and the Republic of Serbia. In defending the Republika Srpska during the Bosnian conflict, Arkan served President Karadžić; in the Croatian War he served President Hadžić of the Serbian Republic of Krajina. That being said, substantial evidence links Presidents Hadžić and Karadžić with the Tigers' genocidal activities. The needs of Hadžić and Karadžić were parallel: to employ and legitimize paramilitary agents to cleanse undesirables from their newly sequestered nations. Arkan's Tigers were invariably their first choice for most cleansing campaigns.

Marshall Harris, U.S State Department's desk officer in Bosnia, informed CNN: "It was clear that Milošević and the people around him were keenly determined to carve out a greater Serbia, the way they were going to do that was to purge that territory of non-Serbs" (CNN, 1997, p. 3).

Ristic (2005) asserted that Hadžić entered into a joint criminal enterprise with Arkan "to ethnically clean Serb-run parts of Croatia [of]...non-Serbs" (para. 4). Hadžić mandated the Army of RSK and ancillary paramilitaries, namely the SDG, to instigate ethnic cleansing in Croatia to safeguard Serbian dominance of the area (U.S Department of State, 1994). The following charge was lodged against Hadžić (2004) during his ICC trial: "[he] established a regime of persecution designed to drive Croat[s] and other non-Serb civilian populations from these territories" (para. 16, i), otherwise assisted by the SDG to precipitate an exodus of tens of thousands declared *personae non gratae* from villages and towns.

At the same time, the Serbian Volunteer Guard was of great benefit to Karadžić in the creation of a "viable Republika Srpska as the first step toward a Greater Serbia" (Baumann, Gawrych, & Kretchik, 1993, p. 25). The Bosnian-Serb parliament drafted the *Six Strategic Goals of Serbian People in Bosnia and Herzegovina* on May 12, 1992. The premise of the document called for the segregation of non-Serb populations in Bosnia. Commander Mladić of the VRS acquiesced: "Further strategic goals...ensur[ed]...the valley of river Drina, next to the border with Serbia [was to be] ethnically 'clean', establishing borders along the rivers Una and Neretva by force and carrying out ethnic cleansing and division of Sarajevo" (Mackic, 2012, p. 22). While Mladić was in attendance he discussed with the assembly the ramifications of the proposed plan: "Do you think you can just move people like that, as if they were a set of keys? What you are asking me to do, gentlemen, is called genocide" (Hodzic, 2012, para. 3). Hodzic (2012) contends this was not said to warn the leaders of the plan's illegalities, but rather to ensure that assenting and non-assenting members in attendance were of the same opinion. As a consequence of the decision arrived at on May 12, the Bosnian-Serb opposition, in concert with the volunteer guard, began to cleanse the territory "they controlled of Muslims...the Tigers played a major role in the ethnic cleansing" (Alverez, 2009, pp. 81-82).

There is a paucity of evidence linking Milošević with SDG campaigns of ethnic cleansing. Patently at this point in time, the researcher cannot connect Milošević with the actions of the SDG.

However, one source confirmed that Milošević's defence minister authorized paramilitary training and funded their equipment and salaries (Cigar & Williams, 1997). Some have maintained that Arkan received orders from Milošević by way of an intermediary, likely a member of the Serbian Secret Police. The researcher was able to identify one direct order from Milošević implicating him in the development of a paramilitary distinct from SDG. Vojislav Šešelj, a notable fugleman from the White Eagles, testified before the International Criminal Court (ICC) that he received direct deployment orders from Milošević to assist Bosnian-Serbs and other Serbian forces. Milošević provided a barracks in Bubanj Potok so that Šešelj could train his volunteers there (Kandic, 1995). While Milošević's need was to dispel and execute non-Serb populations behind the progression of advancing RSK or Republika Srpska armies, he put to work the Serbian Volunteer Guard to cleanse all that the army left in its wake.

Specify Job Performance
The job performed by the Serbian Volunteer Guard was ethnic cleansing. Nadler (1982) defined a job as "the work done by anybody in the organization from the lowest to the highest level" (p. 49). Nabb and Armstrong (2005) advanced that training will be conceived for a job to meet the needs of the organization. Once the performance problem has been identified it is necessary to then ascertain how the job is to be performed (Cookson, 1998). Nadler (1994) recommended that at least one mode of job analysis is undertaken to deduct job performance: (1) task analysis based on observation; (2) analysis based on task simulation; and (3) analysis based on interviews. Testimonies of former SDG, JNA, and SRK officers were helpful in specifying job performance. For the purpose of specifying job performance the following questions beg to be answered: How was ethnic cleansing performed? What were the tasks the Serbian Volunteer Guard trained on? Can it be clear the contribution this job made to the organization(s)? Who was the SDG to cleanse? How did they identify and distinguish these targets from non-target populations?

Since the job is ethnic cleansing, relating SDG activities to the definition of ethnic cleansing should help specify job performance. Bell-Fialkoff (1996) postulated a narrow definition of ethnic cleansing: "population cleansing is a planned, deliberate removal from a certain territory of an undesirable population distinguished by one or more characteristics such as ethnicity, religion, race, class, or sexual preference" (p. 9). Cigar and Williams (1997) have described the SDG role in laconic terms as "limited and episodic"; in short, their function was mainly confined to ethnic cleansing, as "genocide and plunder...have been at the heart of their mission and, in many respects, their *raison d'être*" (pp. 12-13).

The SDG played an indispensable role executing ethnic cleansing in Croatia and Bosnia. However, their genocidal campaigns began in 1991 prior to the outbreak of hostilities in Croatia. They were the principal malefactors of cleansing in Voyvodina; a practice effort to precipitate a small-scale exodus of non-Serbs from the region. Arkan's men, notably one undisclosed lieutenant, harassed Croats on the telephone, instructing them to leave. He remarked that grenades "would drop out of my hands...fall into some Croatian houses". Proud that: "thus [he] forced them out...[The town of] Slamkamen was thus cleansed very quickly" (Cigar & Williams, 1997, p. 193). The SDG were tasked with invoking mass disappearances of non-Serb communities from the new territorial land grabs of forenamed Presidents Hadžić and Karadžić (Cigar & Williams, 1997). Stewart (2007) proffered an insightful description of what Arkan's Tigers performed. To begin, the author articulates clearly that the Tigers "had a methodology to [their] killing and cleansing" (p. 146):

> The process started with relentless shelling from tanks, from airplanes, from sniper roosts; then the Tigers (with JNA and other paramilitary imitators as support) announced themselves; fighting-age men in the town fled through cornfields, through streambeds, and hid in the trunks of cars; those caught were killed; women, children, and the elderly were pushed out of town or sent to camps; sometimes civilians were raped or beaten or shot; religious artifacts and other traces of ethnic groups were burned, defaced, or erased; soon the stealing began; trucks and vans and buses arrived to cart off the booty; which was sold in Belgrade and abroad (Stewart, 2007, pp. 146-7).

Stewart (2007) claimed that foremost targets needed to be identified. The Tigers had to ascertain who were Croats or Bosnians and/or in which communities to concentrate the brunt of their efforts. The author held that state security officials visited regularly with instructions detailing which towns to be sacked. In the town of Tenja: "they took over rapidly and hurried door to door, looking for weapons, asking about ethnicity. Are you Serb? Ustache? Croats who remained were evicted. Men, women, children it didn't matter" (p. 142). Tigers targeted affluent and educated Muslim community members with influence. Muslim homeowner doors were smashed in with hooligan strength, men and women furiously dragged out from their homes onto the street, stripped, severely beaten, and shot. Authors Cigar and Williams (1997) maintain "a Serbian patriot [was] merciless towards the enemy; he does not have the right to spare their children, women, or the aged…" (para. 4).

Dehumanization of the enemy intended for extermination served as a necessity for ethnic cleansing. A requisite aspect of their performance was for the participant to perceive the target as sub-human (Stewart, 2007). Vostrukhov (1992) enumerated the testimony of a Russian mercenary recruited into the SDG. He spoke of his training at Erdut prior to deployment: "the philosophy of brutality [was] drummed into the heads of the fighters" (p. 3). Arkan's men acted in true brutal fashion. For example, in the town of Bratunac, the Tigers performed torture on Muslim males specifically:

> Beating with iron rods and wooden poles. Some prisoners were taken to an "investigation room" where they were forced to trample over their fellow inmates' dead bodies. Mutilation also occurred; ears, noses and genitals were cut off, and the sign of the cross was cut into prisoners' flesh (Cigar & Williams, 1997, p. 146).

Identify the Needs of the Learner

The focus of the identifying the needs of the learner event is on the individual(s) performing ethnic cleansing. The volunteer guard were "instructed on strategies of ethnic cleaning" (Stewart, 2007, p. 152). Cookson (1998) contended that when training and development is deemed appropriate in the specified job performance event, determining the needs of the learner should intently follow. The purpose of the training program as noted by Nadler (1994) "is to bridge the differences between the person and the job, so that individuals can perform in a way that meets the organizational goals" (p. 88). Cookson (1998) posited that the following formula can be exercised to deduce learner needs:

Job performance – Already knows = Need to learn.

The essential information is predicated on who is performing the job, what they already bring to the role, and what they need to know in order to function within the role appropriately. When revisiting the historical record as it pertains to Arkan's Tigers and training, two notable learner groups should be considered: street thugs and convicts, and former JNA members.

Arkan's core group of recruits were young, reprobate, undisciplined street thugs. The learner group identified as *convict* or *street thug* lacked two specific needs: discipline and military acumen. His criminals were hamstrung by a deficit in military skills and discipline. Arkan at first acknowledged that his newcomers were devoid of discipline; therefore, discipline was identified as a learning need. Arkan "insist[ed] on discipline" (Foer, 2011, p. 21), to this end, any recruit who disobeyed or lacked discipline received fifty to hundred lashes on their legs and back. The imbibing days of youth were forced to an end; those caught were humiliated and beaten. Arkan commented: "You know our fans, they are noisy, [and] they like to drink, to joke about...I stopped all that in one go, I made them cut their hair, shave regularly, not drink – and so it began the way it should be" (Foer, 2011, p. 21).

Arkan impressed martial abilities, discipline, and combat tactics upon his SDG "as his first step in transforming these soccer fans into a military style organization" (Alverez, 2009, p. 81). Some were already imbued "with the manner of skilled fighters" (Stewart, p. 154). Hand-in-glove with cultivating discipline, recruits were inveterately instructed in military tactics organized around obeying military command. Arkan expressed the importance of keeping calm under the throes of warfare: "you have to keep your head cool boys...otherwise, you're going to get yourself killed" (Stewart, 2007, p. 156). The Australian Government Refugee Review Tribunal (2010) found that "recruits were trained in weapons handling and techniques, setting and dissembling mines and explosives, first aids and survival skills" (p. 4). Some entrants in Erdut needed to learn how to swim. Mandic, then employed by the Krajina Ministry of Defence, "worked in a compound fifty yards from [Erdut] during the day she witnessed soldiers training in the Danube. Some of them didn't even look like they could swim their dark heads bobbing up and down, disappearing in a fast-moving current" (Stewart, 2007, p. 155). Undergoing military training impelled trainees to reject their civilian identity, which to Arkan emphasized individuality, and replace it with a submissive military identity.

JNA soldiers were moved by the morale that the Tigers exhibited. After the dissolution of the JNA membership in 1992, erstwhile soldiers, identified herein as the second learner group, transferred to the Serbian Volunteer Guard. For JNA transferees some

Serbian Volunteer Guard and the Critical Events Model 43

aspects of the role were likely already in their repertoire of skills, such as: organizing people for mobilization, sorting items, military manoeuvring, handling of arms, and working with explosives. The remaining characteristics of the job, such as the dehumanization of the enemy, needed to be inculcated. They had received no dehumanization education whilst in the ranks of the JNA. Nabb and Armstrong (2005) hold: "Embodied in dehumanization is the idea of morally justified eradication of the subject" (pp. 47-8). I found a source that spoke of a meagre effort by a member of the JNA high command attempting to dehumanize the enemy to Serb citizens. According to McDonald and Swaak-Goldman (2000), Colonel Vukelić characterized Muslims as enemies and cautioned Serbs residing in Bosnia and Herzegovina that they were in need of prompt protection. Furthermore, Vukelić cautioned "Serb members of the JNA to join the struggle to save the Serbs from genocide" (p. 1006). Vukelić's proclamations likely influenced some JNA enrolment in the SDG and the armies of Serbian Krajina and SRK. Before the JNA dissolved, state enemies were forwarded to Arkan's Tigers for liquidation by then-active JNA soldiers. Although cooperation was known to have been fostered between the JNA and the SDG, I accept that the JNA did not serve the purpose of ethnic cleansing as it was not included in their military training. As evinced in the findings of the Australian Refugee Review Tribunal (2010) Erdut's training grounds were "sites of indoctrination for new members, Serb recruits were taught in fighting the enemy, they had no right to spare children, women or the aged" (p. 4). JNA were unaccustomed to this kind of killing. Stewart (2007) claimed, "even [former JNA]…who had gone through military training before described the daily sessions as grueling" and "unlike anything [they've] ever seen or done or heard of" (p. 153). Arkan anticipated that a few recruits, namely JNA, were inexperienced in ethnically motivated murder. Therefore, Stewart (2007) remarked that "Arkan shipped in specialists to discuss the psychology of death, because there were lots of dead people where they were headed" (p. 152).

Nabb and Armstrong (2005) refer to "evidence of similar needs assessment can be seen in the selection of the learner" (p. 47). Arkan enrolled convicted violent offenders competent in violence and intimidation. Stewart noted that many of Arkan's commanding officers were erstwhile underworld partners of his; one being "a convicted murderer", another "a hired assassin" (p. 154). In a similar vein, Mann (2005) attested that Arkan's ranks were replete with criminals released from prison with the express purpose to kill. In recognition of this fact, Arkan's convict recruits were more thoroughly inculcated in the dehumanization of Bosnian-Muslims and Croatian-Catholics than JNA inductees, and more likely to have the moral imperative to remove non-Serbs from Serbian soil than anyone else.

A historiographical trend toward exposing Serbs to a hate-fuelled ideology made it possible for SDG learners to perform their task with reduced capacity for compunction, with apt decisiveness, and without reservation. Media predating the first Yugoslavian war disseminated both anti-Muslim and anti-Catholic messages. A highly charged atmosphere of fear and hatred of the enemy was already fomented in Serbian communities long before the war. In the beginning, Arkan's hooligan recruitment pool received the public prescription of anti-Muslim and anti-Catholic propaganda before acceptance into the SDG. Nearby, Serbian media in SAO Krajina and SRK personified Muslims and Turks as evil land grabbers, as previously experienced in past times. The trend toward ideological insemination continued well into the curriculum designed for training the SDG.

Determine Objectives
The next event to determine in Nadler's (1994) critical events model is the program's learning objectives. The researcher has located no record of any learning objectives in existence. Witness B-129 (2003, April 17) spoke of Erdut's headquarters: "whatever was being done during the day would be destroyed in the evening...papers and documents relating to day-to-day obligations, either of the staff or members of the Serbian Volunteer Guard, after the work was done, would be destroyed" (p. 19058). In recognition of this absence of evidence, general objectives may be inferred from the personal accounts of Tigers, or those who witnessed or participated administratively in Tigers' training.

Cookson (1998) described an objective as a statement "of what is to be accomplished by the training program" (p. 62). The objectives of SDG training can be determined hypothetically from the previous CEM event. Nabb and Armstrong (2005) hold: "learners' needs identified in the previous event must be converted to learning objectives" (p. 35). Objectives can be either general program objectives or specific learner objectives (Nadler, 1989). Cookson (1998) opined urgency as a limitation e.g., "how soon must the training be completed?" (p. 62). From the personal accounts of the SDG we can deduce the length of training and connect it to the 'urgency' with which trainees were trained prior to deployment.

Nadler and Nadler (1989) maintain: "It is necessary to specify the duration of a...HRD program,...Whatever the length, it should be clearly specified so there is no confusion as to when it will start and when it is scheduled to end" (p. 13). Borislav Pelević, instructor of the SDG reminisced: "[training] lasted for three months only after they had been trained for three months was it possible for a volunteer to join the combat group and to participate in operations" (Stanišić & Simatović, 2012, January 14, p. 16334). Pelević himself underwent training for approximately three months, having been recruited in February 1992 by Arkan and sent to Erdut for training until late April of the same year (Ristic, 2012). Pelević remarked that after completing training he was sent to Bijelinja in North-Eastern Bosnia and Herzegovina, where the first documented ethnic cleansing campaign in Bosnia came to fruition.

In Erdut's genesis and period of growth, members of the Special Anti-Terrorist Unit (SAJ) were the Volunteer Guard's first instructors (Stanišić & Simatović, 2013). The SAJ nurtured the foundation of Erdut's educational enterprise. Gagic was amongst a throng of "50-60 men" selected by the SAJ to become Erdut's new trainers. He noted that his training lasted between two and two-and-a-half months before himself and others trained by the SAJ took over the training of the SDG (Stanišić & Simatović, 2013). This is useful for evidencing the urgency of SDG training, because in the beginning, the SAJ trained them for 60-75 days (the equivalent of between two and two-and-a-half months), likely in preparation for combat participation in Slovenia and Croatia. Meanwhile, Pelević commented that 90 days, the equivalent of three months of training, was a requirement for new entrants from April 1992 onward, before deployment to Bosnia. This leads the researcher to ask a further few vexing questions: Was Arkan of the opinion that a better trained and disciplined force was needed for the Bosnian conflict? Did Arkan evaluate the performance of the first SDG group operating in the Slovenian and Croatian conflicts and decide that additional training was necessary for raw recruits to perform optimally in Bosnia? The experiential evidence extracted from the testimony of witness C-047 helps with addressing the first question. The witness underwent two months of training at Erdut, although there is no mention in his testimony of the year. He did note that he participated in the intimidation of Osijek, a town in Croatia known to have endured SDG attacks from August 1991 through to June 1992. If my provisional assumption about the 'urgency' of training is correct, his testimony confirmed that training lasted two months between mid-1991 until early-1992, but as the war deepened training increased to three months before the deployment of the SDG into Bosnian townships.

According to Saks and Haccoun: (2008) "objectives also describe the knowledge and skills to be acquired" (p. 123). Cookson (1998) maintained that "there are many ways to state learning objectives ranging from the specific behavioral to the general philosophical" (p. 63). This event lacks any distinguishable formula for what training objectives should constitute and, most importantly, how to deduct learning objectives from historical curricula. To determine the learning objectives of the SDG, Saks and Haccoun's (2008) formula will suffice. The authors advance:

> Who is to perform the desired behavior? What is the actual behavior to be employed to demonstrate mastery of the training content…? Where and when is the behavior to be demonstrated and evaluated; and what is the standard by which the behavior will be judged (p. 125).

What knowledge, skills, and behaviours did the SDG acquire in their two-to-three months of training? At this stage, the training objectives of the SDG should resemble the needs identified in the previous event. Within that two-to-three months training window, the SDG embraced discipline, carried out orders effectively within a training environment that captured the realness of war-induced anxieties, and abided by military ethos, order, and structure. Secondly, the SDG learned to distinguish Croatian-Catholics and Bosnian-Muslims from Orthodox Serbians. With the assistance of TO and MUP forces, they learned ethnic, culture, and religious identifiers which set each group apart from one another. Thirdly, they developed an emotional detachment from the abuse inflicted on enemy groups and non-cooperating parties. When all previous objectives converged in the performance of ethnic cleansing, including the wanton destruction of cultural and religious symbols and artifacts, they would "sequester and exterminate target groups through the mass execution process" (Nabb & Armstrong, 2005, p. 36). To reiterate, the primary learning objective of the Erdut program, within a 60-90 day interval, was to induce recruits to commit murder, ultimately toward the goal of cleansing lands acquired in the name of an ethnically homogenous Greater Serbia.

Build Curriculum

What Nadler (1982) means by 'curriculum' in this event is the prescription of a lesson plan detailing the knowledge intended to be imparted. Cookson (1998) opined: "As used in the CEM, curriculum is defined as the material that has to be learned and the sequence of that learning" (p. 64). The plan, as Nadler (1982) understood, should be devised to address the determined objectives outlined in the previous event. The core activity in this event is the selecting of content organized by a subject matter specialist (SMS) (Cookson, 1998). A reorganization of the historical record through a CEM lens will show reliably that Arkan required assistance in obtaining a desirable educational model.

Subject Matter Specialists (SMS)

At this stage, the program designer will likely need the assistance of a subject matter specialist (Cookson, 1998). External SMS are brought in to aid content development and to structure the curriculum, in order to achieve the aforementioned learning objectives. Nadler and Nadler (1989) hold: "it is improbable that an organization can provide internally for all the HRD resources that are needed" (p. 45).

Captain Dragan Vasiljković was recruited originally from Australia by Franko "Frenki" Simatović, then head of the Serbian secret police under the authority of Milošević. Dragan had spent six years in the Australian Army reserve unit, 4th/19th Prince of Wales's Light Horse. After serving, Dragan contracted his time as a weapons instructor between Africa and South America. In 1991, Simatović asked Dragan to complete a training manual for the armed forces of Krajina. Dragan testified that Frenki contacted him to prepare a training course: "they asked me if I could write it down. Of course, I did, I wrote it down, a short 21-day course, roughly speaking" (Stanišić & Simatović, 2011, December 14, p. 15721). Simatović asked Dragan: "whether [he] could put [training advice] down on paper and prepare some kind of a manual for training" (Testimony of Dragan, 2003, February 19, p. 16480). He confided in Dragan that he was overseeing the development of a new army in Krajina and a set of manuals would be beneficial to him (Stanišić & Simatovic, 2011, December 14). Dragan channelled his years of military experience into the creation of said training manual. Simatović spoke of the disorganization and lack of discipline evinced by Krajina's armed forces. Dragan's continued testimony to the ICTY noted: "My plan was to form a training camp where anyone issued with any kind of weapon should go through" (Testimony of Dragan, 2003, February

19, p. 16474). He believed that all men circulating through such a camp should be "processed administratively and then be trained professionally" (Dragan, 2003, p. 16474). As a result of undergoing professional training, Dragan stated, they then would be placed under formal military command, with the pay-off being trained formations. As the curriculum designer he sought subject matter specialists to assist in the preparation of a new manual for Simatović and identical manuals for Serbian paramilitary use. From his network Dragan contacted Martin Lynch, an English soldier, requesting copies of training manuals used for developing British infantry: "he needed a military manual for basic infantry training" (Stanišić & Simatović, 2011, December 14, p. 15722). The above rudimentary discussion about Dragan is useful, because he was instrumental in the cultivation of the SDG in camp Erdut (Anonymous, 2004, January 14; Robinson, 2010; Testimony of Witness Nenad Zafirovic, 2004; Partos, 2003; Svarm, N.D). Furthermore, Dragan established his own training centre within Erdut, likely complementing the training program of the SDG in some regard, as will be ruminated later. Perhaps, it was Dragan's involvement in Erdut that was responsible for the extra one month training added to the SDG curriculum in 1992.

In 1991, the SAJ were Erdut's first educators of the Serbian Volunteer Guard. They initially trained 50 - 60 men. The most talented members of the Guard "were later appointed as instructors" (Stanišić & Simatovic, 2013, para. 524). Beginning with SAJ involvement, a new group of instructors were arranged by Arkan to take over the supervision of training activities, including former JNA Colonel Puki, martial arts expert Pelević, and French Legionnaire Milorad Ulemek. The instructors who trained Arkan's SDG will be discussed in greater depth in the CEM event 'Instructional Resources'.

Curriculum Content

Nadler (1994) advanced three ways to view curriculum content in the critical events model: essential, helpful, and peripheral. The 'essential' is: "the absolute minimum that must be learned for the learner to reach the projected objectives" (Cookson, 1998, p. 65). To the SDG, the 'essential' involved invoking dehumanizing scenarios through a curriculum designed to instill hatred toward state enemies, with the intent to induce learners to actively ethnically cleanse. However, such 'essential' learning would not be possible if discipline and military prowess were not also embraced by trainees; described as 'helpful' content believed to "supplement the essential" (Cookson, 1998, p. 65).

It is in the opinion of this researcher that the curriculum was not circumscribed, thus allowing for ongoing modifications and improvements of content whenever Arkan saw fit.

Learners were instructed on how to subdue the enemy during armed-resistance exercises, as armed conflict was bound to be encountered in new villages, townships, or cities that the SDG entered. The blueprint for military training consisted of: A tedious arrangement of physical training and martial arts instruction; hand-to-hand and knife-to-knife combat; handling an array of military equipment and use of fire-arms; installing and dismantling land-mines; first-aid education to provide elementary medical assistance to wounded volunteers and liberated Serbian civilians. The Serbian Volunteer Guard learned to survive the most seemingly insuperable environments, including unfamiliar Croatian and Bosnian landscapes and terrain. The learning objectives of the Arkan's Tigers' training reflect the exigencies of the 'essential' content. The researcher insists that the physical aspects of training constituted the 'helpful' content.

'Peripheral' content falls under a good-to-know category, but is still construed as being necessary for accomplishing the learning objectives. I surmise that the 'peripheral' content of the SDG curriculum was dichotomously religious and nationalistic. 'Peripheral' content complemented the essential and helpful. An apposite example of religious ideology as 'peripheral' content would be the SDG's required signing of affidavits paying reverence to the Orthodox Church. Moreover, SDG training curricula were sacrilegiously virulent, referring to Muslims as wild, savage dogs: "[we are up] against the wild dogs" (Stewart, 2007, p. 173). Arkan's speeches exacerbated fears of an impending Croatian and Muslim genocide of all Orthodox Serbs. Under an Orthodox banner, with the Serbian national anthem playing overhead, Arkan announced to an assemblage of recruits: "the time of the 21st century inquisition has come: they want to kill us and convert us" (Sense Tribunal, 2012, May 11, para. 3). The mere mention of the inquisition lent historical resonance to his ideological banter. Arkan worked diligently to foster an 'us against them' attitude, thereby enhancing 'essential' content.

Arkan introduced a political ideological component early on during SDG training, also indicative of 'peripheral' curriculum content. Before the inception of war in 1991, Arkan's Delije chanted pro-Serbian nationalist tunes while practising street-fighting tactics. Lyrics were couched in official nationalist language and ideas of "fighting for a United Serbian State" (Herbert, 2003, p. 248). Trainees were instructed to dissever themselves from political parties, "because they would be working for the state...their primary loyalty should be to the state" (Testimony of Milan Babic, 2006, February 17, p. 1542).

Sequencing

Once training content has been decided, the program designer must consider the sequence of learning events that need to take effect (Cookson, 1998). It appears as if the sequence of the SDG curriculum went from general to specific; that general knowledge was inculcated first, and then application practice closely followed. The researcher believes that after the Tigers trained in Erdut, they went to desolate small-town streets and surrounding forests to practice. The trainees woke at 5:30 am and by 6:00 am their beds were made; themselves dressed to standard in their green and black uniforms. Arkan then gave his soldiers a studious inspection. By 6:30, physical training commenced, draped in full combat equipment, under orders to run up and down village streets. Being situated close to the Danube, trainees swam for hours, wading neck-high through the river. Stewart (2007) posited "training went on around the clock" (p. 124). In the nearby village of Erdut onlookers observed the 101st Training Centre curriculum as dangersome. Men sparred with bare-knuckles and blunt objects, crawled through serpentine obstacle courses on their stomachs, dashed through tire trails, went on arduous marches, all the while vehemently vocalizing songs of the Serbian Volunteer Guard.

Social learning theory and conditioning

The curriculum "will reflect the learning theories the designer(s) may hold" (Nabb & Armstrong, 2005, p. 36). Nadler (1994) maintains a theory is a "way of explaining something that is essentially abstract, but for which a plausible explanation can be built so it can be used" (p. 126). The authors contend that a curriculum can be fashioned around an individual theory rather than a patchwork of many learning theories. Nadler's (1994) work revisits Malcolm Knowles' (1984) 'organismic and mechanistic' theories of learning. Organismic learning theory is the idea of a learning environment possessing the ability to adapt and change much like a living entity. Mechanistic learning theories "apply the stimulus-response" where learning is synonymously viewed as conditioning (Nabb & Armstrong, 2005, pp. 36-7). "There are many learning theories that can be utilized by the designer" as noted by Cookson (1998, p. 34). However, one learning theory utilized by the SDG becomes readily apparent through the CEM lens: Bandura's social learning theory.

Social learning theory, also known as observational learning, can be inferred through the use of one of three models: live model (demonstrates desired behaviour), verbal instruction (describes desired behaviour), and symbolic or cultural artifacts elucidating desired behaviour (Sims & Manz, 1982). Behaviour modelling is an on-the-job training method where trainees can learn behavioural skills by observation of a model, followed by knowledge sharing if the situation calls for it. The social learning theory attests that individuals learn to engage in conflict or violent behaviours by imitating a model depicting a violent act (Bolden Jr., 2008). Demonstrations of violence amid the SDG's training regimen were two-fold: physical punishment of trainees for behavioural infractions and the forced viewing and partial participation in the torture or execution of captured enemies. The former involved Arkan doling out heavy punishment to trainees found guilty of dereliction of duty caught drunk while on guard duty, or violating any of his resolute rules. Arkan had men tied to a flagpole, stripped and beaten with a baton. He nourished a culture of pain and violence grounded in discipline and animosity for the enemy.

Grossman (1995) poignantly described: "Every aspect of killing on the battlefield is rehearsed, visualized, and conditioned. On special occasions even more realistic and complex targets are used...these make the training more interesting, the conditioned stimuli more realistic" (p. 39). Erdut was unceasingly supplied with Croat and Bosniak POW torture dummies for trainees to practice torture skills (Spiric et al., 2006). The JNA handed captives over to the SDG to be executed or spared for later use for torture (Stewart, 2007). Trainees beat prisoners with iron rods and wooden poles. Tigers exhausted mutilation techniques; removing ears, genitals, and noses. Cigar and Williams (2007) posited: "such behavior was considered accepted practice in preparation for harsh policies as part of the training that Arkan's paramilitary agents received" (para. 20). Sells (1998) maintained:

> The final dehumanization of the perpetrator occurred in ritualized fashion, when young soldiers were forced to watch torture, gang rape, and killings and forced to participate...To participate was to learn to believe that the victims were not truly human anyway (p. 75).

Conditioning was gainfully utilized by SDG instructors to help troops overcome any natural opposition to killing (Encyclopedia of Violence, Peace, and Conflict, 2008). Trainees were prohibited communication with loved-ones in order to stamp out leftover visages of their past believed to be antithetical to the dehumanizing content of their training. Arkan spared no expense in this effort. Nabb and Armstrong (2005) noted "if this dehumanization [did] not occur, killing [was] much less likely to take place" (p. 46). Smeulers and Grunfeld (2011) argue that if delinquent men can be socialized to commit crimes, it might analogously be possible that men can be socialized to perpetrate grandiose acts of crimes against humanity.

Select Instructional Strategies
Cookson (1998) notes that strategies are to include all "methods, techniques, and devices available to facilitate the learning process" (p. 67). During this event the services of an instructional design specialist may be called in. Instructional strategies are responsible for instituting the program. Any number or combination of instructional approaches can be used with any program (Nadler, 1994). Instructional strategies cover a wide spectrum of methods or techniques to aid assisted learning (Nabb & Armstrong, 2005). The researcher found that the following instructional strategies were exercised in the instruction of Arkan's Tigers: Direct instruction (teacher-instructed strategies including lecture, drill, and practice), interactive instruction (role plays/peer-partner), and experiential learning (activity-oriented strategies including simulations and conducting experiments). Much of SDG training went beyond typical cognitive modes of learning.

Direct instruction
Drills and Practice
Iordanova (2001) opined: "In contrast to the regular state army, Arkan's Tigers had…their drills so rigorous that videos of their training sessions have been offered for sale in the martial arts category" in Serbian outlets that rent VHS tapes (p. 181). The researcher viewed two Serbian Volunteer Guard training videos, sourced from Youtube. In one video, the opening scene records the SDG arrayed in battle formation, as Arkan sauntered up and down the line studiously inspecting his group. The following scenes produced images of SDG carrying out drills and practice. Two groups formed. One group laid flat on their backs, stomachs exposed, covering their genitals with clasped hands. The other group trampled over the chests and abdominal sections of those lying down (LudiSrbijanac, 2008). Trainees were seen somersaulting on Erdut's soccer field in threes, rolling upward into a fighting stance. Upon exhibiting readiness to

fight, trainees somersaulted backward, typically in twos, and ran back into a line of formation. In groups of twenty, trainees dropped onto their bellies in unison, hugging the ground, using their bellies and hands to push forward (Otuzniak, 2009). Tigers crawled laboriously over rough terrain, rifles in hand, under barbed wire supported by two-foot high wooden posts. They dove through elevated tire holes, landing in a roll forward shooting them up to their feet again (Otuzniak, 2009). Trainees concluded the obstacle course by jumping from an eight-foot high concaved ladder. Cookson (1998) would likely suggest in this event the learning styles of the SDG be taken into consideration. The author states, "different learners have different learning styles, and are comfortable with some strategies, and antagonistic towards others" (p. 68). When considering the learning style of the bulk of enrollees (previously noted as high-school dropouts, street-thugs, and prison inmates), kinesthetic learning, alternatively known as tactile learning, should be considered here as their learning style (Druian & Butler, 2001). Druian and Butler (2001) hold that most high-school dropouts are kinesthetic learners. The National Dropout Prevention Network (N. D) recorded, "80% of [presumably American] prison inmates are high school dropouts" (para. 11). The kinesthetic learning theory argues that learning transpires when a student engages in physical activity, rather than attending lectures or watching demonstrations.

Behaviour Modelling
Trainees observed the instructor's use of rope. The instructor modelled how to approach the enemy from behind, rope in hand, slowly contort the rope around the neck, and pull the target to the ground. The instructor drove one knee into the neck of the enemy, pinning him, while simultaneously strangling the subdued victim. In one other modelled activity, trainees observed an instructor held at gunpoint by a participant. The instructor demonstrated how to remove the pistol from the enemy's hand, lock his arm with a submission hold, and force him to the ground (Otuzniak, 2009).

Interactive instruction
Peer-partner/Role playing
SDG practised various kicks during martial arts training. Instructed to kick at the height of a peer partner's head first with their left foot and follow through with an ensuing lower body kick from their right foot. Kicking exercises spanned across the length of Erdut's soccer field (Otuzniak, 2009; LudiSrbijanac, 2008). In small groups, Tigers

(trainee group one) crawled undetected in a stealth-manner to a designated point in a field or forest where an unsuspecting group of peers (trainee group two) awaited. To simulate sneaking up on the enemy, the exercise required those in practice to pounce on a trainee in group two from behind. Trainee group one, when broaching the target closely jolted to his feet, forced trainee group two from behind to the ground. A light punch to the jugular ensued. In a similar exercise, a peer approached his partner from behind, grabbed his ankles and pulled his legs out from under him. A quick kick to the genitals followed, accompanied by a punch to the back of the neck.

Experiential learning

Simulations

Erdut's firing range supplied trainees with first-person shooting experience. Firing ranges were supplanted with diverse obstacles. In the video-taped simulation observed by this researcher, three metallic barrels narrowly filled the gap between the trainee and the paper target on the opposite end of the range. The shooter darted from barrel to barrel shooting at the target, finally when no barrels were left to take cover behind, trainees ran quickly to the target, delivering a final shot to the head.

War-time simulations occurred on two fabricated landscapes: the forest and the city streets. In the forested landscape, trainees manoeuvred in-and-out from behind trees, adorned in full equipment, accoutered with an assault rifle and ammunition. The SDG were instructed to push forward into enemy territory unnoticed. As live mortar fire encircled them, Tigers sprinted across vast fields, no cover provided. The fields were soggy and densely-riddled with mud and rocks. In the urban landscape, presumably a derelict part of Erdut, the streets destitute of citizens served experiential learning well. The streets resembled a perceivably emptied town harbouring snipers. Trainees took cover behind burnt cars, dashing down the streets, avoiding rapacious gun fire aimed in their general direction. In other simulations, trainees were led by a sergeant down a narrow street, one-by-one, dust escaping from under their black boots, providing them a faint gossamer of cover. Trainees ran closely crouched to the ground (Otuzniak, 2009; LudiSrbijanac, 2008).

Rehearsal/Experimentation

Torture education required trainees to be both subject to and subjugator of torture. This education inculcated Tigers in torture techniques to convert them into "docile fighters to be sent to combat"

(Spiric et al., 2004, p. 155). To become as "merciless towards the enemy" as Serbian patriots should be, as noted by (Vostrukhov, 1992, p. 3), Arkan organized torture sessions for neophytes to rehearse and experiment in unreserved brutality. The dehumanization of the enemy, an anxiety-provoking condition of learning was integral to SDG's education. Erdut torture training, like an efficacious drug administered for brutality, was the cure necessary for continued life in the Serbian Volunteer Guard. This education was contrived to abrogate any preexisting despondency to entering war. Matriculation in discipline and torture often lasted a month, at minimum a week. An estimated 5,000 Tigers experimented in cruelty; the precursor for exacting unmitigated violence in the field. As a result of this education, SDG members felt morally justified in their actions. Nabb and Armstrong (2005) posited: "in order for people to be effective killers of other people they must see their targets as something other than human" (p. 46).

Obtain Instructional Resources
The obstacle to this event is to ensure there are proper instructional resources for program implementation. Cookson (1998) maintains that the physical resources necessary to introduce a new program should give due consideration to the "equipment, materials, and facilities needed based on the program" (p. 70). Equipment comprised of items anticipated to be used recurrently (Cookson, 1998). Material items are foreseen to expend during the conduct of training. Facilities depend on various factors. Learning facilities may strategically be located "off ranch" away from the work environment, while others may embrace closer proximity to the workplace. Training interventions can at times operate at probable high expense. Programs can be costly, so the procurement of adequate financing should be considered (Cookson, 1998). Nabb and Armstrong (2005) state: "equipment and materials are acquired, financing is secured, the people necessary to implement the training…are gathered and all is coordinated for enactment" (p. 37). Through the CEM lens, facilities, equipment and materials, instructors, and other assets in Arkan's employ will be contemplated and analyzed separately below.

Facilities
Erdut (101st Training Centre)
In August 1991, the cynosure of the Serbian Volunteer Guard command relocated from Belgrade to a military facility near the village of Erdut in the Osijek district of Eastern Croatia, once

Slavonia. This land of vegetation, farms, and a litter of villages and small cities surrounding it were given life by the Danube. Camp Erdut, otherwise known as the 101st Training Centre, was operated by the JNA until their disintegration in early 1991. The control of Erdut was then transferred to Arkan (Stanišić & Simatović, 2009, June 30). Alongside the SDG other paramilitary groups and TO members trained here concurrently. Members of the Serbian Krajina Army were reported to have received training here in three-day intervals.

Robinson (2010) contended: "The training center at Erdut was established with the significant [financial] support of the Serbian DB (Interior Ministry)" (para. 5). Evidence affirms that operational costs of Erdut incurred in 1991 were covered by the Ministry of Defence for the Serb Autonomous Region of Slavonia, Baranja, and Western Srem (SO SBZS). An invoice numbered No. 29/92 produced by Dalj, was issued on January 22, 1992, to the defence minister "for the costs of the training center in Erdut for the year 1991, which amounted to 1,001,550.70 dinars" (Stanišić & Simatović, 2013, p. 47994). On January 17, 1992, Dalj issued Arkan an invoice amounting to 3,448,033.40 dinars, exorbitantly higher than the invoice issued to the defence minister. Arkan outright refused to cover the expenses, insisting the costs of operating Erdut should be incurred between the SO SBZS and the TO Centre for Special Training. Unbeknownst to the researcher is whether such costs represent monthly, quarterly, or confounded annual expenses. Nonetheless, the evidence deduced through the CEM lens demonstrates that the entire fiscal burden of operating Erdut as a training centre was not entirely covered by Arkan himself.

Arkan's recruits, originating from all over the country, were immersed in the camp by the hundreds; bus loaded and brought in by jeep to undergo immediate discipline and fighting development. Every core member of the Tigers underwent military training in Erdut (Marjanovich, 1997). A daily Serbian newspaper, *Borba*, reported that well over 10,000 draftees trained at Erdut (Marjanovich, 1997). One testimony avouched a high demand to get into Erdut. Many sought membership into the SDG and vigorously gave their best to get in.

Mount Tara

A paramilitary boot camp was conceived along the border of Serbia and Bosnia near Mount Tara. While only a few of Arkan's members trained here, they were placed under the authority of Serbian military trainers and "trained by regular army officers" (Alverez, 2006).

Evidenced in the case against Milošević, training for Tigers at Mount Tara slated members for combat in *Velika Kladuša* in Western Slovenia. Training commenced here for a period of seven days. Simatović asked Arkan for 40 soldiers to assist in Western Slovenian operations. The small group of 40 presumably went through Mount Tara. When one witness was asked: "were they [SDG] untrained for war operations, those men that you just mentioned? Were they men who needed training", he replied: "no" (Oppenheim & Van der Wolf, 1997, p. 222). This leads the researcher to believe that trained SDG from Erdut went to Mount Tara for continuous development or perhaps to cultivate a skill or behaviour not common to the curriculum in Erdut. Moreover, the researcher assumes that those who served in *Velika Kladuša* had undergone SDG training at Erdut, predominately in the technical aspects of ethnic cleansing; whereas the extra seven days of training at Mount Tara was to assimilate SDG members into outfits organized by the army. In recognition of this, Mount Tara played a minute role in the training and development of Arkan's Tigers. However, it is known that the Serbian Volunteer Guard trained at Mount Tara later in 1995, in preparation for an offensive coined the 'Paux Operation'.

Equipment/Materials
Uniforms, ammunition, firearms, and projectiles

Camp Erdut was resourcefully contrived into Arkan's private training compound. The JNA abandoned equipment and armaments, leaving numerous supplies in Erdut's depots to avail Arkan's fledgling empire. When the training centre was granted to Arkan, it was also furnished with arms by the local Territorial Defence (Sense Tribunal, January 24, 2012). Dimitrijevic opined that, in the case against Stanišić and Simatović (2012, January 17), the warehouse at Erdut was stockpiled with an assortment of weapons for training and combat purposes: "it contained automatic rifles, M-70s, semi-autimatic rifles; hand-grenades; Zoljas; Osas and ammunition" (p. 16066).

The camp's grounds were "transformed into a contemporary facility comparable with the best international centres of this kind" (Radović, 1995, p. 1). Here, two adjacent soccer fields were retrofitted as obstacle courses, complemented by firing ranges. On the firing range a cacophony of machine gun and assault rifle projectiles were fired freely. According to witness JF-050: "Most of our equipment was a copy of the foreign legion equipment" (Stanišić & Simatović, 2010, p. 12189). Novices were issued firearms upon arrival into Erdut. Weapons were carried on person throughout the training day (Testimony of B-1738, 2003, March 17).

Each training session in Erdut could accommodate 1,000 men. The men were given two types of uniforms for training; green in the daytime, and black clothes with ski masks (balaclavas) at night (Simons, 2003). They were issued an olive-drab uniform, a pair of military-issue black boots, an automatic rifle, and an M-70. Ammunition was granted on request prior to training exercises and generally requested two to three times a week "because a lot of ammunition was used for training" (Stanišić & Simatović, 2012, p. 16331). In a day's training, recruits could fire roughly 60 bullets equating to two rounds of clips. Permission was needed by the Territorial Defence (TO) office for Zoljas, grenades, and hand-held rocket-launchers for use in training (Stanišić & Simatović, 2012). Pelević, chief instructor for the Serbian Volunteer Guard noted that he personally trained the SDG in the afternoons how to operate Zoljas and fire rocket-launchers. Erdut's training grounds were distinctly separate. One such area was designated as a shooting range "where the troops were trained and taught how to use those weapons. So ammunition was something that was constantly needed in the course of the training provided" (Stanišić & Simatović, 2012, January 17, p. 16066). Contrary to what many erroneously believe, the Serbian Volunteer Guard never used AK-47s.

Accountability of materials and equipment
As reflected in Dimitrijevic's ICTY testimony, there existed a system of checks and balances specifically concerning the handling of Erdut's materials and equipment. As logistics coordinator, Dimitrijevic managed the munitions depot in Erdut. When ammunition or artillery was requested for use through his office, the injunction was relayed to workers in the repository. Dimitrijevic followed up with the depot to verify that what was received on paper was in "every respect in accordance with what was in the depot" (Stanišić & Simatović, 2012, January 17, p. 16180). Dimitrijevic remarked that operations within Erdut ran errorlessly; mistakes were never made in the operations' administration side or within Arkan's combat units. "Any error, any mistake, would have been punishable", opined Dimitrijevic (Stanišić & Simatović, 2012, January 17, p. 16180). Dimitrijevic stated that he did not physically take stock of the ordinances day-in/day-out due to the magnitude of stock stored in Erdut, nonetheless, he remained confident that "It was impossible to have any discrepancies, either surpluses, however minor, or any

minuses, again however minor" (Stanišić & Simatović, 2012, January 17, p. 16181).

Human beings as targets

For the objective of learning ethnic cleansing and genocide, Erdut was endlessly supplied with POW torture dummies for exploitation; for trainees to practice torture skills on and to desensitize the trainees to the gore and pain of their victims (Spiric et al., 2004). One witness ascertained that over fifty non-Serb detainees were held at Erdut for this express purpose. As discussed later in greater detail, Captain Vasiljković was observed using Muslim men as live targets, while overseeing training exercises at Erdut (Robinson, 2010).

Instructors

It is imperative to state outright who SDG instructors were not: neither Serbian DB nor MUP trained SDG members. Gagic (2013, February 15) remarked that it would have been "quite unnatural for them to do so, since the police and the state security, given the nature of their work, were not military units and knew nothing about warfare" (Stanišić & Simatović, para. 525). Likewise, Pelević confirmed it would have been irregular to receive instruction from either Serbian DB or MUP forces. Only instructors derived from a military background trained the SDG (Stanišić & Simatović, 2012, January 24, p. 16344).

Gow (2003) enumerated that "Arkan had some 100 instructors who were reported as inducting about 1,000 volunteers per month in October 1991" (p. 84). Through the combined CEM and HRD lenses many types of instructor have been identified. In light of this, the following instructors were either former military or those who skyrocketed through the SDG ranks by demonstrating advanced military aptitude through a mentoring arrangement.

Special Anti-Terrorist Unit (SAJ)

The SAJ, previously introduced in the 'Build Curriculum' event, were the first group of instructors identified to train SDG members. When 50 to 60 of the Serbian Volunteer Guard's finest emerged from the first cycle of training, Arkan appointed them as trainers, ceding the instructing responsibilities of Erdut to them (Stanišić & Simatović, 2013). To determine the experience that SAJ instructors brought to the role as SDG trainers, it is necessary to look at their training backgrounds. They were typically chosen from among Serbia's police force. An extensive vetting process was involved in the selection of

SAJ members. They were considered exceptional students, athletic, and prepossessing ideal physical characteristics deemed suitable for service (Testimony of Stalevic, 2010). After an onerous selection process, passing the requisite physical check-up and medical examination, the SAJ then underwent training. After performing satisfactorily during training, novices could become members of the MUP's Special Anti-Terrorist Unit (Stalevic, 2010). The SAJ set the standard for all policing and military outfits operating in Serbia. They were an elite unit, well-trained and "capable to act as an elite unit of the MUP of the Republic of Serbia" (Testimony of Stalevic, 2010, p. 13846).

Gvozden Gagic and Borislav Pelević

Upon entry into the SDG, Gvozden Gagic endured two to two-and-a-half months of training. He took over the training of the SDG, which he claimed "lasted for 3 months and, once completed, the Guard members had joined combat units" (Stanišić & Simatovic, 2013, para. 525). Pelević concurred with Gagić's testimony of three months being allotted for SDG training: "Only after they had been trained for three months was it possible for a volunteer to join the combat group and to participate in the operations" (Stanišić & Simatović, 2012, January 24, p. 16344). Pelević correspondingly served at Erdut as a chief instructor, after having undergone two or two-and-a-half months of training himself as an introductory SDG member. Pelević explained that after fifteen-days into his training, he was asked by an undisclosed SDG lieutenant to assist in the training of physical exercises. He noted that on the twentieth day he began training people. He was a self-described martial arts expert, physically sound, and "knew how to prepare troops, so [he] assumed responsibility for physical training, for training in martial arts" (Stanišić & Simatović, 2012, p. 16344). Pelević exacted high standards for physical development, expecting that soldiers could be excellent shooters, and knowing that if members were not physically primed for combat, they would serve no purpose militarily to Arkan. Throughout 1992 Pelević continued to train SDG recruits, and was later conferred the rank of an SDG officer. In the mornings he trained the SDG "in…martial arts. And in the afternoon [he] trained the troops how to use Zoljas, hand-held rocket-launchers" (Stanišić & Simatović, 2012, p. 16360).

Milorad Ulemek (Legija aka "Legion")

Dimitrijevic (2012) performed background checks on prospective SDG members for admission. He remarked that an erstwhile French

Legionnaire, named Milorad Ulemek: "seemed a good guy and kept a steady progress in the unit...was a very active instructor at Erdut" (Šarić, 2012, p. 2). Ulemek, a former french sergeant of four years, with past involvement in theatres of war in Chad and French Guyana, made him an ideal candidate for enlistment. Even Captain Dragan was in awe of 'Legija', whom he noted as: "militarily the most educated person out of all who were with Arkan...Very soon it was clear that Legija knew a lot, and that's why he was made into one of the main instructors" (Svarm, N.D). His nom de guerre 'Legija' was derived from Legion. Legion was at the forefront of 101st training instructors. Gagic noted that Legion arrived in the SDG as a foreign recruit in April 1992, and was appointed as an instructor later that year. Pelević confirmed Legion's arrival in April (Stanišić & Simatović, 2012, January 24).

Yugoslavian People's Army (JNA) Colonels
JNA Colonels also served as educators in Erdut. A former JNA Colonel named 'Puki', short for the Serbian translation of colonel 'pukovnik', acted prominently as an SDG instructor (Stanišić & Simatović, 2013, February 15). Pelević (2010) described Puki as an army colonel, and he was addressed as such when instructing the SDG. Puki continued to wear the uniform of the JNA (Stanišić & Simatovic, 2012, January 24). Other colonels who instructed the SDG were all easily identifiable by the former Army of Yugoslavia uniforms which they donned while training the Serbian Volunteer Guard (Stanišić & Simatović, 2012, January 24).

Captain Dragan Vasiljković
Dragan was contracted by Simatović to design a training program for the professional development of paramilitaries and support forces in Krajina (Armatta, 2010). I have found through the CEM lens that he was provisioned the necessary funding to establish his own network of training institutions, cited in ICTY testimonies as 'Alpha' centres. His vision was for all weapons-carriers to circulate first through his training centres to guarantee proper handling and maintenance of firearms (Testimony of Dragan, 2003, February 19). Dragan remarked that all men circulating through such a camp would be "processed administratively and then be trained professionally" (Testimony of Dragan, 2003), and placed under some form of military control. Ultimately, Dragan was recruited to improve the training infrastructure of irregular Serbian forces. Simatović commissioned Dragan to train paramilitary forces under the TO of Krajina, thus

spawning a network of training camps under the Alpha umbrella. An Alpha centre was erected in Bruska, near Knin in 1993. When Rade Rašeta, a retired colonel, arrived in Bruska he was imminently aware that "Dragan Vasiljković was commander of the Alpha Center...for training of Special Forces" (Testimony of Rade Rašeta, 2006, p. 3922). An elite group of 28 soldiers formed a network of train-the-trainers who would oversee the day-to-day operations of Dragan's 26 Alpha centres in Bosnia and Croatia.

Dragan was appointed commander of Golubić in April 1991. Golubić was an abandoned vacationing centre for youth. Dragan procured funds through Nikodin Martic's assistants and the commander of the Territorial Defence to finance the construction of Golubić into a state of-the-art training compound. Dragan's first batch of trainees consisted of: "some 80, maybe 100 men...wearing different uniforms, various weapons ranging from hunting rifles to Kalashnikovs, diverse insignia and markings" (Testimony of Dragan, February 19, 2003, p. 16482). Martic arranged the introduction between Dragan and Golubić's first batch of trainees. He was introduced as their instructor and they were told to obey him. Dragan chose Golubić's optimal performers as determined by their performance in the training program, and transferred them to a fortress in Knin "for advanced training and training to be instructors themselves" (Testimony of Dragan, 2003, p.16481). Golubić graduates advanced to instructorial positions under Dragan, or moonlighted as intelligence specialists ascribed a variety of names e.g., Red Berets, Knindzas, or the Original 28, recognized as the 28 elite trainers who oversaw the educational expansion of Dragan's 26 Alpha Centres (Stanišić & Simatović, 2013, February 11). The researcher found that Stanišić and Simatović (2013, February 11) suggest that the Original 28 were primarily responsible for training Red Berets and developing anti-terrorist platoons who would serve as trainers in paramilitary camps. Nonetheless, the training imperatives of Dragan's Golubić were reminiscent of Arkan's Erdut. Witness Milan Babić (2006, February 17) visited Golubić twice after its inception in April 1991. Babić remarked that a number of constituents from different municipalities, either members of a police force or not having "underwent training for some time...acquired military skills, obtained weapons, and underwent ideological training" (p. 1542). When Babić was asked to comment more on Golubić's ideological training and the constitution of Golubić's curriculum, he recounted: "people were taught not to be too strongly attached to political parties because they would be working for the state involved in defense"

(Babić, 2006, p. 1542). Recruits were told that their residual loyalty must be unswerving to the state. Golubić's ideological curriculum inculcated trainees to be loyal to the state not to political parties (Martic, 2007, June 12, p. 52). However, training at Golubić was "predominantly military" (Martic, 2007, June 12, p. 52), "trainees wore blue camouflage uniforms" (Martic, 2007, p. 52), and "training groups consisted of between 40 and 100 trainees per group" (Martic, p. 52), trained over a period of 20 days. Martic explicated that weapons training included artillery use, mining, sniper shooting, and target practice. In addition to an intensive physical exercise regimen, there was "training in the securing of persons, self-protection and abseiling...the training was classical police training" (p. 52). Furthermore, Golubić trainees "received training on fitness, mopping-up techniques...various kinds of shooting, scouting, and searching or taking over houses" (Stanišić & Simatović, 2013, February 28, p. 48473).

Novices who trained at Golubić were educated to develop and train units in their home municipality. On June 23, 1991, Dragan discerned that Golubić's main objective was to militarily transform men, so that after they completed training, they could return home and create miniature training grounds to nourish the development of new forces to thus thwart the "rise of Ustashahood in Croatia" (Stanišić & Simatović, 2013, February 28, p. 48484). Golubić trainees "[could] be traced through the establishment and formation of other camps and through the movements and activities of its core members" (Stanišić & Simatović, 2013, p. 48484). Dragan and other prominent instructors toured the field, proffering advice on the cultivation of new units. His unit, wherever they went, followed the precise developmental model established at Golubić for training Serbs (Stanišić & Simatović, 2013, February 28). This explicitly gave rise to Dragan's famed Alpha Centres.

Golubić is believed to have served an ethnic cleansing purpose. Witness JF-039 observed a group of graduates from Golubić who were sent to cleanse Ljubovo of non-Serb populations. The Ljubovo operation satisfied the graduation exercise component of Golubić's training curriculum (Testimony of Witness JF-039, 2013). Much like Arkan, Dragan had a known reputation for his nefarious training techniques. Witness B-161 (May 22, 2003) expressed that Dragan used Muslim captives as training tools. He vividly recounted: "he captured [three] Muslims and said that he would release them, but actually he's train[ed] his soldiers using them" (Testimony of Witness B-161, 2003, p. 21035). Captured men were used as targets for torture training. He described how one captive was driven at gunpoint into a river, where one of Dragan's instructors proceeded to use the man for target practice. Extending his accusations against Dragan, witness B-161 claimed that Dragan personally confirmed that "target practice should be done using live men as targets" (B-161, 2003).

Dragan and his Red Berets instructed the Serbian Volunteer Guard and, to some extent, other genocidal paramilitary groups operating in Croatia and Bosnia under the aegis of Milošević's manifold state agencies (Partos, 2003). Undeniably, Dragan independently augmented the effectiveness of Erdut's curriculum (Svarm, N.D). I find it probable that SDG members circulated through at least one of Dragan's many camps, as I have determined with certitude: "one individual…trained at Golubić joined the SDG in 1991" (Stanišić & Simatović, 2013, February 28, p. 91). This said individual was likely among the first to graduate from Golubić, and was then sent to Erdut to assist as an instructor or perhaps in program design. From the testimony of Anonymous (2004, January 14) as a witness in the trial against Milošević: "confirmed…he saw Dragan Vasiljković, aka Captain Dragan, carrying out tactical maneuvers with Arkan's Volunteer Guard" (para. 6). On Dragan's first visit to Erdut, Arkan escorted him around the compound on a personal tour: "I remember that Arkan lead me through the bedrooms, and in one of them he said: 'In this one, there is 250 years of prison'" (Svarm, ND, para. 12). A confidential report circulated by Major-General Babić on October 25, 1991, confirmed Dragan's involvement as trainer of the SDG (Robinson, 2010). The 101st Training Centre housed an Alpha encampment, the location and materials fashioned from the preexisting wine facility in Erdut. In early 1992, Nenad Zafirovic recounted as a formative observation while touring Erdut, that passing "along the road going past the Alpha center [her] and some colleagues would see Dragan Vasiljković engage[ed] in tactical exercises with members of the Serbian Volunteer Guard of Arkans" (Testimony of Witness Nenad Zafirovic, 2004, p. 30714). Dragan's barbarity in Erdut, is consonant with his behaviour in Golubić; Robinson (2010) noted: "Mr Vasiljković was observed using a Muslim man as a live target during training exercises at Erdut" (Robinson, 2010, para. 7). In the same way, SDG instructors found utility in this training approach.

Conduct Training
The final event in Nadler's (1994) critical events model signifies the conclusion of program design and relinquishing control of the

program to the learning facilitator; as noted by Cookson (1998) to be the instructor(s) of the program. Evaluation and feedback during this event, Cookson argued, can comprise several evaluations. Job performance cannot be adequately evaluated until the trainee is delineated to perform a task (Nadler, 1994). Nadler concluded that there is but one basic purpose "to conduct the training program previously designed" (p. 207). Nabb and Armstrong (2005) proclaimed evaluation is natural in this event. Through the CEM lens, SDG training and development went on as discussed. Training took place under regimented, simulated conditions designed specifically for the SDG to commit ethnic cleansing. Through the CEM lens, SDG training in Erdut was mechanistic, well-oiled, and effective at churning out agents of ethnic cleansing.

Gagic discerned that Erdut's first cycle of recruits was trained by the SAJ. The most promising group of 50 to 60 men were winnowed out of the initial pool by a selection committee to train prospective SDG members. At first, training lasted "two-to-two-and-a-half months" (Stanišić & Simatović, 2013, para. 525), confirmed by witness C-047, himself having undergone two months of training. While the learning program remained in its incipient stage, the duration increased to three months, which is consonant with the testimony of Pelević. By early 1994, approximately 10,000 genocidaires underwent training at Arkan's base (Pavlovic, 1994).

Stewart (2007) holds that training continued around the clock. The author states: "Soldiers in black or green could be seen sparing, crawling on their stomachs, running through tire trails doing marching steps, chanting Tigers' fight songs or emptying rounds of assault rifles and machine guns" (p. 152). The SDG were thoroughly cultured in all aspects of warfare: "trained and capable of every form of infantry combat" (Srpskenovine, 2010). Radović (1995) observed that Erdut was filled with the workings of a fully-functioning military unit, likening it to a US Army training depot:

> It is busy like a bee-hive every morning since 6 'o' clock, when a new working day begins. There are morning calisthenics, breakfast and inspections. The trumpeter plays the Serbian anthem and a new day starts. A strenuous training awaits them...Sunday is a day off. They attend the mess in the church, play sports on various play-grounds, go out...but everything is deserved, because disrespect of the rules of this stoic school of humanity can bring the old

Serbian measure: 25 strokes on the buttocks, in front of the entire ranks (Radović, 1995, p. 13).

Witness B-1738 claimed that the Serbian Volunteer Guard exercised quite heavily, and every few days ran distances of up to 25 kilometres (Testimony of B-1738, 2003, March 17). The running curriculum took place principally outside the camp, as traffic passed, day or night, with weapons carried at all times. Witness C-047 described that his unit underwent training every day and were continually immersed in fitness exercises. He indicated that an integral component of the curriculum was sustained at night. One such activity involved taking position around Osijek, to demonstrate their forces' skills, and to practice tactics in provocation (Testimony of Witness C-047, 2003, June 4). ICTY probed witness B-1738 to describe the training he encountered while in Erdut. He emphasized discipline: "The training was in discipline with a lot of running and training in the use of all types of firearms and explosives" (Testimony of Witness B-1738, 2003, March 17, p. 5).

Sources detailing rewards and compensation that the SDG received are scarcely known to exist. Dimitrijevic, senior logistics coordinator for the SDG, testified that members "were never paid or compensated in any way for the time they spent in the Serbian Volunteer Guard" (Testimony of Jovan Dimitrijevic, 2012, January 17, p. 16098). Dimitrijevic continued: "[SDG] never receive[d] any payments or any remuneration of any kind from 1991 through 1995…We never gave them any money. They volunteered. They were not there for the money that was in the job" (Stanišić & Simatović, 2012, January 19, p. 16265). However, in the case against Stanišić and Simatović (January 19, 2012), the ICTY prosecutor argued that inducements to fight were adroitly arranged by the Serbian DB, conceding hundreds of payments to SDG members, "at least from the end of 1994 throughout 1995" (Stanišić & Simatović, 2012, January 19, p. 16273). Correspondingly, Witness B-129 noted that in 1995 the DB issued money to Arkan to distribute to his soldiers as salaries (Testimony of Witness B-129, 2003, April 16).

Stewart (2007) suggested that forced conscripts were paid wages as low as $7 a month, paltry in comparison to the $1000 a month the SDG were in receipt of. The SDG had apt incentive to ethnically cleanse. Propositioning rewards, Arkan had known, would elicit a higher level of compliance. By the same token, many SDG members favoured looting by way of recompense. B-129 recounted that on St. Nikolas Day in 1995, Arkan issued pistols to his officers, symbolizing his outward appreciation for their merits. Each pistol issued had a personalized inscription on it; additionally, a license and permit was awarded, giving the bearer the right to possess it (Testimony of Witness B-129, 2003, April 16).

Implications for research and practice
A joint HRD-CEM lens was used to explore the extent to which the SDG were trained and, moreover, how the historical record pertains to the SDG and learning. As noted in Procknow (2014): "HRD can be used to organize and explicate historical educative or learning events differently from a perspective that's not education specific" (p. 384). The principal implication of this research is to demonstrate how an HRD program design model can be used to reorganize historical curricula to obtain a holistic understanding of what SDG training entailed from inception to implementation. Furthermore, the CEM lens can be used to develop new prerogatives of how genocidal regimes utilized training and development as a way to include genocidal content in their curricula. The limitations are arguably most similar to Procknow's (2014): "few readers may egregiously mistake the…subject matter as proffering potential strategies for augmenting the performance of genocidal agents" (p. 385). Others may mistake the views in this work as providing an HRD model to educate citizens for violence. Although stark contrasts exist between the present work and Procknow (2014), the implication here is that the CEM can be used by historians of educational policy for organizing historical research. It also offers what I believe to be the most signal feature of the CEM lens; it can provide structure to secondary or post-secondary history lessons through its application to organize in-class lessons for students of history.

Recommendations for future research
Traditionally, the CEM has in the past been revered by HRD and adult education academics and has been commonly selected as a program design model of choice. The researcher holds high regard for the CEM, and quite rightfully believes that any endeavour undertaken to analyze past curricula would benefit immensely by organizing historical sources according to the eight-step, programmatic CEM approach to program design. The overriding recommendation for future research is to apply the CEM to a historical educative event, other than a genocidal curriculum, perhaps dated earlier than the 20th century. Procknow (2014) encouraged "cross-fertilization or collaboration of other academic disciplines such as education and

business to see the merits in relating their experience to genocide research" (p. 385). This work is a complete fusion of two distinctly different areas of research: comparative genocide research and human resource development. Although previously occupying two separate spheres, I have demonstrated that they can coexist mutually to avail both fields. Lee (2002) held: "HRD has learnt from other disciplines, so I suggest other disciplines can learn from HRD" (p. 18). In the same breath, Alagaraja and Dooley (2003) comment: "In the field of HRD, there is a great need for high-level collaboration with other disciplines" (p. 84). Through the CEM, the past suffuses the present so simply, through the reorganization of historical data by use of a modern-day conceptual model. By not pursuing a structured and deductive approach to understanding, the past denies historicity. The CEM can be used to elucidate the intricacies involved in training, development, or education thus unveiling new perspectives and, as I recommend, can be applied to any aggregate of past educational events.

Conclusion
Through the application of a CEM lens, primary and secondary sources were reviewed and reorganized by the eight-sequential events of the CEM as they pertained to training and developing the Serbian Volunteer Guard. The historical record, as it existed, advanced uncertain and conflicting interpretations of how learning interventions were organized for Arkan's group. We can make certain that more factive conclusions can be deduced when the purview of the CEM is applied. Through the CEM lens the researcher was able to fill the gaps, from inception to implementation in the SDG historiography relating to learning. Serbian Volunteer Guard training began in 1991. The SAJ were Erdut's first instructors. The lens allowed the reorganization of the historiographical timeline to conclude that, in its inchoate phase, training under the SAJ was two months. It continued to be two months until early 1992, when the SAJ were replaced and the curriculum was modified to permit a month's extension, to total three months. Moreover, through the CEM lens, I inferred that a train-the-trainers program was first introduced by the SAJ to train future SDG instructors. Not to mention, training increased mere weeks before the Bosnian conflict erupted, which led this researcher to conclude that Arkan desired a finer-trained group for ethnic cleansing activities in Bosnia. At the same time, a historiographical trend toward additional dehumanization training occurred concurrently with the escalating participation of the SDG in Bosnia.

The CEM lens assisted the researcher in categorizing the dearth of research on the SDG under Nadler's proposed critical events e.g., instructional strategies and curriculum building. By thematizing key curricular data through the CEM lens, one uncovers the depth of organization, planning, and financing necessary to train genocidal agents. Participation of hundreds of instructors (a few sourced internationally), the degree of SMS involvement in curriculum and facilities design, and the network of training centres scattered throughout Serb controlled lands indicates some degree of mobility of trainees for developing requisite behaviours and skills to ethnic cleanse. To this end, the CEM assisted the researcher to identify the hallmarks of SDG training, what the Erdut curriculum constituted, the equipment and materials used in training, the learning environments, and, particularly salient, the instructional strategies employed, e.g., direct instruction, interactive instruction, and experiential and observational learning.

CHAPTER THREE:
Differentiating Rwanda's perpetrators through the training lens

Introduction

A single undertaking of Rwanda's learning amid the 1994 genocide has not yet been discussed anywhere in the entire corpus of published literature. Little information on how the *National Republican Movement for Democracy and Development* (MRND) instructed its Hutu populace to kill Tutsi has been brought to light. Through comparative analysis, the historical record relating the relationship between civilian defense (CD) and Interahamwe during the Rwandan Genocide will be reorganized and reviewed through a training lens, to discern the differences between these two perpetrator groups. When looking at Rwanda's genocide through a training lens, particularly the historical record relevant to the learning programs contrived for CD and Interahamwe forces, discrepancies can be discerned between the two groups. Varied *International Criminal Tribunal for Rwanda* (ICTR) testimonies relay trouble differentiating between civilian defense and Interahamwe forces. Then Prime Minister Kambanda endorsed "the Interahamwe was a militia separate from Civil Defense" (Bagosora, Kabiligi, Ntabakuza, & Nsengiyumva, 2008, December 18, para. 481). On the whole, it may fairly be said, ICTR evidence refers to a sizable "overlap between political party militias, such as the Interahamwe and the civil defense system. This does not necessarily mean that all members of the Interahamwe were part of the Civil Defense system" (Bagosora, et al., 2008, December 18, para. 494).

Statement and Significance of the Problem

In the long run, testimonies have confused which training was organized for either group. In the case of Bagosora, Kabiligi, Ntabakuza, and Nsengiyumva (2008, December 18), the prosecutor maintained "it is not clear whether this training was directed at training the Interahamwe as such or whether some members were trained as part of the civil defense system" (para. 458). Organizing the data on CD through a training lens allows us to differentiate much more clearly between civilian defense and Interahamwe by analyzing the underlying content constituting civil defense learning. Furthermore, it becomes much more complicated when looking at the learning accorded to each group by the government. The prosecutor in the case against Bagosora et al., (2008) inferred:

> There is a significant body of evidence concerning the training of civilians in many cases identified as Interahamwe, which may have been part of Rwanda's civilian defense system, given the similarities in training locations attributed to the civilian defense system (para. 489).

When the historical record pertaining to training of Rwanda's Interahamwe and civil defense were reorganized and reviewed through the training lens, it became evident that many defense and prosecutorial witnesses were uncertain which groups they observed engaged in training exercises. Through the lens, as will be shown in this work, we can better identify errors in the historical record, e.g., when witnesses erroneously claimed that they observed Interahamwe training; however, after reviewing the context of the source through the training lens, their testimony suggests they actually observed CD.

The significance of this research is threefold: The field of Human Resource Development (HRD) requires more historically oriented manuscripts (Callahan, 2010); HRD perspectives, theories, and ideas have not contributed to the growing discourse in comparative genocide research on Rwanda; and the field of genocide research itself has in the past had trouble differentiating between civil defense forces and Interahamwe, and vice versa, proving further a difficult task, given their symmetrical training curriculums.

Sources and Research Methodology

Primary sources for this present historical research study were gleaned from *International Criminal Tribunal for Rwanda* (ICTR) documents, e.g., summaries, sentences, and judgments. Cumulative testimonies of those accused of crimes against humanity and genocide, prosecution and defense witnesses, and those acknowledged as outside spectators have proved fruitful in this work. Thick descriptions derived from over twenty-five court documents are offered to ease the transferability of this chapter's conclusions and findings. Moreover, primary sources relating to civil defense, entitled 'Civil Defense documents' or otherwise known as 'directives,' five in total, issued to all prefects and bourgmestres during April, May, and June of 1994 were of import: two of which were published on May 25, 1994, by then Prime Minister Kambanda: *(1) The Directives of the Prime Minister to all Préfets on the Organization of Civil Defense of 25 May, 1994;* and *(2) Directive of Jean Kambanda to all Préfets on the organization of the Civil Defense 25 May, 1994.* The other three: *(1) Letter to all Préfets from Jean Kambanda regarding Instructions to Restore Security in the Country of 27 April 1994; (2) the Ministerial Instructions to the Préfets of the Préfectures on the Use of Funds Earmarked for the Ministry of the Interior and Communal Development for Civil Self-Defense of mid-June 1994;* and *(3) The letter to Commandant du Secteur Anatole Nsengiyumva from Karemera regarding the Opération de ratissage á Kibuye of 18 June, 1994.* The latter three directives issued by Interior Minister Karemera were of less significance to the present work. The 'Civil Defense documents,' as they have been referred to in the literature, were made readily available momentarily after various cabinet meetings jointly attended by the interim government and the MRND steering committee. The case against Nahimana, Barayagwiza, and Ngeze (2003, December 3) claimed that "in the chambers view, these documents concern the formal implementation of the CD program on a national scale" (para. 445). Correspondingly, the prosecution bemoaned that the 'Civil Defense documents' delineated a definite schema for supporting the implementation of the genocidal CD plan (Karemera & Ngirumpatse, 2012, February 2).

Other principal documents consulted were communications published by Rwanda's media, e.g., newspapers and radio over which MRND had foremost control. Party speeches recorded during committee meetings and rallies also contributed to the vast dearth of primary sources. Verwimp (2004) noted that all of Habyarimana's speeches and interviews "were published during his reign by his office and the office of Information of Rwanda (ORINFOR)" (p. 25). Secondary sources factored prominently in this research. Newspaper, television, and radio broadcasts beyond Rwandan borders were useful, e.g., the combined works of Des Forges (1999) and Hirondelle News (2005).

Research Limitations

Limitations and shortcomings are worth mentioning. There is scant information on the contemporaneous education of Interahamwe and civilian defense. All sources consulted for the present work were carefully ruminated; all in all, the researcher feels confident that a cornucopia of supplementary sources detailing the civil defense curriculum or the learning structure for Interahamwe exists beyond what was used here. A critical limitation of this work was that inextricable differences between the two perpetrators were discerned only through comparative analysis of both groups' learning curriculums. Though it should be noted there was a dereliction of traditional schooling: the interim government closed both elementary and secondary schools in the days leading to the genocide. However, incontrovertible evidence differentiates that these two groups were not educative specific, i.e., Interahamwe wore uniforms sporting insignias, whereas civilian defense wore traditional Hutu garb. More so, the results of this study are unlikely to be confirmed, as no similar studies exist or have been published by comparative genocide research or HRD academia. Furthermore, verbatim transcription has not been used in all cases, as many summaries, sentences, and judgments resembled précis, not court transcripts. Testimony is not contemporaneous with the period in which the actual crimes occurred, leading to what the researcher believes to be lapses in memory of those testifying. Furthermore, when learning is discussed in the sources, it is commonly described as training, not education, development, or human resource development (HRD), which makes it difficult for any researcher categorizing learning events as education, training, or development. Another limitation is penetrating the hegemonic advantage present in the scholarship on Rwanda's genocide. Lastly, the ICTR trials are still ongoing, so perhaps not all of the information pertinent to this research has yet surfaced.

Rwandan Genocide (1994)

The Rwandan genocide was a class-based genocide happening along antagonistic ethnic polarizing lines. Rwanda, prior to the genocide, segregated the 14 percent Tutsi affluent landowners from the 85 percent Hutu proletarian population. Class demarcation served as the stimulus for Hutu groups to spout anti-

Tutsi sentiments. A growing Tutsi opposition was surreptitiously gaining momentum within Rwanda, reaching far into Uganda and other neighboring countries. The 2500 strong Tutsi-led Rwandan Patriotic Front (RPF), forged in 1987, invaded Northern Rwanda in 1990, in an attempt to oust the Hutu government. In preparation for the Rwandan advancement, the RPF numbered four thousand troops. The troops, principally second-generation Tutsi, were well-trained by the Ugandan army and had previously experienced warfare in the Ugandan Bush War.

The RPF invasion culminated in the start of the Rwandan Civil War. The Hutu regime, backed by Francophone Africa and France, defended territorial autonomy against the primarily Ugandan backed RPF. The Civil War was fought in two phases: the first phase from October 1, 1990 to August 4, 1993, and the second phase from April 7, 1994, through to July 18, 1994. The protracted second phase was used as a veneer to hide the genocide of Tutsi during the conflict.

In the first phase, the numerically superior RAF, equipped with armored cars and helicopters, failed to thwart the RPF's growing territorial advancement. For the first few days of the offensive, the element of surprise worked favourably for the RPF. Only through Zaire's and France's intervention would the RPF onslaught be quelled. Since 1975, France continued to honour the defense pact signed with Rwandan President Juvenal Habyarimana, proffering military aid, artillery, equipment, and mortars, becoming Rwanda's largest foreign-military contributor. By the week's closure, the RAF began counter-offensive actions against the RPF, forcing them into Akagera National Park bordering Tanzania. The Rwandan government initiated a false flag campaign on October 4, 1990, staging numerous forays on Kigali, igniting fires, firing off rounds, and triggering explosions in or around the city; the destruction was attributed to RPF sympathizers. Tutsi were encouraged to cooperate with local Hutu police to identify RPF supporters in their communities. Over the course of the following week, 10,000 Tutsi were arrested, the village of Bahima was ethnically cleansed, and their homes were plundered and burned down under the advisement of Major Ntabakuze; hundreds were slaughtered in a period of 48 hours (Malvern, 2000). The RPF effort subsided to allow them to reorganize and rebuild their command structure. The enrollment of

RPF continued to grow, attracting Tutsi caught up in the diaspora. When the RPF invaded in 1990, membership was only 9,335. In 1991, the army's numbers swelled threefold to 27,913; however, as Alverez (2009) maintained, "most of these new recruits were poorly trained and ill-educated young men" (p. 87). As noted in the case Bagosora, Kabiligi, Ntabakuza, and Nsengiyumva (2008, December 18), the RAF resorted to lowering "its recruiting and training regimen" (p. 33) to facilitate expeditious growth and relegating training in military operations to one year.

By early 1991, the RPF accepted members from Tanzania, Zaire, Burundi, Europe, and the United States, augmenting their size from 5000 to 12,000 in 1992. Their numbers continued to grow to a staggering 25,000 during the second phase of the Civil War (Prunier, 1995). After regrouping in 1991, the RPF, in January of the same year, carried out hit-and-run skirmishes and guerrilla warfare along the Northern Rwandan border. A series of ceasefires and failed attempts at amelioration proved fruitless until July 12, 1992, when the *Arusha Accords* were signed in Tanzania, only stonewalling conflict until February 8, 1993.

The RPF resumed their offensive on February 20; the threat of French intervention once again forced the RPF into a peace agreement, lasting until April 1994. On April 6, 1994, President Habyarimana, upon returning to Rwanda on his presidential jet from negotiations in Dar es Salaam, was fired upon, causing his plane to crash. Dallaire (2003) recalled in the hours after the President's death that Habyarimana's Presidential Guard "conducted an obviously well-organized and well-executed plan-by noon on April 7" (p. 232). The surviving remnants of authority within the MRND were consolidated under the Rwandan territorial administration by the Ministry of Interior and military command structure, under the aegis of the Ministry of Defense and RAF (Karemera & Ngirumpatse, 2012). Defying the peace agreement ushered in the start of the second phase of the Civil War, most ordinarily referred to as the Rwandan genocide, spanning three months and culminating in the deaths of 937,000 Tutsi. Hutu deaths were paltry in comparison.

President Habyarimana, his closest political myrmidons, and his ruling MRND Party from 1975 to 1994 ultimately succumbed to the surmounting pressure of the RPF. In response, the MRND organized ideological and military preparations, linking ideology and military preparedness together in a program designed for "youth wings in order to defend their Party's interests and coercively increase support" (Alverez, 2009, p. 83). Habyarimana cautioned Hutu of an impending Tutsi plan for perpetrating mass genocide: "they are going to exterminate you until they are the only ones left in this country, so that the power which their fathers kept for four hundred years, they can keep for a thousand years!" (Des Forges, 1996, p. 48).

The MRND were primarily Hutu, and consisted of Habyarimana's political circle known as the Akazu, elsewise known as the Little House. As RPF efforts receded, the Akazu campaigned against the RPF, calling for mass Rwandan support. The Party began ruminating on options to protect Hutu civilians, as well as their sway on political power in Rwanda. Two options were selected: a civil defense (CD) program, a national human resource development (NHRD) endeavor to militarily train citizens in arms and defense, and the organization and education of irregular paramilitary forces, e.g., the Interahamwe.

Civil Defense

The forming of civilian self-defense programs ultimately militarized society and precipitated the increased speed by which Tutsi were killed (Malvern, 2006). Civilian defense was about arranging Hutu groups together to train for the purpose of exterminating Tutsi (Totten, 2011). Civilian defense refers to preventative initiatives designed to sustain and safeguard the defense of civilian populations from extraneous military action (Arnold and Wiener, 2012). The idea of civilian defense was first promulgated in 1989 by the then Rwandan ambassador to Zaire who proposed to the then foreign affairs minister the utility of CD for protecting Rwanda from external attackers (Malvern, 2006). He urged Hutu civilians to organize "in a programme of Civil Defense...to counter communities where there was a majority of Tutsi" (Malvern, 2006, p. 20). Civilian defense preparations began in September of 1991, when Hutu officials learned of the RPF's multiplied recruitment efforts expanding beyond the Ugandan border, surpassing the RAF in military strength by the hundreds (Des Forges, 1999). Des Forges' account, in my opinion, is largely confined to Northern prefectures. Civil defense began with the erection of roadblocks, checking identification cards, and engaging in neighborhood patrols in October of 1990 as a counteroffensive action to RPF attacks, particularly in Northern prefectures, e.g., Ruhengeri and Byumba (Nahimana, Barayagwiza, & Ngeze, 2003, December 3; Bagosora et al., 2008, December 18). In July of 1991, Colonel Augustin Ndindiliyimana counseled Habyarimana on the strategic advantages of creating a "trained militia in all of Rwanda's communes" (Malvern, 2006, p. 21). This was likewise affirmed by the prosecutor in the case against Ndindiliyimana et al., (2007, September 11): "from as early as 1991, the government of Rwanda elaborated an ethnically-oriented civil defense programme, the main components of which included training civilian Hutu men in military tactics" (para. 18). A security council was created in each of the ten prefectures to investigate the feasibility of citizenry self-defence. The spawning of CD programs throughout Rwanda had escalated exponentially after the Kibuye meeting on May 3, 1994 (Karemera & Ngirumpatse, 2012). The meeting was convened by the interim government and led by Kambanda; Kambanda addressed the congress and propositioned civilian defense as a means to checkmate the RPF. He commented that "the war was in all communes in Rwanda" (Karemera & Ngirumpatse, 2012, para. 947).

  Contrarily, Caddick-Adams balked about the civilian defense documents and said "that there was nothing sinister in Rwanda's civil defense planning and that it was consistent with those of other western countries" (Bagosora et al., 2008, para. 484). He attested that all states have, in some shape or other, hatched a civilian defense contingency plan to ready citizens, during moments of peace, for a forthcoming civil crisis. Rwandan CD resembling those found in European times foregone, Caddick-Adams continued, primarily served as an auxiliary unit, and, more so, it was to maintain a "military structure with a central hierarchy overseen jointly by the Ministries of Defense and Interior" (Bagosora et al., 2008, para. 485). Somewhat of an anomaly in my opinion, Caddick-Adams conveyed that the interim government systemized civilian self-defense to ultimately achieve good and to assuage the fears of affrighted Hutu, rather than what the consensus believes: to exterminate Tutsi. At any rate, the testimony of witness number 1279 resonated with Caddick-Adams commentary; by the same token, he found that civilian defense was integral to the defense of Rwanda and that "one cannot incriminate Rwanda's system up-front as a programme to kill remaining Tutsis in Rwanda simply because they tried to put a civil defense system into place" (Bagosora et al., 2008, para. 1049).

Karemera's intent was to concoct a collective CD plan that would be structured, easily governable, and directed, "not something wild and out of control" (Nahimana et al., 2003, para. 649). Prosecution acknowledged that the principal malefactors of the genocide were namely the Interahamwe and other MRND controlled militias, gendarmes, and RAF in cahoots with the Ministry of Defense. All in all, the ICTR prosecutor claimed that civilians inducted into civil defense organized by a territorial administration under the advisement of the interior minister also served as perpetrators of the genocide.

Civilian Defense Structure

To relate the disparities between civilian defense and Interahamwe, it is essential to elaborate first on the command structure of the CD. It was the shared opinion of its forefathers that civilian defense be presided over by government officials and the RAF (Nahimana et al., 2003). The following ICTR cases enumerate that it was the responsibility of each prefecture to steward their own civilian self-defense. The Ministries of Interior and Defense represented the national level of CD, deriving its upper-echelon from the MRND party (Karemera & Ngirumpatse, 2012, February 2): "this was a government activity" (para. 1062). One testimony avowed that subsidiary Ministries managed civilian defense forces: the Ministries of Primary and Secondary Education, Youth and Sports, Family Affairs, and Tourism (Bagosora et al., 2008). Kambanda outlined in his May 25, 1994 directive a hierarchal framework for how CD committees should be configured at the sectoral, communal, prefectural, and, more so, at the national level (Karemera & Ngirumpatse, 2012). His proposed outline for CD provided that committees be arranged to coordinate CD "at every level of government from the national to the sector level" (para. 470). Decisions on appointments to the national coordinating committee were overseen by the defense ministry and at times deliberated with the Ministry of Interior. Nevertheless, prefects were advised by the national committee to harmonize civilian defense committees at the sectoral, communal, and prefectural level. Committees were responsible for the administration of CD training, infusing discipline, and "providing weapons and logistical support" (Bagosora et al., 2008, para. 478). Both defense and interior ministries generated lists of available reservists and gendarmes, residing within each prefecture, to direct the physical development of civilians. Beyond urban domains, well into surrounding rural regions, military personnel were sought after as instructors (Bagosora et al., 2008, December 18). Prefects circulated the lists of reliable reservists and citizens to the administrators of CD who would voluntarily work closely with RAF to defend neighborhoods (Bagosora et al., 2008). CD, for two or more prefectures, could be administered by one prefect; as an example, Nsabimana presided over CD for both prefectures of Gikongoro and Butare (Simba, 2005, December 13). Conversely, the interim government presided over the Cyangugu prefecture civilian defense (Munyakazi, 2010, July 5).

In like manner, bourgemestres, otherwise known as mayors, were prominent organizers of civilian defense within prefectures (Simba, 2005, December 13; Setako, 2010, February 25). Bourgemestres were asked by prefects to devise a militarily-themed program for training citizens within their respective communal boundaries. A germane example comes from the testimony of witness FAI in the case against Kanyabashi (2008, February 15). The accused was a bourgemestre in Butare prefecture. He was asked by prefect Nsabimana to create a standardized plan to train Butare's civilians in military maneuvers. FAI further recollected a government program to annihilate Tutsi being discussed by the bourgemestres of the Butare prefecture. Communal councillors occupied the lowest level of the hierarchy (Des Forges, 1999).

Local military reserves worked with communes and served as relief instructors, administering guidance and rendering strategies conducive to improving trainee performance. As evidenced by the prosecutor in Simba (2005, December 13), Gikongoro reservists, communal police, and two drivers with military backgrounds were noted by the accused to conduct the trainings of civilian defense. In the same vein, the *Prime Minister's Civil Defense Directive of May 25, 1994* stated that "communal police and reservists were responsible for providing training in each locality" (para. 478). Already noted in Ntagerura et al., (2005, February 25), two gendarmes were recruited to assist in instruction at Shagsha Tea.

The historical record relaying recruitment of civilian defense has variably been referred to in ICTR cases as beginning at different times in different prefectures. In the cases of Nahimana et al., (2003, December 3) and Bagosora et al., (2008, December 18), recruitment for occupying roadblocks began in 1990, namely, in Northern prefectures. Authorities had little difficulty recruiting men for civilian defense training: "people fought for the opportunity to participate" (Des Forges, 1999, p. 404). Colonel Nsabimana recommended nominating one male from "each unit of ten households" to be trained and armed (Des Forges, 1999, p. 83), the equivalent of sixty men, to safeguard their commune. The ultimate decision as to which citizen to arm was made by the communal council. In December of 1993, communal conferences in Nkuli and Mukingo were organized towards the recruitment of CD; RAF Generals were at the helm of hand selecting citizens to undergo training (Ndindiliyimana et al., 2005, December 2). Kambanda remarked in his May 25, 1994 directive that any able-bodied and physically fit Hutu male prepossessing "high moral character" (Des Forges, 1999, p. 83) "of good conduct, who lived in the same neighborhood, cellule, or secteur" (para. 1276), ideally aged between twenty-five and forty years, would be considered for recruitment (Munyakazi, 2010, July 5; Des Forges, 1999). In a similar vein, recruits were ideally between twenty-five and forty (Des Forges, 1999). By the same token, Hutu with Republican leanings, assured of the need to participate in irregular civil defense activities, were inducted (Bagosora et al., 2008). In the later stages of civilian defense, bourgmestres "sent councilors and their subordinates from house to house to sign up all adult males, informing them when they were to work" (Des Forges, 1999, p. 234).

Purpose of Civilian Defense

To a large extent, ICTR testimonies were themed, allowing the researcher to identify four purposes of CD: to support RAF, to defend Hutu localities, to flush out Tutsi and obviate the risk of them fleeing, and to exterminate Tutsi.

One purpose of civilian defense was to assist soldiers in front-line combat: "to support soldiers at the battlefront" (Munyakazi, 2010, July 5, para. 152)..."to reinforce the armed forces" (Munyakazi, para. 157). In the same vein, the cases against Kanyabashi (2008, February 15) and Nahimana et al., (2003) likewise confirmed that the express objective of CD was to advance the work of the Rwandan Armed Forces and to reinforce their formations. As an example, Karemera instructed Nsengiyumva to provide civilian reinforcements to RAF operating in or around Kibuye, namely the Bisesero region (Bagosora et al., 2008). Moreover, the RAF operating in Kigali was allocated the lion's share of Nsengiyumva CD command.

In his May 5, 1994 directive, Kambanda expressed that the overarching purpose of the civilian defense design was to, first and foremost, guarantee the preservation of the Hutu people and to embolden Hutu to defend themselves, their kindred, and households against RPF attacks (Ngirumpatse, 2012). Noted in Bagosora et al., (2008, December 18) as early September 1991, Colonel Nsabimana proposed to the Minister of Defence to provide "one gun for every 10 households and 1,760 guns for Muvmba, Ngarama, Muhara and Bwisige communes....the government distributed 500 Kalashnikovs to civilian authorities" (para. 509). In any event, Hutu populations were vulnerable or incapacitated; able-bodied Hutu were encouraged to assist their neighbors and nearby Hutu communities. Kajelijeli, the bourgmestre of Mukingo commune, nurtured the development of a civil defense project that came to be known as the 'Virunga Force'; the force was entrusted to safeguard the commune's population (Kajelijeli, 2003, December 1). CD also made arrangements for the safe-conduct of Hutu displaced by the war effort or derived from areas liberated by the RAF (Nahimana et al., 2003). The case against Ntagerura, Bagambiki, and Imanishimwe (2005, February 25) has provided that not all civilian defenses were coordinated for citizen protection but were additionally to protect Hutu business interests. In January of 1994, the factory manager of Shagasha Tea was approached by two of the defendants. They informed him that Tutsi had attacked Rwanda and that members of his workforce should be ready to thwart any attack on the factory that could inadvertently disrupt production. Thirty employees were known to have undergone training from January until March of 1994. They were shown how to handle firearms so that at the right time they could defend themselves and workplace cohorts.

A few ICTR testimonies deduced that the principal purpose of CD was to exterminate Tutsi, e.g., Ndindiliyimana et al., (2007) "the militia were being trained in preparation for the mass killing of Tutsi civilians" (para. 18) and Kanyabashi (2008, February 15). Gahima (2013) elucidated the "so-called civil defense system whose declared mission was self-defense, but whose real mission was to carry out massacres of members of the Tutsi community" (p. 44). One witness added disparately that "the training was not within the framework of civil defense, because after that people went to kill Tutsi" (Nahimana, Barayagwiza, & Ngeze, 2005, January 12, p. 24). Conversely, Karemera and Ngirumpatse (2012, February 2) stated the contrary. Witnesses corroborated in the forenamed case that it would be egregious to consider that civil defense programs had been designed to eliminate Tutsi.

Claimants have avouched that civilian defense forces were entrusted to prevent Tutsi from fleeing Hutu-controlled zones. The cases of Nahimana et al., (2003), Rwamakuba (2006, September 20), and Karemera and Ngirumpatse (2012, February 2) give credence to the claim that Tutsi were forbidden to leave Rwanda en route to Zaire or other neighboring refugee destinations. CD manned roadblocks to single out Tutsi and forestall their escape and "to inflict harm upon them" (Karemera and Ngirumpatse, 2012, February 2, para. 326; Rwamakuba, 2006, September 20), or, as regarded in the Meetings of the Consuls of Ministers on April 27, 29, and 30, 1994, to unmask the enemy and his accomplices (Bagosora et al., 2008) and to "identify and kill Tutsi" (Ngirumpatse, 2012, para. 1081). CD scoured forests in search of accomplices (Kanyabashi, 2009, January 14). CD administrators slated Hutu civilians to gather intelligence on the presence and movements of Tutsi within their commune and, to a greater extent, denounce RPF collaborationists and Tutsi infiltrators within their larger prefecture.

Length of Civilian Defense training and number of participants

The record posits that civilian defense training lengths varied, differing by the number of weeks or months. Moreover, the purported number of civilians undergoing training at one time is incongruous among the vast spectrum of testimonies. An observer reported that "in some places, one cycle of training immediately followed another...one group of trainees in a town comprised about 400 men...in the end several thousand men were trained" (Des Forges, 1999, pp. 402-403). As already mentioned, training start dates in the Northern prefectures of Ruhengeri and Byumba were decidedly earlier, dating back to 1990, and taking place until 1994 (Ndindiliyimana et al., 2007, June 18).

It is my opinion that CD training began in other prefectures as early as January 1994 up until April 1994 (Ntagerura, Bagambiki, & Imanishimwe, 2005, February 25; Karemera & Ngirumpatse, 2012, February 2; Simba, 2005, December 13). Prosecution in the case against Kajelijeli (2003) inferred that "people began training in 1991...training continued until 1994" (para. 335). Concurring with my argument is Ntagerura, Bagambiki, and Imanishimwe (2005, February 25) which has demonstrated that CD training commenced as early as January 1994, ongoing until March 1994, for thirty employees of the Shagsha Tea factory. Similarly evidenced in the case against Karemera and Ngirumpatse (2012, February 2) on March 29, 1994, an organized group of civilians in Kigali were trained in traditional weapons use. Corresponding namely with Ntagerura et al., (2005, February 25) in the case against Simba (2005, December 13), prosecution witness YF attested that CD training for thirty Hutu entrants lasted from January until March of 1994 in Rukondo, Gikongoro prefecture: twice a week from 10.00 a.m. to mid-day. Simba (2005, December 13) is compatible with Ntagerura et al., (2005, February 25) on two points: training lasted three months, e.g., January to March 1994 and involved thirty trainees per session. Witness YF in Simba (2005) estimated that twenty-four training sessions were conducted over the span of these three months. YF was present during training on two occasions and observed other training sessions from a nearby location.

In Setako (2010, February 25), one attestant suggested that civil defense training was two weeks, beginning sometime between April 20 and April 25, 2004. One other witness remarked, "450 to 500 civilians...received military training from soldiers at Mukamira camp in April 1994" (para. 327). This training was believed to have lasted less than 20 days. Witness SLA of the same case asserted having undergone CD training in Nkoli commune on April 12. With 500 other recruits, SLA "began one-and-a-half to two weeks of training at Mukamira Camp" (para. 322). The evidence in Setako (2010, February 25) is consonant with the *Prime Minister's Civil Defense Directive of May 25, 1994*. The directive "called on people to join the army...[with the explicit] need to organize...people and train within the next 15 days" (para. 477). However, this directive proffered "detailed instructions on the urgent organization of CD in Kigali, Kigali-rural, Byumba, Ruhengeri and Gisenyi prefectures" (Bagosora et al., 2008, para. 472), to be completed over a fifteen day period.

Civilian Defense Training Environment
Civilian defense forces were trained at the local level (Des Forges, 1999). Explicating the training locations of both Interahamwe and civilian defense will illuminate additional doubtless differences between these two perpetrators. This section details the diverse environments in which CD forces were trained. Youth members of the CD were "trained on the roads of their communes" (Munyakazi, 2010, July 5, para. 157), trained in communal offices (Simba, 2005, December 13), and, specifically in the case of Ntagerura, Bagambiki, and Imanishimwe (2005, February 25), employees of the Shagsha Tea factory were trained on the fields surrounding the factory; the neighboring Nyungwe forest was converted for training use. Des Forges (1999) described how hundreds of men converged on football fields and in stadiums to receive training. Few testimonies suggested a lack of training locations to accommodate citizen demand. One commune in Butare reportedly became weary when the territorial administration neglected developing additional camps to address this demand. Percipient witnesses in the area implied that men were rushing to local training grounds to receive firearms and subsequent training on how to use them. A similar issue was reported of Nyakizu commune; community members bandied together, teaching themselves combat skills, inviting neighbors to participate.

Civilian Defense Training Content
The Party's approach to civilian defense training was dichotomous: Party ideology, imbued with anti-Tutsi precepts, and rudimentary

military training, emphasizing defense with traditional weapons (Bagosora et al., 2008). As reminisced by one witness of his two weeks of training, the Party drilled lessons teeming with anti-Tutsi hate messages into their students (Setako, 2010, February 25). He alleged that they were taught that "Tutsi and their accomplices were the enemy" (para. 327) and taught "to obtain information on the actions and presence of the enemy in the commune and cellule" (Ngirumpatse, 2012, para. 1081). Anti-Tutsi indoctrination texts and meetings were integral for fuelling the violence of the civil defense. Bagosora customized propaganda campaigns distinct to each commune's Tutsi situation. Sensitization meetings were held immediately after training that, namely, reiterated parallel themes of killing Tutsi. However, they did serve additional means. Orators instructed CD to "give their full support to their government and to collaborate with the Rwandan Armed Forces" (Ngirumpatse, 2012, para. 1030). The prosecutor in Karemera and Ngirumpatse (2012) rebuked sensitization speeches; "instead of halting the genocide the speeches and documents actually intensified the genocide" (para. 1030). Meetings gave instructions on how to ferret out uncensored propaganda material on the radio and, at the same time, enemy coordinates.

Verwimp (2004, June 22) suggested that Habyarimana's ideology glorified the peasantry; the author holds that Habyarimana identified himself as a peasant. Tutsi were contrasted to occupying a feudal position within Rwanda; they refused to till land and were likened to colonist occupiers. When an authoritative power is legitimized by a peasant ideology, the author contemplated that "genocide becomes a political option (and indeed almost a necessity) because a peasant society does not tolerate the existence of non-peasants" (p. 25). Revolutionary-laden ideology was the linchpin of Rwanda's genocide, justifying Hutu aggression against oppressive Tutsi. The contrast between Khmer Rouge's Democratic Kampuchea and Habyarimana's Rwanda, the author contends, were salient. He maintained that Habyarimana's forced cleansing of Kigali was analogous to or modeled on Pol Pot's emptying of Phnom Penh. Habyarimana's campaign of forced ruralization allowed him to gain control over the mobility of citizens.

There exists an apparent discord in ICTR accounts about the instructional resources used in training. On the one hand, traditional weapons were mentioned, e.g., machetes, bows and arrows, spears, and swords (Karemera & Ngirumpatse, 2012, February 2; Simba, 2005, December 13; Bagosora et al., 2008) as a consequence of there being a deficit in firearms: "insufficient firearms available" (Karemera & Ngirumpatse, 2012, February 2, para. 636), and on the other hand, advanced weapons were mentioned, e.g., firearms and grenades (Simba, 2005, December 13; Ntagerura, Bagambiki, & Imanishimwe, 2005, February 25; Bagosora et al., 2008). Witness LAO commented on receiving military training in the manner of handling firearms and explosives in the name of civil defense (Karemera & Ngirumpatse, 2012, February 2). Coincidently, in testimony against Kajelijeli (2003), prosecution witness GAO testified to receiving training in firearms as early as 1991: "civil defense members were trained in the use of firearms" (para. 335).

Apart from the apparent rupture in ICTR testimonies, Bagosora, as cited in Des Forges (1999), noted CD training as constituting instruction on the use of hand grenades, rifles, bows and arrows, and spears. This CD was known to have fashioned targets out of "empty tins with bull's eyes painted on or marked with chalk" (p. 107). Demonstrations on how to properly discharge firearms were, for few, the principal objective of their training. They were shown how best to achieve the furthest trajectory when hurling spears and launching bows (Des Forges, 1999). Through awareness campaigns, Hutu populations were advised to locate traditional weapons such as arrows, spears, and bows, as prosecution in Karemera and Ngirumpatse (2012, February 2) regarded such weapons as "cutting and thrusting weapons" (para. 1070). In the opinion of the researcher, both traditional and advanced weaponry were used for training, the latter used when firearms were readily available and more toward the end of the genocide, when the RAF was in dire straits.

Interahamwe Origins and Structure

The Interahamwe had their genesis namely in the commune of Mukingo, in Kigali prefecture in 1991 (Kajelijeli, 2003, December 1). They were established as the youth wing of the MRND at first, to proselytize communities, in order to build awareness of the MRND agenda (Kajelijeli, 2003; Munyakazi, 2010). Prosecution witness GDQ commented that "the youth wing of the MRND was called the Interahamwe and that it existed since the formation of the MRND Party by President Habyarimana" (Kajelijeli, 2003, para. 350). Dr. Bangamwabo exclaimed that an MRND member by the name of Murenzi Desiree forged in 1991 "the Interahamwe as a think-tank for young people, to create political awareness among the youth" (Kajelijeli, 2003, p. 14). Moreover, he alleged that the Interahamwe were often referred to as "young civil servants who were brought together to carry out a political or ideological aim" (Kajelijeli, p. 14). Worth mentioning further, Dr. Bangamwabo pointed out that Interahamwe means those who "have the same view because they are together, people who have the same height, gait and possibly the same objectives, and it means that they stand in solidarity" (Kajelijeli, p. 14).

In a similar way with CD, the shared occurrence, succinctly highlighted in few ICTR cases, was that Interahamwe were created to serve manifold purposes: to assist in communal security and activities (Munyakazi, 2010; Nchamihigo, 2008, November 12; Karemera & Ngirumpatse, 2012, February 2; Kajelijeli, 2003), "to fight for the defense of the country" (Munyakazi, 2010, para. 141), to protect MRND officials as remarked in Karemera and Ngirumpatse (2012) toward the end of 1993, and to ready MRND youth to support the front-line activities of the Rwandan Armed Forces (Karemera & Ngirumpatse, 2012, February 2, para. 276). In my view, MRND youth formally organized under the Interahamwe banner (translated as, 'those who stand together' or, alternatively, 'those who fight together') were mobilized toward the objective of ethnically cleansing Rwanda's Tutsi population (Kamuhanda, 2003, January 22; Kajelijeli, 2003). Likewise confirmed in the case against Bikindi (2001, July 4), the prosecutor derided the accused, as well as other MRND who knowingly deployed militias to exterminate Tutsi.

From its inception, the Interahamwe elected eleven leaders in total, five of whom formed the National Committee, with the remaining six members serving as advisors. Robert Kajura was elected first Interahamwe president. Georges Rutaganda acclaimed as his vice president. The Interahamwe were organized at each level of government; the Interahamwe leadership was modeled after the MRND's own structure, with officials at the national, prefectural, and communal levels (Muhimana, 2004, April 11):

circumstantiated additionally in Mpambara (2007, August 9) and Kajelijeli (2001, January 1), "there were organs at préfecture, commune and cellule levels" (section 4.2). Interahamwe leaders were sourced from within the Interahamwe apparatus (Munyakazi, 2010, July 5). Each sector and commune acquired its own group of Interahamwe; however, Interahamwe leaders were, at times, at the disposal of bourgmestres (Kajelijeli 2003, December 1), or, as demonstrated in Mukingo in 1994, Joseph Nzirorera was positioned as Interahamwe president, while concurrently holding the office of bourgmestre (Karemera et al., 2005, August 24).

The MRND structure held considerable governmental and political sway over the Interahamwe. Matthieu Ngirumpatse was the residing President of the MRND during the weeks leading up to and during the genocide (Karemera & Ngirumpatse, 2012, February 2; Malvern, 2006). Ngirumpatse entered domestic politics in 1991. His first appointment was as Chairman of the Kigaliville prefecture. In May of 1992, he accelerated to the position of National Secretary of the MRND and to National Party Chairman and Chairman of the MRND Executive Bureau in July of 1993. He occupied both positions until 1994. Ngirumpatse held de jure authority over MRND dealings and "was the individual in Rwanda with the most de facto power and influence and authority over the Interahamwe during the genocide" (Karemera & Ngirumpatse, 2012, para. 1546). Elucidated in the case against him, prosecution held that "the principal group responsible for coordinating the military training for the Interahamwe was the Executive Bureau of the MRND" (para. 279).

Interahamwe Recruitment

In its inaugural stage, Interahamwe were derived from Hutu-Akazu football clubs. The contemporary image evinced by Interahamwe recruiters appealed to young misguided youth. As early as 1990, 'Hutu Power' leaders jetted around on motorcycles, donning dark sunglasses, pop hairstyles, and peacockish pajama suits, attracting raw Hutu youth recruits to their fledgling movement (Gourevitch, 1998; Munyakazi, 2010). MRND youth wings had to compete against rival political youth movements to recruit Rwanda's best and worst. Interahamwe recruited between the ages of 18 and 35 (Munyakazi, 2010), however, "if a 40-year-old was strong and able-bodied he could be a member of the youth wing of the MRND, but this was uncommon" (para. 93). A trusted party background and the ability to be implicitly relied on to store secrets were requisites for selection (Karemera & Ngirumpatse 2012, February 2). Any recruit, merely on the account of him being Hutu, strong, healthy, and male, was accepted (Nchamihigo, 2008, November 12). Enlistment guidelines during the second phase of the Civil War were broadened to expand the recruitment horizon of Interahamwe; this marked the departure of youth joining the Interahamwe for ideological reasons, in my opinion.

Multiple accounts insisted that members of the Interahamwe "consisted of unemployed illiterate youths, who were involved in many violent incidents, particularly during and after political rallies" (Karera, 2007, December 7, para. 40). In like manner, the evidence adduced from the case against Karemera, Ngirumpatse, and Nzirorera (2005, August 24) shows that, "over time, the MRND Interahamwe "youth wing" attracted and incorporated unemployed, delinquent youth that often engaged in illegal activity" (section 24.1). The MRND sculpted them from unintelligent thugs to disciplined and politically-educated killers. Gourevitch (1998) regarded recruits as atrophied youth, "wasting in idleness and its attendant resentments" and had likely perceived the opportunity of genocide as nothing short of an extemporaneous carnival (p. 93). Promises of intoxicants, a military identity, and a steady provision of food incentivized scum to swell the ranks of the Interahamwe. Rallies were forged as a result of word-of-mouth advertisement. Interahamwe spokespersons attracted a throng of youth by coaxing them with free alcohol. Rallies were followed by bibulous marching and enticing, truculent speeches (Alverez, 2006). Prunier (1995) commented that "a lumpen-proletariat of street boys, rag-pickers, car-washers, and homeless unemployed," (p. 231) swarmed around Interahamwe recruiters. Rwanda's economy during the 1980s and early 1990s was substandard, compared to other African nations. Poor economic performance culminated in rampant unemployment. Many still affected economically or displaced by the first phase of the Rwandan Civil War resided in temporary makeshift camps near Kigali. Interahamwe recruiters pamphleteered these camps, inciting displaced youth to participate. Des Forges (1999) estimated that sixty percent of Rwandans were younger than twenty years of age, giving thousands of Hutu scant hope "of obtaining land needed to establish their own households or the jobs necessary to provide for a family" (p. 11). The opportunity to get even with Tutsi bourgeoisie "was the best thing that could ever happen to them...[to] take revenge on socially powerful people as long as they were on the wrong side of the political fence" (Prunier, 1995, p. 231). The MRND promised farmers and land cultivators propriety over Tutsi land, property, farm animals, materials, and building and housing equipment, e.g., roofs and windows, in exchange for active membership. To Hutu entrepreneurs, spendthrifts, and elitists, home ownership and control over Tutsi businesses, vehicles, and TVs was their impetus for involvement (Des Forges, 2009).

In Moore (2009), an erstwhile Interahamwe disclosed why he swore fidelity to the MRND. It was not what the Hutu government informed him of, he continued; it was what he intercepted on an RPF radio broadcast. The claimant commented: "They broadcast the names of my neighbors, saying that they had blocked Tutsi from getting water at the wells...This was true, but how did they know that? I became convinced there were Tutsi informers among us" (para. 16). Nonetheless, Interahamwe formations steadfastly increased in membership and continued to attract profiteering opportunists once the genocide commenced. By 1992, Rwandan paramilitaries were provisioned with 580,000 machetes and an accompanying 85 tons of heavy weaponry. Lists of Tutsis were compiled and distributed as early as January 1992. Hutu police and soldiers slandered the reputation of those participating in the genocide for purely profit-driven motives.

Embroiled in the impending genocide were 700 to 1500 Presidential Guards and a larger Hutu RAF contingent comprised of 50,000 troops. At any rate, the enrollment of Interahamwe in the moments leading up to the genocide still required augmenting. Mueller (2001) provided a summative assessment on Interahamwe motivations for entering the training program; however, Mueller's remark about "foreign drifters who had chiefly signed up not for ideological reasons" (p. 114) should be carefully considered:

> Most of them hastily recruited in the previous few years from landless peasants, the urban unemployed, and foreign drifters who had chiefly signed up not for ideological reasons, but rather for the guaranteed food and

drink (each man was entitled to two bottles of beer a day, a luxury by Rwandan standards) and for the opportunity to loot, because pay was low and irregular (Mueller, p. 114).

Radio and print communications were fundamental in the registration of Hutu youth. Published print materials encouraged youth enlistment, namely, the famed-publication *Kangura*, translating in English as "to wake others up" (Malvern, 2004). According to the Montreal Institute for Genocide and Human Rights Studies, two radio stations precipitated Tutsi hate propaganda: Radio Rwanda and Radio Television des Milles Collines (RTLM). Félicien Kabuga, in conjunction with Kangura magazine, bankrolled RTLM's activities. The purpose of the RTLM was to safeguard Hutu power. The station broadcasted, from July 8, 1993, to July 31, 1994, primarily anti-Tutsi rhetoric infused with a language of hate and belligerence. Ethnic nationalism or ethnicism resulting therefrom was sent teeming throughout Hutu tribes. RTLM targeted Rwandan youths as audience members by playing cotemporary Zairean music, unlike other radio outlets, and it introduced humour. The station played to the prejudices of Hutu animosity toward Tutsi. Even Bagosora proposed that the RTLM play songs spewing anti-Tutsi lyrics, outwardly imitating Hutu's famed national singer, Bikindi (Des Forges, 1999). Broadcasts rallied Hutu youth to protest peace talks between Habyarimana and the RPF. At times, the primary purpose of the station appeared to be a tool to aggrandize the president; RTLM glorified Habyarimana as a martyr of the Hutu people on the day of his demise on April 6, 1994. On this day, the RTLM led the vocal castigation of Tutsi rebels and implored Hutus to exterminate Tutsi and initiate the final war; the code word "cut down the tall trees" played on a looped transmission signaling to Hutus to start the 100-day bloodletting of Tutsi. During the second phase of the Civil War, the station divulged the locations of fleeing Tutsi and advised Hutu audiences to apprehend them. Yanagizawa-Drott (2012) estimated that the RTLM broadcasts were responsible for an estimated 9.9 percent of the participation in the violence perpetrated against Tutsi, suggesting reliably 51,000 Tutsi deaths. By and large, the interim government did not intervene nor moderate the station's vulgar anti-Tutsi stance, nor did it insist that the station tone down their reckless encouragement of violence toward Tutsi.

Interahamwe Training and Development
Training of Interahamwe was part of the conspiracy in which to murder Tutsi (Kajelijeli, 2003). The MRND initially established the Interahamwe as a "military training organization for training MRND youth" (Muhimana, 2004, April 11, p. 2). MRND youth in receipt of military training metamorphosed into militias capable of slaughtering innocents. Quoted from the following case against Bizimungu, Ndindiliyimana, Mpiranya, Nzuwonemeye, and Sagahutu (2002, November 14), in order for the MRND to execute a mass-scale extermination of Tutsi with speed and ease, "it was necessary to create a militia that was structured, armed, and complementary to the Armed Forces" (section 4.13).

Interahamwe training start dates and locations were not systematically synchronized across all prefectures. In Northern Rwanda, e.g., Mukingo, Interahamwe training began in 1991 (Kajelijeli, 2003; Malvern, 2006). The researcher is unsure whether civilian defense training in Ruhengeri and perhaps other Northern prefectures predate Interahamwe training in the north. In 1991, a branch of MRND, entitled *Civil Defense*, known alternatively as *Virunga force* or *Amahindure*, came into existence (Kajelijeli 2003). This researcher believes that *Civil Defense*, underscored in Kajelijeli (2003), singularly represents that Interahamwe began training in 1991 and was not CD. Amahindure were trained to operate firearms, e.g., R4s, Chinese-made grenades, and M26s; this is another indicator that these were Interahamwe trainees, not CD. The case also stated that Amahindure was the name given to the Interahamwe residing in the Mukingo commune, as well as possibly the entire Interahamwe representative of the Ruhengeri prefecture. Malvern's (2006) research confirmed that Interahamwe training started as early as January of 1991; however, it was overseen by French instructors for Interahamwe leaders and RAF instructors of Interahamwe (Malvern, 2006). An incompatible viewpoint was that bourgmestres and sector councillors in Ruhengeri began administering Interahamwe training in 1992 (Kamuhanda, 2003, January 22). Moreover, in the cases of Karemera and Ngirumpatse (2012, February 2) and Karamera et al., (2005, August 24), congruent with the research findings of Malvern (2006), it was stated that Interahamwe, in the prefecture of Kigali, were militarily trained in Gabiro, Bigogwe, and several other sectors in Kigali, beginning training sometime between March and July of 1993. Likewise, Interahamwe in Bugarama, Cyangugu prefecture were trained between October of 1993 and April of 1994, "on diverse dates at diverse locations in and around Bugarama commune" (Munyakazi, 2010, July 5, para. 135). Kajelijelil (2003) and Setako (2010, February 25) contend that few Interahamwe in Mukingo began training in January of 1994; Setako (2010, February 25) has also shown that training commenced here on April 12, 1994 and continued throughout the genocide. This latterly provided training, as described in Setako (2010, February), was urgent – a resultant decrease in military training from mere months to a measly two-week learning experience, allowing Karorero to instruct 150 Interahamwe only at the commune office. Their training concluded when supervising instructors were of the opinion that the trainees attained competence as shooters.

Despite these incongruences, and lack of incontrovertible evidence proving that training of Interahamwe youth began in 1991 or 1992, it is in my opinion that training began for most Interahamwe youth in 1993. A letter written by Ngirumpatse on February 15, 1993 to Habyarimana evincing the author's urging of "secret training of civilian youth" (Karemera and Ngirumpatse, 2012, February 2, para. 275) is the clinching evidence needed to patently confirm that the organization of the Interahamwe training program began as early as 1993.

Interahamwe Instructors

The present researcher opines that the majority of instructors for Interahamwe training were gleaned from the Rwandan Armed Forces. However, there was no official link between the Rwandan Armed Forces and the Interahamwe (Muhimana, 2004, April 11). Numerous oral histories have corroborated the use of RAF in conducting training of Interahamwe (Simba, 2004; Muhimana, 2004; Alverez, 2009; Kajelijeli, 2003; Bizimungu et al., 2002, November 14; Munyakazi, 2010, July 5; Malvern, 2006; Hirondelle News, 2005).

According to Alverez (2009), "President Habyarimana's Rwandan military openly trained, armed, and supplied the militias," as well as coordinated forays with the Interahamwe to "maximize their genocidal reach" (p. 87). RAF members were temporarily discharged from service to assist in the military training of Interahamwe (Kajelijeli, 2003). To serve as an example in Kigali: "government buses turn[ed] up at the barracks in 1992, carrying certain soldiers to secret places where they would train the unemployed" (Malvern, 2006, p. 26). Bizimungu, Chief of Staff for the Rwandan Army, collaborated with other military leaders across Rwanda, conducting training "simultaneously in several prefectures around the country: Ruhengeri, Cyangugu, Gisenyi and Butare, as well in the Mutara Sector" (Bizimungu et al., 2002, November 14, p. 4). He ordered Colonel Nkundiye, in 1993, to supervise the training of Mutara Interahamwe in conjunction with Major Mpiranaya, "who sent him some of his subordinates for this purpose" (Ndindiliyimana et al., 2002, September 25, section 4.17). Major Francois Uwimana of the Bigogwe camp spearheaded the militaristic training of the Bigogwe Interahamwe (Malvern, 2006). Prosecution witness DA argued that Interahamwe, ordinarily in the area of Gabiro, were "trained by Rwandan soldiers" (Hirondelle News, 2005, para. 2). In a continuation of witness DA's account, a throng of 500 to 600 enlistees were ushered into training coordinated by RAF instructors. Christophe Nyandwi, Interahamwe President of Cyangugu, presided over the training of Cyangugu-based Interahamwe with Sergeant Major Ruberanziza (Nchamihigo, 2008, November 12). All in all, the irrefutable evidentiary materials, seen through a training lens, indicate a high degree of collaboration between Interahamwe leaders and RAF in the training of Interahamwe.

During military training sessions, more than one instructor's presence was required (Kajelijili, 2003; Munyakazi, 2010). Comparatively, in the case against Munyakazi (2010), Aziz, the Interahamwe leader in the Bugarama commune, also moonlighting as his Interahamwe's resident weapons instructor, was always accompanied by two other trainers. Notably, a pattern emerged after having reviewed ICTR transcripts that trainers of Interahamwe came in threes. Coinciding with the testimony of GDD, prosecution witness GAO testified that Karorero, then "a sergeant in Habyarimana's army and a person of Nyiramakuba, as well as two corporals named Musafiri and Bimenya...conducted the training" (Kajelijeli, 2003, para. 361). Furthermore, training across two or more communes or prefectures could oftentimes be directed by one person (Nchamihigo, 2000). As evidenced by the case of Ntagerura, Bagambiki, and Imanishimwe (2004, February 25), the accused Ntagerura trained Interahamwe in the Karengera commune and other communes within the bounds of Cyangugu as early as January of 1994 and up until July of 1994.

Members holding both bourgmestre and Interahamwe portfolios were responsible for inculcating ideological change in recruits. Noted in Kajelijeli (2001; 2003), the accused, then bourgmestre and leader of the Interahamwe in the Mukingo commune, lectured on the ideological proclivities of the MRND to his fraternity. In the same way, sensitization meetings were held for civilian defense; in like manner, they were held for Interahamwe. After military exercises, meetings were held to ready young Hutu psychologically for combat (Kajelijeli, 2003). Kajelijeli, with forenamed Karorero, at times trained together Interahamwe. Karorero likely served as second-in-command under Kajelijeli. A hierarchy among instructors for Interahamwe training became apparent to the researcher. The lead instructor, in this case Kajelijeli, shepherded ideological development, and a supporting instructor, Karorero, oversaw physical development. Karorero himself served as the primary instructor of military training, attended by two Corporals.

Professors were also under the employ of military camps (Nchamihigo, 2000). The researcher has inferred that here they assisted with the educative earmarks of the genocide. A group of Interahamwe in Murangi were instructed by Nchamihigo, and, moreover, he "sought the support of Professors Razare and Aimable Twagirayezu" (Nchamihigo, 2008, November 12, para. 42). In a different vein, communal policemen (Simba, 2004), gendarmes (Munyakazi, 2010), and Presidential Guards (Malvern, 2006) held instructor positions in the Interahamwe. As an example, in Camp Kigali as early as 1992, Nkundiye, a Belgian trained Presidential Guard, accompanied by Colonel Nzabanita and with the moniker Gisinda, was responsible for training Interahamwe (Malvern, 2006).

Train-the-trainers of the Interahamwe

I wondered if training camps served separate purposes. Were there train-the-trainer locations explicitly designed to educate trainers? Furthermore, did political leaders who arranged training for Interahamwe receive their training at a location to which Interahamwe youth were forbidden access? Having rearranged the historical record through a training lens, six train-the-trainer centres became apparent: Kabuga (Karemera & Ngirumpatse 2012), Gabiro (Malvern, 2006; Bikindi, 2008, December 2; Hirondelle News, 2005, January 13), Club Jaly (Bikindi, 2001, July 4), Mukamira (Kajelijeli, 2003, December 1), CIPEP in Gikongoro town (Simba, 2005, December 13; Simba, 2004, May 6), and Bigogwe (Kajelijeli, 2003, December 1).

The principal instructors of Interahamwe trainers were French forces (Malvern, 2006; Bikindi, 2008, December 2; Des Forges, 1999). The French played a pivotal role in training RAF soldiers, "who would in turn serve as instructors for [Interahamwe]" (Des Forges, para. 70). There are a number of incongruences in the historical record relating to when and where French forces began training Interahamwe leaders and RAF instructors of Interahamwe. The earliest account was Malvern (2006), who maintained that French forces trained Interahamwe leaders in Gabiro as early as January of 1991. I found no sources confirming the January, 1991 start date. However, two sources, Bikindi (2008, December 2) and Hirondelle News (2005, January 13), confirmed Gabiro as a military train-the-trainer location beginning toward the end of 1992. In the case against Bikindi (2008, December 2), the accused confirmed the existence of a military training centre in Gabiro, as well as admitting to personally assisting French instructors in the military training of a small group of Interahamwe around 1992-1993. Conflicting testimonies were posited in this case against Bikindi. In one testimony, a former RAF member noted that he received training in Gabiro and that Gabiro was sui generis reserved for RAF only, and absolutely no Interahamwe trained here (Bikindi, 2008, December 2); another testimony, congruous with Bikindi's own, corroborated that Interahamwe leaders, unskilled in military combat, received training here in 1992. Witness DA likewise affirmed that French instructors drilled Interahamwe politicos in Gabiro on survival techniques and in the use of firearms

(Hirondelle News, 2005, January 13, para. 2). French instructors continued training RAF instructors well into the month of January, 1994 (Bikindi, 2001, July 4). The accused, in close collaboration with French instructors, trained RAF instructors at Club Jaly, located in Kigali (Bikindi, 2001, July 4; Karemera & Ngirumpatse, 2012, February 2).

Prefects, bourgmestres, councillors, and others politically responsible for arranging Interahamwe training required training themselves, as evidenced in Karemera and Ngirumpatse (2012), Simba (2005, December 13), Simba (2004, May 6), and Kajelijeli (2003, December 1). As an example, prosecution witness HH reminisced being invited in 1993 to the Kabuga Building, alongside sector and neighboring commune leaders of Kigali. HH and the others were placed by the MRND into training cloaked in secrecy, "prior to beginning the selection of youths to undergo training" (Karemera & Ngirumpatse, 2012, para. 282). His statement highlights that in 1993, Kigali leaders at the prefectural, communal, and sectoral levels were ideologically and militarily trained before the mainstay of Interahamwe youth. While here, the witness received training from a quondam Presidential Guard member named Gaparata. One testimony in Karemera and Ngirumpatse (2012) maintained that senior Interahamwe and MRND officials were also given training here and sent to Gabiro, likely for military training, congruous with DA's testimony in Hirondelle News (2005, January 13) and Bikindi's (2008, December 2); and Bigogwe confirmed in the case against Kajelijeli (2003, December 1) that the accused was the founder of Mukingo's Interahamwe and trained in Bigogwe. In like manner, the triumvirate of Gikongoro in March 1993: Aloys Simba; Laurent Bucyibaruta, then prefect of Gikongoro; and Captain Sebuhura of the RAF orchestrated a learning program intended to train trainers of future Interahamwe, including both MRND and Interahamwe leaders, bourgmestres, councillors, and others politically responsible in the Gikongoro region (Simba, 2005, December 13; Simba, 2004, May 6). Aloys Simba held alleged "de facto control over the military, the Interahamwe, [and] the gendarmes" in both the cities of Butare and Gikongoro (Simba, 2005, December 13, para. 24). Remarked in the case against Simba (2005, December 13), training was contrived for communal leaders of Interahamwe as late as January of 1994 at CIPEP in

Gikongoro. Their training emphasized military tactics less, focusing mainly on instructions of how to administer censuses and register people. Two types of registers were instructed: one intended for registering Hutu and the other for Tutsi.

In addition to Gabiro and Bigogwe, Interahamwe trainers received an education in weapons use in Mukamira camp. In the case against Kajelijeli (2003, December 1), the prosecution attested that these trainers correspondingly "led youth at [the] Eager School on exercises training in the handling of weapons, particularly the Kalashnikov" (para. 362). However, witness GAP of the same case interpolated a mismatched version at Mukamira, claiming that the camp was used for military practice, not training. If Mukamira served Interahamwe leaders as principally a practice environment, this speaks volumes to the forethought that went into the educational framework and infrastructure of Interahamwe training.

Interahamwe Ideological Training Content
Underpinning many curriculums with genocidal content involves the dyadic interaction of military exercises and ideological insemination. From discrediting the Arusha Accords to slandering Tutsi, Hutu Power ideology pervaded the masses, either ignorant or educated. In Gisenyi, with an audience of 4,000, the authenticity of the Arusha Accords and the terms and conditions stated therein were publicly denounced (Karemera, Ngirumpatse, Nzirorera, 2006, June 16). Ideological sessions spanned three weeks (Alverez, 2009). Hate propaganda escalated between 1991 and 1994, resulting in steady increases in MRND membership. In Bikindi (2001, July 4), the prosecutor maintained that the accused's group of Interahamwe imbibed on his virulent antagonism toward Tutsi; he vilified impartial Tutsi and members of the political opposition, typifying them as RPF accomplices in the press. After socializing his troupe in matters of the Party, he spurred his Interahamwe on throughout training to decimate all suspected accomplices. Since birth, Hutu parents told their children that "they could tell who the Tutsi were because of how they were shaped" (Moore, 2009, para. 9). Accomplices were described by Hutus as unknowns who spoke Kinyarwandan poorly or as "persons who openly declared their affiliation with the RPF" (Karemera & Ngirumpatse, 2012, para. 286). A tradition began in

1992, where Hutu organizers began gluing banana leaves above Hutu front doors so Hutu residences could easily be distinguished from Tutsi.

The 'Hutu Power' movement was developed as an ideology under the MRND, the ideological precepts pioneered by Leon Mugesera, Ferdinand Nahimana, and Hassan Ngeze (Nyirubugara, 2008). The 'Hutu Power' political platform was oblivious to the mainstay of inductees; as for these murderous Hutu, the ideological aspect of the genocide was far too esoteric (Nyirubugara, 2008). For weak-minded neophytes, simple instructions on how to encroach upon Tutsi and murder in manageable proportions sufficed.

To a large extent, the desensitization of Hutu to violence through a Hutu Power ideology, I believe, is unrivaled as a reason for the genocide - a parallel view shared by Verwimp, as he bemoaned this exclusionary ideology as "culminat[ing] in the implementation of the genocide plan" (p. 7). Nyirubugara (2008) identically hold Hutu-Power ideology responsible for the genocide. The ideology of Hutu Power has been alternatively referred to as the other "name given to the genocide ideology in Rwanda" (Nyirubugara, 2008, para. 2). The author argued that genocides need an established ideology, referencing previous genocides, e.g., the Holocaust and the scope and extent ideology played. Hutu Power ideology permeated Hutu discourse beginning in December of 1990, when *Kangura*, the mouthpiece of the MRND, published *the Ten Commandments of the Hutu* (Prunier, 1995; Des Forges, 1999). This commentary on Hutu society suggestively had a circulation of 10,000 and was printed at no cost to the MRND (Hutu Hate Propaganda, 2009). The commandments were transmitted to Hutus through the mediums of radio and print newspapers (Des Forges, 1999). Adelman and Suhrke (2000) hold that "these commandments were supposed to appeal to and guide the supporters of the Habyarimana regime in how to deal with their enemy, the Tutsi" (p. 75). The Ten Commandments elaborated below were excerpted from the December, 1990 issue of *Kangura*:

> 1. Every muhutu should know that a mututsi woman, wherever she is, works for the interest of her Tutsi group. As a result we shall consider a traitor any muhutu who

marries a mututsi woman, makes a mutusi woman his concubine, employs a mututsi woman as secretary or makes her his dependent.
2. Every muhutu should know that our bahutu daughters are more suitable and conscientious in their role of women, spouses and family mothers. Are they not beautiful, good secretaries and more honest?
3. Bahutu women, be vigilant and try to bring your husbands, brothers and sons back to reason.
4. Every muhutu should know that every mututsi is dishonest in business. His only aim is to enhance the supremacy of his ethnic group. As a result, we shall consider a traitor any muhutu who forms an alliance with batutsi in business, invests his money or government's money in a mutusi enterprise, lends or borrows money from a mututsi, gives favors to batutsi in business, such as obtaining import licenses, bank loans, construction plots, public markets, etc.
5. All strategic posts, be they political, administrative, economic, military or security must be entrusted to bahutu.
6. The education sector (pupils, students, and teachers) must be majority Hutu.
7. The Rwandese armed forces must be exclusively Hutu.
8. The Bahutu should stop having mercy on the batutsi.
9. The bahutu, wherever they are, must have unity, solidarity and be preoccupied by the fate of their Hutu brothers. The bahutu, both inside and outside Rwanda, must constantly look for friends and allies for the Hutu cause, starting with our bahutu brothers; they must constantly counteract the Tutsi propaganda; the bahutu must be firm and vigilant against their common enemy.
10. The 1959 social revolution, the 1961 referendum and the Hutu ideology must be taught to every muhutu at all levels. Every muhutu must spread widely this ideology. We shall consider a traitor any muhutu who will persecute his muhutu brother for having read, spread and taught this ideology (Source: Hutu Hate Propaganda, 2009, p. 1).

The historical record is in agreement concerning the negative implications stemming from these ten Hutu ordinances.

The pursuance of policies structured around the ten commandments' philosophy and the Hutus' unhealthy consumption of a hate ideology staked on ethnicity ultimately gave rise to the atrocities in Rwanda (Adelman and Suhrke, 2000). Correspondingly, Grunfeld and Huijboom (2007) surmised that the commandments fanned "the flames of ethnic hatred, resentment and fear against the Tutsi population and Hutu political opponents who supported the Tutsi ethnic group" (p. 23).

Members of the interim government attended rallies, vocalizing Hutu Power concepts. Rallies and meetings multiplied Hutu involvement in the violence. After the assassination of the Burundian president, "the tone and intent behind the speeches…took on a more sinister tone" (Karemera & Ngirumpatse, 2012, February, para. 1016). In a similar fashion, evidenced in the case against Gatete (2011, March 31), the accused instructed an audience to begin desensitizing others "to the killings" (para. 153). Attacks on Tutsis grew more intense in the hours after Gatete's public spectacle; as a result, Interahamwe in attendance marshaled further reinforcements for the attacks. Whilst still in their dormancy, military authorities invited Interahamwe to attend MRND meetings at the local and national levels. Energetic Interahamwe careerists took the stage to make pedantic showcases of their dedication to the Tutsi annihilation: "they took the floor to demand ruthless action against Tutsis and those who helped them" (Des Forges, 1999, p. 226). The prosecutor in the case against Karemera, Ngirumpatse, and Nzirorera (2005, August 24) deduced that public meetings and rallies were sites of indoctrination, which in turn "led propaganda efforts to accelerate the genocide" (p. 20). Similarly, the researcher herein refers to meetings and rallies as frequent, knowledge-imparting events, at times arbitrarily imposed on communities, thereby necessitating my claim that these events were educative. Furthermore, MRND cleverly utilized music, song, rhyme, and beats to convey Hutu Power ideology. The powers of song and lyrics have been identified here as training tools. In the same way songs were parroted during rallies, "songs were sung during training whose import was that the Tutsi should be exterminated" (Bagosora et al., 2005, February 2, para. 36); and "singing "Tubastembatsembe" (we will kill you all)" (Moore, 2009, para. 15).

Verwimp (2004) reckoned that an overlooked and oftentimes neglected aspect of the genocide was Habyarimana's ideology of agrarian economics. The author delved into speeches made by Habyarimana, dating from 1973 through to 1994, to explore how Habyarimana's macro-economic policies played, if any, an integral role in the genocide. The underlying economic principle endorsed by Habyarimana was that the Hutu way of life was to tend to the fields (The New Times, N.D). This oft-discounted ideology restricted rural migration to Kigali. Government authorization was needed for changes in residency, and "permission was rarely given" (Magnarella, 2002, p. 33). Moreover, Habyarimana made meager attempts to diversify Rwanda's economy. He had created no viable alternative sectors, for he continually persisted on pursuing agri-centric policies (Magnarella, 2002). Relating Habyarimana's economics with the ideology of 'Hutu Power', Tutsi were likened to aristocratic enslavers of the native Hutu peasantry (Magnarella, 2002). In Verwimp's view (2004), Hutus decried Tutsi feudalism, referencing the historical servitude of the Hutu peasantry. The Hutu ideology told that, "they [were] always plotting against the Hutu and working for the benefit of their own ethnic group" (p. 7). Multiple ICTR cases document the extent to which abusive verbiage was used, referring to Tutsi: "training of the Interahamwe included the use of incendiary language illustrative of an intent to exterminate the Tutsi population" (Kajelijeli, 2003, p. 94). Tutsi were censured as being "dangerous plants IGISURA that must be uprooted" (Ndindiliyimana et al., 2005, December 2, para. 17) or as "bad grain [to] be separated from the good grain" (Ngirabatware, 2012, December 20, para. 1312). The ideology fervently decried Tutsi as subhuman. It upheld Tutsi as alien invaders or as *inyenzi* (cockroaches) citizens and never truly considered Tutsi as citizens to the fullest extent of the word (Magnarella, 2003). Aside from an agrarian ideology, a religious ideology further deepened the demarcation of Tutsi and Hutu. Religious ideology "contributed to the country's deepening demographic problems" (Magnarella, 2003, p. 33). Catholicism was the religious centerpiece for the majority of Hutus. Tutsi historically refused the attempts made by missionaries for their conversion. Purportedly, demons found refuge within RPF guerillas (New Times Rwanda, N. D). The demonization of the enemy and thereby their wanton destruction the MRND promised perpetrators celestial rewards (Magnarella, 2002).

Military Training of Interahamwe

Habyarimana envisioned all Hutu persons benefiting from military training. He even mandated his top confidants, bearers of graduate degrees, to attend re-education of sorts to solidify their obedience and unwavering support on policies likely concerning the Tutsi problem (Des Forges, 1999). Military training was a versatile mechanism, adopting many faces to accommodate the learning needs of MRND youth. All Interahamwe received an education in military foundations; however, there is a patent rupture in the historical record pertaining to for how long raw Interahamwe recruits were trained. Four sources refer to the length of military training being four months (Ntagerurua, Bagambiki, & Imanishimwe, 2006; Zigiranyirazo, 2008, December 18); three months (Munyakazi, 2010); and for one month (Karemera & Ngirumpatse, 2012, February 2). The incongruencies are less significant when contrasting the number of trainees inducted into each military training program; in late 1993, 600 people, gleaned from different communes, trained in a military barracks in Bigogwe (Zigiranyirazo, 2008, December 18). This figure is likewise confirmed by the case against Kajelijeli (2003): "600 or 620 members of the Interahamwe from Mukingo and Nkuli communes began to train at the commune office" (para. 365); and in July 1993, 700 were trained at an undisclosed location in Kigali (Karemera & Ngirumpatse, 2012, February 2). However, as inferred in Setako (2010, February), when training lengths decreased to a meagre two weeks as a result of Hutu engagement in the second phase of the Civil War, groups of 120 were hastily trained, namely in firearms use.

Habyarimana demanded that the location and knowledge of training environments be withheld from the wider public (Karemera & Ngirumpatse, 2012, February 2). Soldiers were taken to secret training destinations, thereby requiring inordinate logistical supports to get them there (Malvern, 2006). The structural mainstays of training centres were constructed in rural areas adorning the deserted countryside. Habyarimana rejoined to his critics that the RAF was training these men to become National Park Guards.

Military training of Interahamwe materialized in Kigali, Byumba, Gisenyi, and Kigali, notably at Ruhengeri, Gako, Gabiro, Mukamira, and Bigogwe camps contiguous to neighboring forests, including Akagera in Umutara and Gishwati in Gisenyi (Karamera et al., 2005, August 24; Karemera & Ngirumpatse, 2012, February 2). Training had been conducted simultaneously in several prefectures around Rwanda: "Ruhengeri, Cyangugu, Gisenyi and Butara, as well as in the Mutara sector" (Ndindiliyimana et al., 2002, September 25, section 4.15; Bizimungu et al., 2002, November 14). In Malvern's (2006) account, "there were several training places" (p. 26); however, she hones in on two: one situated near Kigali International Airport and the other in a camp near Gisenyi. Des Forges (1999) perceived that the two dominant military training encampments were Gabiro (located near Akagera Game Park) and one other located in the North-Western forest of Gishwati, close to the Habyarimanian-owned Hotel Mont Muhe. Gishwati trainees resided in tents. Instructors welcomed reputable men of inspiration and prestige as guests into the camp. They toured the compound, inspiring motivation and proffering verbal encouragement. Respected MRND and business officials ventured from Kigali to offer support. In January of 1993, staff from the Hotel Mont Muhe slaughtered and roasted a cow in honour of the trainees: "the tired and sweaty recruits came out of the forest fifteen or so at a time to enjoy the barbecue and plentiful beer" (Des Forges, p. 101).

In Dorn and Matloff's (2000) research, the authors posited that Interahamwe leaders "trained their subordinates not to defend territory, but rather in commando tactics such as the use of knives, machetes, rope trapping and binding of victims and silent guns so as to kill people" (para. 33). Before the inauguration of genocide, Gourevitch (1998) opined that "paramilitary drills were conducted like the latest hot dance moves" (pp. 93-4). Oftentimes, the president and his wife would observe student drills, applauding their ostentatious displays of learning. While Interahamwe members converged in private, they "organized themselves into small neighborhood bands, drew up lists of Tutsis, and went on retreats to practice burning houses, tossing grenades, and hacking dummies with machetes" (Gourevitch, 1998, pp. 93-94). Interahamwe were inculcated in infiltration tactics to penetrate behind RPF's housed frontlines. During traditional weapons practice, students "slic[ed] through a banana tree with only one cut" just as they presaged to do with Tutsis (Moore, 2009, p. 32). In Nyamata, this practice was observed to simulate tearing through human flesh and bone (Moore, 2009). Recruits were shown how best to handle a machete. Instructors provisioned trainees "with human-shaped dummies" (Alverez, 2009, p. 90). They were trained "to handle weapons and use explosives and then later they were taught to kill, with the emphasis on speed" (Malvern, 2006, p. 26). To assist in a swift killing, Interahamwe were instructed to sever the Achilles heel, so as to immobilize the victim (Malvern, 2006). Practice in advanced weaponry, particularly firearms, was often one week long and involved target practice within designated forested training zones (Ntagerura et al., 2006). In Bugarama specifically, training was conducted on two adjacent football fields on site and "at the CIMERWA football field all [sic] of Bugarama Commune" (Munyakazi, 2010, July 5, para. 135) off Tenth street. The witness implied that training accommodated on occasion ten trainees per session. Prosecution witness BWW asserted that the training took place "at locations called Kibangira and Ninth Avenue" (Munyakazi, 2010, July 5, para. 142). Recruits were provisioned with pieces of wood fashioned into the same shape as rifles for practice (Munyakazi, 2010, July 5). Interahamwe were "trained to handle M26 and Chinese-made grenades, Kalashnikovs and R4's" (Kajelijili, 2003, p. 75) and ML4 rifles. They did not have the outward appearance of soldiers, testified Emmanuel in Moore (2009); notwithstanding, they were "young men trained to fight with machetes and guns" (para. 24). Trainees were also provided with grenades to throw into homes to burn (Alverez, 2009). The Rwandan press published on March 17, 1992 that the Interahamwe were described as "well trained killers" (Mubangutsi, 1995, p. 55).

Interahamwe were provisioned with uniforms and weapons "as a sort of graduation from training" (Kajelijeli, 2003, para. 375; Setako, 2010, February 5). Interahamwe uniforms were of mixed colours, bearing resemblance to camouflage; breast pockets were affixed with MRND insignia (Bagosora, et al., 2008). Interahamwe were easily distinguishable by their Kitenge uniforms, e.g., "an African garment often wrapped around the waist" (Karera, 2007, December 7, para. 40). When training ceased, Interahamwe were assigned cloak-and-dagger names, e.g.,

Kuwait or Zulu (Hirondelle News, 2005) and permitted to return home. Mueller (2001) opined that there was an estimable 1,700 Interahamwe who received uniforms and sufficient training prior to the genocide; however, in my opinion, that number may reflect the amount of Interahamwe trained in both Ruhengeri and Kigali prefectures only.

There are two moot points I would like to comment on before entering my analysis. As training of Interahamwe continued into 1994, it became more overt and more notorious over time: "on some occasions be seen training in public places or on their way to the training sites" (Bizimungu, Ndindiliyimana, Nzuwonemeye, & Sagahutu, 2002, November 14). A second unexpressed point and rather removed from the available literature is that centres additionally existed as outposts for continuing learning and development. As noted in the case of Ngirabatware (2012, December 20), as early as March of 1993 within the commune office in Nyamumba, there was a "center for commune development and continuing training" (para. 125).

Comparative Analysis
When reviewing the record through HRD lenses, I have deduced new insights when looking more in-depth at the learning sessions contrived for two perpetrators of Rwanda's genocide. The primary objective of this present research was to use the training lens to reorganize the historical record to further discern the differences between civilian defense and Interahamwe. This research reflects an analysis of history through a training lens; moreover, rearranging the historical curriculums relaying the learning of two historical groups can elevate an HRD academic to the role of historian. The present research holds that armed civilian defense forces and Interahamwe were culpable as malefactors in the Rwandan genocide (Nahimana et al., 2003; Kanyabashi, 2008, February 1; Gahima, 2013; Rwamakuba, 2006). Suffice it to say, my research has shown that civilian defense was about organizing Hutu communities together to train them militarily for the purpose of cleansing Rwanda's Tutsi population (Tottten, 2011; Ndindiliyimana et al., 2007, September 11). Likewise, Interahamwe training was organized to convert politically-motivated citizens into militias (Kamuhanda, 2003, January 22; Muhimana, 2004, April 11) for the express purpose of exacting

genocide and crimes against humanity against Tutsi (Kajelijeli, 2003; Kamuhanda, 2003; Bikindi, 2001, July 4). It should be duly noted that the researcher has inferred no instance or claim where civilian defense forces trained Interahamwe; however, few sources hold that Interahamwe trained civilians in civil defense (Karemera & Ngirumpatse, 2012, February 2).

One of my conclusions is that the Interahamwe evaluated post-training performance; as for civilian defense, the researcher has not found any clinching evidence indicating otherwise. Meetings were held between prefects and Interahamwe figureheads to "assess the advancement of the killings" (Kanyabashi, 2009, January 14, para. 32). Notwithstanding, they carried out evaluations of how Tutsi killings proceeded to guarantee an efficient extermination strategy. *Prima facie* evaluation of the extermination strategy appeared to have only been related to Interahamwe genocidal actions, not civilian defense. One case affirmed my provisional conclusion. In Ntagerura, Bagambiki, and Imanishimwe (2006, July 7), one of the accused, Bagambiki, was known to have evaluated training of Interahamwe in Gashirobwa.

Many other differences persist, relating to how the organization of training for either group was implemented. Through the training lens, when viewing who prepared and implemented training at the prefectural level, novel discernible differences can be ascertained between the two perpetrators. Prefectural and sectoral MRND leaders (Nahimana et al., 2003) and prefectural and sectoral Interahamwe leaders, although in a few instances they were one and the same, had organized training for Interahamwe (Simba, 2004, May 6; Simba, 2005, December 13). Furthermore, civilian defense training was presided over by prefects (Bagosora et al., 2008), bourgmestres (Kanyabashi, 2008, February 15; Bagosora et al., 2008), and the ministries of interior and defense (Nahimana et al., 2003; Karemera & Ngirumpatse, 2012, February 2), with the express financial backing of the interim government.

Training Sites and Learning Environments Differed
Through the training lens, I have further discerned more disparities between the two perpetrators by the significance that they accorded to the location of their training. The record signaled that

Interahamwe trained in prefectures other than their own; more so, they killed Tutsi in prefectures other than their home prefecture. Civilian defense forces trained in the same area in which they killed. No anonymity was required. Interahamwe members were recruited from their home communes and shipped off to train in seclusion far from home. By and large, CD training was open and easily viewable (Munyakazi, 2010, July 5; Des Forges, 1999). Civilian defense training, unlike that which the Interahamwe received, served a genocidal intention in their home commune and neighbouring communes (Simba, 2005, December 13). CD was already familiarized with their neighbours and the surrounding environment; being trained on their stomping grounds reinforced neighbourly dependence and maintained continued relations among Hutu brethren. The mainstay of Interahamwe training sites were surreptitious and kept from the public eye at the request of Habyarimana (Malvern, 2006), elsewhere remarked as the "secret training of civilian youth" (Karemera and Ngirumpatse, 2012, February 2, para. 275). Interahamwe trained in remote rural areas: forested domains requiring the residing of trainees in tents (Malvern, 2006) and in military compounds in Kigali, Byumba, Gisenyi, and Ruhengeri, notably at Gabiro, Mukamira, and Bigogwe camps (Karemera et al., 2005, August 24; Ndindiliyimana et al., 2002, September 25; Karemera & Ngirumpatse, 2012, February 2). As training of Interahamwe continued into 1994, it became more overt and less surreptitious over time; "on some occasion [Interahamwe could be] seen training in public places or on their way to the training sites" (Bizimungu et al., 2002, November 14).

Length of Training Differed
Through the training lens, it is possible to reorganize the historical record pertaining to training length of both perpetrators, to infer which group proffered longer training sessions. Civilian defense training was suggested to have been two weeks (Setako, 2010, February 25; Bagosora et al., 2008), a matter of fifteen days (Bagosora et al., 2008), or a period of three weeks (Simba, 2005, December 13). The length of training hinged on the prefecture and the likelihood that the said prefecture could come under RPF attack. In Ntagerura et al., (2005, February 25), Shagsha Tea employees, under the aegis of civilian defense, participated in

military training for a period of up to three months, twice a week, from 10 am to mid-day.

After a careful review of the available sources, few Interahamwe training times were deduced. For the most part, not many training times enveloping the entire Interahamwe learning experience were provided - only the length of time given to either ideological development, e.g., three-weeks as noted by Alverez (2009), firearms training, e.g., two weeks (Setako, 2010, 25 February), or one week (Ntagerurua, Bagambiki, & Imanishimwe, 2006). Likewise, Interahamwe training was noted as being four months in some cases (Ntagerurua, et al., 2006), three-months (Zigiranyirazo, 2008, December 18), and one month (Karemera & Ngirumpatse, February 2), decreasing to a meagre two weeks beginning on April 12, 1994, (Setako, 2010) in the days preceding the beginning of the genocide. Training for both Interahamwe and civilian defense forces were known to have declined in length amid the genocide. Training was an urgent matter for both perpetrator groups during the protracted second phase of the Civil War. Through the training lens, I conclude that CD would not need to be long; why would it be, when CD were only trained on how to kill most efficiently unarmed Tutsi, not armed Tutsi rebels?

Instructional Resources Differed
Further inextricable differences between the two perpetrators were inferred by thematizing the training resources allotted to the learning of either perpetrator during training. Interahamwe were in receipt of technical weaponry for practice. Civilian defense forces were provisioned with mainly traditional weapons. Interahamwe were instructed on how to use R4s, Chinese-made grenades, M26s, and mines (Kajelijeli, 2003; Moore, 2009). Some sources detract from the validity of my conclusion; Interahamwe were also trained in the use of traditional weapons, machetes, bows and arrows, spears, and swords (Gourevitch, 1998; Setako, 2010; Dorn & Matloff, 2000; Karemera & Ngirumpatse, 2012, February 2; Ntagerurua, Bagambiki, & Imanishimwe, 2006; Des Forges, 1999). Notwithstanding the similarities, civilian defense forces were trained in the use of traditional farming tools for fighting, e.g., scythes, shovels, and machetes. The use of traditional weapons in a training environment as training resources led to my legitimate inference that civilian defense can be distinguished from

Interahamwe, by looking at the resources employed to train either group.

Acknowledging civilian defense use of traditional weapons as instructional resources as the evidence through the training lens suggests, civilian defense groups were trained to: repress attacks by Tutsi civilians and target unarmed Tutsi infiltrators or accomplices other than RPF. In the case against Bagosora et al., (2008, December 18), the prosecutor opined that "arming Civil Defense forces with traditional weapons indicated that their target was civilian rather than military" (para. 484). Providing traditional weapons for post-training performance, Caddick-Adams claimed, likely discouraged civilian defense from engaging "better trained troops where they would certainly lose" (Bagosora et al., 2008, para. 486).

Instructor use Differed
Through the training lens, the instructors utilized to train civilian defense differed dramatically from those training Interahamwe. The Interahamwe training network borrowed instructors from the Rwandan Armed Forces (Alverez, 2009; Kajelijeli, 2003; Simba, 2004; Muhimana, 2004; Bizimungu, et al., 2002, November 14; Munyakazi, 2010, July 5; Hirondelle News 2005; Malvern, 2006), French military personnel (Malvern, 2005; Bikindi, 2001, July 4; Bikindi, 2008; Hirondelle News, 2005, January 13), Presidential Guards (Hirondelle, 2005; Malvern, 2006), communal police (Simba, 2004), and, to some extent, university professors (Nchamihigo, 2008, November 12) to assist principally with the ideological components of the curriculums. French lecturers were also utilized to instruct RAF who, in turn, trained Interahamwe; there was no recorded instance of this applying to CD. In like manner, Interahamwe trainers at the prefecture, sectoral, and communal levels were militarily and ideologically trained, foregoing training of Interahamwe youth. Civilian defense received instruction by gendarmes (Ntagerura et al., 2005, February 25; Simba, 2005, December 13) and army reservists (Ntagerura et al., 2005, February 25; Simba, 2005, December 13). Bourgmestres were informed that "there should be training in each sector and that reservists and communal police should conduct the trainings" (Simba, 2005, endnote. 38). Conversely, one witness spoke of his experience while a member of the Bugarama

Interahamwe, that he was "trained by soldiers and gendarmes belonging to a detachment" (Munyakazi, 2010, para. 142) close to Munyakazi's residence; evidently this contradicts my provisional assumption that gendarmes only trained civilian defense.

Interahamwe had a heavier ideological component
Interahamwe curriculums involved a more cumbrous ideological component than CD. Civilian defense training interventions did incorporate Party ideology; nonetheless, since training times were noted three weeks at most and dwindled steadily during the genocide, CD learners likely encountered less ideology in their training than Interahamwe (Setako, 2010, February 25). Sensitization meetings were held for civilian defense routinely upon exiting the program (Setako, 2010; Karemera & Ngirumpatse, 2012, February 2). For both groups, sensitization meetings supported MRND objectives by propagating anti-Tutsi beliefs (Kajelijeli, 2003). Verwimp (2004) contended that Interahamwe's learning of anti-Tutsi ideology drove the genocidal plan home (Nyirubugara, 2008). Through song, music, and dance, Interahamwe evinced their hatred of Tutsi. Public meetings and forums as avenues for indoctrination were frequented more by Interahamwe than CD (Karemera et al., 2005, August 24). Alverez (2009) contended that Interahamwe received upwards of three weeks of political indoctrination, whereas the entire CD learning experience military and ideology training combined was, at most, three weeks. The researcher has found no sources confirming Alverez's claim of a three-week indoctrination session.

Civilian Defense a National Human Resource Development (NHRD) undertaking
Civilian defense can easily be discerned from Interahamwe in the historical record, when viewing training organized by the MRND as a national human resource development (NHRD) undertaking. Through the training lens, civilian defense framed exclusively for Hutus is reminiscent of an NHRD initiative purported to uphold the safety of Hutu citizens from perceived Tutsi aggression. NHRD connotes a national agenda (McLean, 2004). Kim (2012) referred to NHRD "as the development of a national policy to improve the well-being of its citizenry and is normally devised by governmental departments, has been accepted as one of the frame-

breaking developments in HRD" (p. 242). In the case against Nahimana et al., (2005, January 12), the accused claimed that "Civil Defense should be in the domain of public authority, whereas the Interahamwe and other such militias were in the domain of political parties" (para. 649). More to the point, McLean (2004) regards NHRD as going "beyond employment and preparation for employment issues to include health, culture, safety and community" (p. 269). The researcher wishes to draw attention to McLean's use of "safety" and "community" in his definition for the purpose of the following discussion. NHRD, in the same manner shared with contingency planning, can organize and institute strategies to safeguard Hutu safety, and, more so, engineer preventative measures to ward off unwanted threats. Civilian defense and the training interventions underpinning such defense initiatives underscore safety and survival education. Kim (2012) implied that problems faced by a specific community that share "demographic, economic, social, or other characteristics have been addressed by HRD interventions" (p. 243). The Hutu, a community bound by social and economic parallels, faced an enemy outside their purview of affiliation, the Tutsi, primarily wealthy, land-holding peoples. Through the NHRD lens, "well-targeted awareness campaigns and educational strategies serve as the platform for preventative measures" (Mace, Venneberg & Amell, 2012, p. 338). The NHRD intervention identified here is that MRND used the educative strategy of civil defense preparedness to safeguard Hutu survival. In the same vein as the Soviet Union preparing Russian citizens during the Cold War, MRND civilian defense was grounded on two analogous principles: first, it was organized at the territorial level to protect the entire nation through continuous training on safety measures, and, second, "civil defense called on the mobilization of material and human resources of the nation as a whole" (Arnold & Wiener, 2012, p. 34). Consonant with Arnold and Wiener (2012), the researcher here acknowledges that at the national level, MRND reached out to its human resources by proffering military training to avail their safety.

Rwanda had already documented a history of utilizing the populace through an NHRD program called Umaganda, i.e., community service. Umaganda first originated on February 2, 1974, under the authorship of President Habyarimana. Umaganda required Rwandans to "perform unpaid collective work one day per week" (Verwimp, 2004, September 12, p. 18). In the same breath, Des Forges (1999) commented that Umaganda "allowed national and local officials to mobilize and control the labor of the entire Rwandan adult population one day every week" (p. 234). Rwandans voluntarily sacrificed a day's labor to improve the well-being of their collective - a practice that continues today takes place every last Saturday of the month. Umaganda extended to bourgmestres and prefects the necessary experience to quickly organize and mobilize citizens to action. Des Forges, as well as Verwimp, maintain that parallels exist between the organization of civil defense and Umaganda. Both authors had steadfastly argued that, in Umaganda, bourgmestres used "their authority to summon citizens for communal projects, as they were used to doing for Umaganda" (Des Forges, 1999, p. 234). The MRND superimposed civilian defense on the Hutu populace. MRND-controlled media fervently reminded Hutus of the necessity of the program by underscoring safety and community as the foci of civilian defense. MRND proposed civilian defense as a national endeavor, financed, organized, and implemented by the territorial administrations, to assist in the CD plan fully being realized (Karemera & Ngirumpatse, 2012).

By analyzing the historical record through a training lens, it is comprehendible that the Hutu government advocated this bestial NHRD policy to serve a second aim: to ethnically cleanse Tutsi (Ndindiliyimana et al., 2007; Kanyabashi, 2008, February 15; Gahima 2013; Nahimana, Barayagwiza, & Ngeze, 2005, January 12). In support of this viewpoint, Verwimp (2004) proposed that young people aged 14 and 25, "Habyarimana demanded...engage themselves actively in the national development enterprise, who would do a lot of killing during the 1994 genocide" (p. 32). The Hutu Power ideology of the MRND likened the murder of Tutsi to performing a state service: "killing people was considered as doing a job...[telling] youngsters...they were working for the development of the country when they participated in the killing campaign" (p. 32).

Verwimp's (2004, September 12) work explored the likeness of decisions made by the MRND regarding Umaganda in 1982, 1984, and 1986 that bore similarities to the civil defense program. Verwimp contended that this juxtaposition: "shows how a policy of forced unpaid work, designed to control and exploit the peasant population and to enable local and national officials to mobilize the population for collective ends, can be turned into an efficient extermination machine" (p. 30). A recognized comparison between the two programs was that the 1982 meeting accentuated the completion of projects: "accumulation of unfinished projects or not useful projects must be avoided" (Verwimp, p. 28). This notion, in turn, resonated in MRND propaganda, urging "peasants to finish the project, meaning that nobody should escape" (Verwimp, p. 28). This being said, the similarities are remarkable as national development programs, both beyond question NHRD projects. To further accent the commonalities here of Umaganda and civilian defense, Verwimp indicated that Umaganda as a national works undertaking required that the successes of one prefecture be shared with other prefectures. MRND directives to this effect stressed that Hutu peasants should embrace the killing of Tutsi, as killing was "already going on in the rest of the country" (p. 29).

Su's (2011) work into the collective killings perpetrated during the Cultural Revolution proves fruitful to this discussion. The author contended that "when communities kill, they define the target as either an unredeemable criminal or an enemy" (p. 5). The Hutu community collectively identified Tutsi as the enemy. With the full backing of the state, the author continued, "a community willing to kill collectively exists in the context of state institutions" (p. 5). The large-scale killing of the enemy, Su maintained, "result[s] from the state's sponsorship, acquiesces, or simple failure to stop them, or some combination of the three" (p. 5). MRND aided and abetted the mass extermination of Tutsi, evidenced by their passive stance to quelling the massacres. At any rate, the state fostered an environment for killing by providing violent education to Hutu civilians.

When reorganizing and reviewing the historical record pertaining to Rwanda's civilian defense in the months leading to the genocide through a training lens, the parallelism between the MRND's use of NHRD programs in the past, e.g., Umaganda and civilian defense, becomes evident. The researcher deduced that civilian defense accelerated under the guise of being an NHRD program to serve a two-fold purpose: improve community security and guarantee community security through the *in situ* destruction of the enemy. Umaganda gave bourgmestres and prefects the requisite experience to facilitate quick and precise organization of Hutu for collective means. During the genocide, Umaganda was adroitly converted into a funnel to feed the growing massacre with more killers.

Implications for Research and Practice
Perhaps the primary implication of this research is that when more than one perpetrator of crimes against humanity and genocide are active in one genocide, analyzing the relationship between how each perpetrator group trained and performed their duties, more so, who they killed, and how they killed, can result in the proper identification of the perpetrator responsible for such atrocities. It may seem insignificant to look at training lengths, locations, and the trainers used in the training of genocidal soldiers; however, as this research has demonstrated, when Civilian Defense and Interahamwe were contradistinguished, I was able to form new perspectives on the organization, structure, training, and command of these two groups that have otherwise been absent or neglected by authors of Rwanda scholarship. The primary implication for practice that this chapter, in addition to the two preceding chapters, has shown is how an HRD practitioner, such as me, can venture outside the rigidly accepted and comfortable confines of the never-evolving field of HRD and that we can explore other subject fields by applying a training, development, or human resource development lens to other academic domains such as history, geography, art theory, etc.

Recommendations for Future Research
As this present work has shown, two distinctive groups, oft-times confused to be one and the same, through a training lens can be confirmed - and held accountable for atrocities in Rwanda - as separate perpetrating entities. I hold the opinion that, first, the training lens can be used to hold perpetrators of crimes against humanity and genocide culpable for their actions, and, second, that the training lens can be used to put to rest the confusion as to which perpetrating group participated in what capacity. Future research could look at distinguishing the manifold Serbian paramilitaries, e.g., The Scorpions, White Eagles, or Arkan's Tigers, involved in the wholesale slaughter of Croats or Bosniaks,

amid the dissolution of Yugoslavia or, likewise, Bosnian paramilitaries, e.g., Mosque Doves or Green Berets responsible for the numerous deaths of Bosnian-Serbs. Future research could look more myopically at the four Einsatzgruppen (A-D) that were tasked by Himmler's SS to track down and murder eastern European Jews. An important recommendation for future researchers that continue to discern discrepancies between Interahamwe and CD is that they should revisit this subject matter five, ten, and fifteen years from now. I say this because a limitation of this research is that ICTR activities are still ongoing, and, perhaps, new information pertaining to how either CD or Interahamwe were trained will surface. Most importantly, more research is needed to explore how Rwanda's Civilian Defense resembles a national human resource development (NHRD) undertaking, further reminiscent of Rwanda's Umaganda program. With that said, there is ample NHRD scholarship that could possibly help shed light on how a national human resource development program was utilized to organize and train Hutu civilians toward enacting a genocidal plan against Tutsi. One reviewer of this work had commented that Civilian Defense as an NHRD program only benefited Hutu; therefore, it would in fact be anti-NHRD, as it benefited Tutsi none.

Conclusion

Over twenty-five ICTR cases were reviewed for content documenting how either Civilian Defense or Interahamwe trained. Information pertaining to training of either group was first thematized and, second, comparatively analyzed. Interahamwe training included a more cumbrous ideological element; the location where Interahamwe trained was secluded and withheld from the greater public; Interahamwe training occurred in a prefecture distinct from their own. Civilian Defense training was localized, open, and easily viewable in their communities. Interahamwe training lengths far exceeded the length of training given to CD. Training for Interahamwe was, at times, as long as four months; in contrast, CD typically ran two weeks. However, the length of training depended namely on how likely a commune or prefecture was to come under rebel attack. Another dissimilar feature was that Interahamwe were documented to have been involved in the training of CD, whereas Civilian Defense was in no way involved in the training of Interahamwe. The trainers selected to usher in the development of CD differed from those chosen for training Interahamwe. Trainers of the Interahamwe underwent an arduous and specialized train-the-trainers program for the express purpose of training Interahamwe. Interahamwe were trained by Rwandan Armed Forces and French Legionnaires, whereas CD were trained by army reserves, gendarmes, or communal police. Another markedly different aspect of the Civilian Defense program from that designed for the Interahamwe were the instructional resources allocated to training either group. CD trained with traditional weapons, e.g., machetes, scythes, while Interahamwe trained with technical weaponry, e.g., firearms and automatic rifles. Lastly, Interahamwe were known to evaluate post-training performance; Civilian Defense, as I could not find any record to support, had not evaluated post-training performance.

CHAPTER FOUR
Genocidal Youth Movements: A Comparative Analysis of Political Learning Curriculums

In this research, the genocidal movements of Khmer Rouge (KR) youth and Hitler Youth will be comparatively assessed through a human resource development (HRD) lens to compare the similarities and disparities between the two movements' use of political learning curriculums. Both movements have been described as perpetrators of crimes against humanity: the Khmer Rouge in the Cambodian Genocide and the Hitler Youth in the many genocides enacted against groups considered undesirable in Nazi Germany, e.g., Gypsies, homosexuals, and Jews. The commonalities and discrepancies in political pedagogical curriculums designed for children and youth learners will be the cynosure of this research.

The methods used to obtain an optimal degree of reliability for the Khmer Rouge portion of this present research were three-fold: Communist Party of Kampuchea (CPK) documents that survived Democratic Kampuchea (DK); *Revolutionary Flags* and *Revolutionary Young Men and Women*, two of three magazines published by the Khmer Rouge; and textually-rich accounts of a few who survived the Khmer Rouge. The Party documents I speak of were derived from Chandler, Kiernan, and Boua's (1988) work. The three authors translated (from Khmer to English) eight Party documents and published their translation accordingly in *Pol Pot Plans the Future: Confidential Leadership Documents from Democratic Kampuchea, 1976-1977*. Two of the documents translated were consulted, as they pertained to education and indoctrination of Khmer children: *"The Party's Four-Year Plan to Build Socialism in All Fields, 1977-1980"* and *"Preliminary Explanation before Reading the Plan, by the Party Secretary"*. Secondary sources were sparingly used, limited to newspapers, foreign broadcasts, academic journals, and a few online sources.

The following four sources utilized in the Hitler Youth subsection are of significant historical provenance: Hitler (1939), Rust (1938), and Ziemer (1941 and 1972). Hitler's (1939) seminal publication, *Mein Kampf,* provided the researcher with verbatim descriptions of Hitler's utopian view for Nazi Germany. His work provided Nazi Germany's first outline for moulding the minds of Germany's children to help usher his ideology into existence. Rust's (1938) *Education and Instruction, Official Publication of the Reich and Prussian Ministry of Knowledge Education, and National*

Culture outlined the standards by which elementary, secondary, and post-secondary schooling were to be modeled, not to mention the structured rules for teachers and students to follow in class. Ziemer's (1941 and 1972) magnum opus, *Education for death: The making of the Nazi*, is the best empirical account of life in Pimpfe, Yungvolk, and the Hitler Jugend that I have found.

This research will be a valuable contribution to HRD scholarship, as political and ideological curriculums and primary/secondary school education under the Khmer Rouge and the Hitler Youth have been explicated very little. Ayres (2000) opined in *Tradition, Modernity, and the Development of Education in Cambodia*, "there are few scholarly books or articles dealing with Cambodia's development of social policies and even fewer seriously addressing education" (p. 440). Ayres (1999) further postulated in *The Khmer Rouge and education: Beyond the discourse of destruction*, that "the task of attempting to examine education in Cambodia during the period is heavily reliant...on those transactional records of the regime's upper echelon that have come to light in recent years" (p. 221). Party policies were safeguarded under the DK, culminating in an insufficiency of academic materials of the time surviving, except one geography and one arithmetic textbook, which Clayton (1998) claimed "have not been analyzed...[and] are among the archives of the Tuol Sleng Documentation Center in Phnom Penh" (pp. 9-10). Ayres acknowledges a Ministry of Education existing in DK. However, we cannot patently shine light on its activities, other than a limited production and distribution of textbooks "intended to guide teachers" (p. 109). Ministerial documents have either been lost or never existed, "while education statistics were certainly never compiled" (Ayres, 2000, p. 109). More so, it is unknown to the researcher if a comparative study of politically-themed curriculums between two genocidal groups exists, especially between the Hitler Youth and Khmer Rouge youth.

These two genocidal groupings were not contemporaneous, they existed decades apart. Another limitation of this research is that only subjects with politically-themed curriculums educating either group will be discussed. Moreover, the available literature on Hitler Youth aged 14 through 18 is saturated, with scant published work on Pimpfe and Jungvolk. One other limitation of this research was that the Hitler Youth excluded females; conversely, the Khmer Rouge youth allowed female membership.

Morris and Sweeting (1991) contend that "control of the school curriculum has long been perceived as a primary tool for

HRD of Genocidal Youth Movements 121

maintaining and legitimating political power and the ideology of those in power" (p. 249). The authors differentiate political indoctrination from political education, which for all intents and purposes is important to distinguish, as both terms are used synonymously in Hitler Youth and Khmer youth literature. The authors suggest that political indoctrination warrants a "deliberate use of all socialization agencies to transmit a single ideology as the truth...Political education refers to the attempt to create a critical awareness of political phenomenon by open and balanced discussion of a range of evidence" (p. 249). The researcher maintains that Hitler Youth underwent political indoctrination, and so had Khmer youth. In recognition of this, the work will intentionally avoid using political training, political education, or political development and use instead political indoctrination throughout; Procknow's (2014) work demonstrated the distinction between the three, and he suggested further exploration of political learning amid genocides should carefully consider the uniqueness of the terms and not use them interchangeably.

Connell (1970) asserts when investigating the significance of political learning in schools that "it's necessary to go beyond a study of the schools themselves" (p. 155). Connell's work targets political education, which she claimed raised few empirical questions. The author asks: How are the political ideas of children cultivated? What purveying influence do schools play in their development? To extend her findings, the author advances an additional couple political questions: What forces are at work controlling political education? If political education is undertaken, what will it constitute, and on what grounds will it be planned?

Khmer Rouge, 1975-1979 in Democratic Kampuchea

In Pol Pot's Democratic Kampuchea 1975-79, parents exerted little if any authority over their children. The Khmer Rouge severed family bonds, turned family members onto each other, and destroyed any semblance of loyalty that children had for their parents. The research purpose of this chapter will be addressing the subject matter and impact of Khmer Rouge indoctrination. This contribution looks to discuss the core curricular lessons of the political indoctrination that KR contrived for children.

In 1962, Cambodian Communists organized in secret the grassroots *Alliance of Democratic Khmer Youth*, later rebranded as *the Alliance of Communist Youth of Kampuchea*. Pot held in the highest regard the alumni of *the Alliance* as his loyal circle, which

Ross (1990) maintained he utilized to usurp the Kampuchean Communist Party centre. Recruiting Khmer children was integral for Pot and his coterie of French-educated elite to institute their revolution. Prior to April 17, 1975, Khmer Rouge cadres were tasked with recruiting children from impecunious villages and towns that littered the Kampuchean countryside. Few children were eager to relinquish old societal constructs, out of resentment for having little worth in it. At first, Pot's recruitment of children operated in the same vein as Mao Zedong's campaign enrolling Chinese youth into his Red Guards. After April 17, reluctant Khmer children were conscripted into the Khmer revolutionary army, uprooted from their home villages, and placed into indoctrination camps. After this date, and to a large extent, Khmer children voluntarily embraced Khmer Rouge precepts and sought membership.

Induction of child soldiers and cadres was common during 1975-9, and Khmer children launched their military careers at the age of 12 (Sihanouk, 1980). KR fledglings were typically most savage between 12 and 15 years of age (Pran, 1997), though children as young as five were being trained as cadres (Child Soldiers International, 2001). They continued to recruit boys and girls until 1998 in residual zones still under their control. Aside from the children used in ancillary roles, e.g., ammunition carriers and cooks, many did engage in combat. A KR defector from the area of Pailin confirmed receiving military training at the age of five, and she recounted her membership in a group of 200 to 300 hardened 14 year-old girls. The KR supplied these girls with weapons and prepared them for front-line combat (Child Soldiers International, 2001).

Cambodia made myriad advancements in restructuring education following independence in 1953 (Royaume de Cambodge, 1967). The schooling structure's prodigious post-independence growth was driven in part by Sihonouk dedicating an average of 20 percent per annum of the national budget to broaden primary and secondary school access to all Cambodians. By 1969, 3200 primary schools, 161 secondary schools, and nine universities were founded. To Ayres (2000), this was a "collective increase of over 130% on the number inherited from the French 16 years before" (p. 207). Government funding for schools abated immediately after Lon Nol ousted the Sihonouk government in 1970. In 1971, a year after the transition of power, the government subsidized only 1064 primary schools, with half of the country's 148 colleges determinedly closed (Whitaker, 1973).

In April 1975, when the CPK ousted the Republicans from power, Pot denounced the 'feudal' system of education left by Sihanouk and Lon Nol. Between 1975 and 1979, the Khmer Rouge nullified, dismantled, and destroyed 90 percent of all school buildings, libraries, and equipment (Barron & Paul, 1977). Seven of nine higher education institutions were demolished (Ol, 1979). Seventy-five percent of primary and secondary school teachers and 91 percent of university faculty were summarily executed under Pot's leadership or hastily fled Cambodia before Pot's power-grab (Ministry of Education, 1984). Many of the schools were converted into barracks or retrofitted as prisons. Both Republicans and Communists adopted a decidedly original pedagogical format by converting buffalo stables to classrooms, holding class instruction outdoors under trees, or arranging for public education in community halls. Out of resentment for their putative imperialist undertones, the liquidation of all western-produced textbooks and school materials was ordered by the KR. Books were purloined from libraries and schools and carelessly piled under trees, exposing them to blistering tropical weather conditions and Khmer mistreatment, e.g., starting fires to cook with or used for rolling cigarettes.

Pot believed children over five years should acquire basic literacy. Further, children were to gain experience in interscholastic fieldwork (Vickery, 1984). One teenage girl recollected that schools for children aged six to seven existed in Damban 3. She further remarked that, in every cooperative she visited, above all dreaded cooperatives, schools were still created for eradicating illiteracy (Vickery, 1984). Damban 4 also had had organized primary education for children, where pupils studied two to three hours daily. On some days, basic school would be attended the entire morning, while the afternoon was reserved for manual work in the fields. Foreign Broadcast Information Service (FBIS) (April 18, 1977) and FBIS (May 5, 1977) posited: While pupils digested studies full-time, the remainder of the day would be used for hands-on experience in the fields. With little effort to relieve the plight of children in rural areas still under development, having inadequate access to food and enduring poor living conditions had deleterious effects on their learning.

Political indoctrination of Khmer youth

The Khmer Rouge readied children to serve as the cornerstone of the Party's agrarian and self-sustaining future. The KR created a structured instructional curriculum to indoctrinate Kampuchea's young: that the future the CPK proposed was the correct future. The nation-wide objectives for political indoctrination of children were three-fold: attract their loyalty, incite agitation and violence towards class enemies, and deepen their revolutionary character. Curriculums were conceived separately to achieve each objective. Instructional strategies varied; lectures, radio broadcasts, reading of short-texts, and behavior modeling were most conducive to their learning. Instructional strategies were not limited to one per learning event.

The October 1976 issue of *Revolutionary Young Men and Women*, a prominent KR propaganda communication, explicated that "from the very beginning, the Party determined to take the work of political consciousness as the most important work of all" (p. 1). Pot believed that a young mind was blank and unprejudiced. He envisaged Khmer children approaching the revolution with a mental *tabula rasa*. Pot and his brotherhood were cognizant that their ideology would be easier to impress upon children than upon adults. For this reason, Sihanouk (1980) in *War and Hope: The case for Cambodia*, posited that the KR bestowed upon children the honorary title of "the dictatorial instrument of the party" (p. 27). In 1977, in celebration of the 17th anniversary of the CPK, Pot spoke highly of the revolutionary possibilities of Khmer children:

> [Childhood] is a period of life in which there are very rapid changes...It is a time when consciousness is most receptive to revolution and when we are in full possession of our strengths...This then, is a general directive of our party...It is the youth of today who will take up the revolutionary tasks of tomorrow (Revolutionary Flags, 1977, pp. 48-49).

How children embraced ideological indoctrination was dependent on the region, teacher, and potential rewards for attending. One such region where political learning was met with success was the South-West. Van, a survivor from Damban 35, a locality in the South-West, holds that schools were contrived to brainwash adolescents to evolve into revolutionary zealots. In the South-West, youth excitedly attended propaganda (or livelihood) meetings (Vickery, 1984). Upon their return, observers described that they beamed with optimism and enthusiasm. Van's detailed account, as documented by Vickery (1984), resonates with Quinn's (1976) observations. At a time before April 17, 1975, a group of teenage boys from a South-Western destination returned from a two-to-three week political indoctrination event. Quinn noted that the boys returned "fierce in their condemnation of old ways; rejected parental authority, were passionate in their loyalty to the state and party; were critical and contemptuous of customs; and had a militant attitude" (p. 13). I have identified five prevalent political and ideological indoctrination lessons contrived by the KR for children: loyalty to Angkar, abolishing individualism, self-reliance, the exploitation of the peasantry by oppressive imperialists and city people, and the school of cruelty.

Loyalty to Angkar

Children were instructed to give their unwavering obedience to Angkar, the State (Teng, 1997). Luong Ung recollected a KR educator lecturing children about their duty to Angkar: "Your number one duty is to Angkar...You are the children of Angkar! In you lies our future...Angkar loves you above all else. That is why Angkar gives you so much power" (Marston, 1994, p. 110). In addition to students, lecturers modeled subservience to Angkar to pupils in class.

The CPK viewed family relationships as undermining a child's loyalty to Angkar. Indoctrination would be useless, if family attachments and the tradition of filial piety continued to negate Angkar's influence. An objective of indoctrination was to destroy the family structure from within. Teng (1997), in the *End of childhood*, recounted: "At the re-education meetings, I believed the Khmer Rouge soldiers when they told us that our families did not love us" (p. 158). Families were partitioned into separate camps. Visitations were limited and an earned privilege. If such a privilege were granted, it was customary do so only once a month. Each visitation was supervised. Displays of affection were proscribed by the Party.

Children were instructed to be Angkar's eyes. Adding to the omnipotence and otherworldliness of Angkar, this required children to report on traitorous activity to Party cadres. In one version of the affair, a child named Khel recalled a friend's burning commitment to Angkar:

> Angkar was the one who had done the greatest kindness for them, not their parents...so they should do anything for the revolutionary party...If Angkar pointed out a traitor, they should dare to destroy that person without hesitation, even if the traitor was their mother or father (Hinton, 2005, p. 131).

Children demonstrated their loyalty to Angkar by verbally castigating and physically assaulting family members in front of their KR counterparts. Chuong (1997) recollected a child having witnessed his mother stealing a potato from the collective garden. The boy, with volcanic suddenness, pounced on his mother and beat her senseless. The boy, apparently proud, proclaimed that he was not beating his mother – but a thief. A section excerpted from the May 1977 issue of *Revolutionary Young Men and Women*, titled, "*But what does being truly loyal mean?*" outlined four qualities that the Party deemed necessary of a loyal student:

> 1. One must be completely loyal to every aspect of the party's political line, consciousness line, and organizational line, all the time.
> 2. One must always execute every aspect of the party line accurately.
> 3. One must struggle to defend the party line so that it is always accurate and pure. Thus, the revolutionary young men and women must not only work hard to execute the line accurately but also always observe and obey the application of the party line at every place.
> 4. One must struggle to clean up hidden enemies burrowing from within and to purify various bad compositions so that they are completely gone, cleansed from inside the ranks of our revolution, Party, and revolutionary youth. Thus it is necessary for our revolutionary young men and women to join together to struggle to clean up hidden enemies burrowing from within and for various groups whose composition isn't in good order to completely cleanse them from inside the ranks of our party, our Revolutionary young men and women, our revolution, and our people.

Abolishing individualism
Pot's policies on individualism bear considerable resemblance to initiatives undertaken by Mao. In parallel to Mao, Pot believed that in order for full communism to persevere, individualism needed to be stricken from the collective Cambodian psyche. The Party's Four Year Plan asserted: "In our educational system there are no examinations and no certificates; it is a system of learning through the collective and in the concrete movement of the socialist revolution and the building of socialism in specific contexts, especially co-operatives…" (Chandler, Kiernan, & Boua, 1988, p. 114). As individualism pertained to schooling, Pot believed that conferring

pupils with certificates or diplomas would promote a competitive attitude. Competition, of course, was antithetical to egalitarianism.

Self-reliance
Indoctrination sessions proffered varied reasons why the new regime endeavored to avoid foreign dependency (Ngor, 1987). The primary reason for self-reliance: "the key concept for the new society, as we were told all the time in propaganda sessions, was independence-mastery...One word made out of two, independence-mastery" (Ngor, 1987, p. 197). Ngor noted that independence-mastery entailed more than economic independence; it also entailed cultural independence and being free of influences which distract 'us' from work. The CPK, overly weary of a burgeoning western influence in South-East Asia, led Pot to exclaim, "we are building socialism without a model...We do not wish to copy anyone" (Ayres, 2000, p. 212). In line with education, previous pedagogical plans developed under Sihanouk were scrapped. In 1978, Pot dictated that "there are no schools, faculties or universities in the traditional sense...because we wish to do away with all vestiges of the past" (Clayton, 1998, p. 3). Khieu Samphan proclaimed that the old education system was inefficient for adequately educating students in natural sciences. Samphan opined that students were oblivious to how rice was sown or transplanted. Samphan's diatribe continued: "everything was done according to foreign books and foreign standards...therefore, it was useless and could not serve the needs of our people, nor could it be of any help in building our nation" (Jackson, 1989, p. 74).

Oppressor vs. Oppressed
Prior to the inauguration of genocide, the Khmer Rouge distributed leaflets offering rudimentary explanations of oppressive themes. Hinton (2005), in *Why did they kill? Cambodia in the shadow of Genocide*, claimed that one leaflet advanced capitalists: "[they] live in affluence at the expense of the working class and the masses, who live in misery, bled by them" (p. 73). Before the ushering in of the revolution, political pamphleteering on oppressive themes lacked formal structural reinforcement. However, after April 17, the Khmer Rouge controlled all national means of communication. Political indoctrination could now be actualized on a nation-wide level.

The political curricula introduced new revolutionary terms and words into the lexicon of Khmer children. These children subscribed to the prevailing tenets of communist theory articulated in class. Cultivating political consciousness entailed learning Leninist voluntarism and Mao's exegesis of Marxist writings (Hinton, 2005). The Party believed that children obtained absolute political consciousness when they could comprehend and recite the Party's agenda in addition to understanding the basic teachings of Marx and Lenin. The Khmer Rouge instructed children on class exploitation: pitting the oppressed farmer against the oppressive imperialists and "Phnom Penh" capitalists. Youth learned about class struggle, traits, and contradictions. The overriding objective of this curriculum was non-educational, in my view; it was rather to awaken feelings of class hatred and class fury within its intended audience. Political classes aroused anger and resentment within both child and adult learners. Instructors likened enemies of Marxism-Leninism, e.g., imperialists, feudalists, and capitalists, to Cambodia's erstwhile Lon Nol regime and city people (Carney, 1977). Propaganda positioned the relationship of the oppressed and the oppressor as an unbridgeable chasm; the latter's influence could only be subdued by violence and "smashing". Hinton posited that Khmer youth would "study a number of documents, including ones on Class struggle and Revolutionary hate" (p. 73). He further suggested during revolutionary meetings that artistic performances depicting a funeral and the eulogy of a fallen comrade were organized to "foment revolutionary violence so that the attendees burned with hatred toward the enemy" (p. 73). Constant exposure to violent propaganda and imagery dehumanized class enemies and desensitized Khmer children to violence.

School of cruelty
Khmer children were hijacked as adolescents and taught to hate and to exact unmitigated violence on Party enemies (Jackson, 1989). A resultant unsuspected brutality emerged from Khmer children thoroughly indoctrinated in violence. Sihanouk (1980) witnessed violence perpetrated by youth while in captivity. Sihanouk claimed that the Khmer Rouge created a 'school of cruelty'. He bemoaned: "Pol Pot and Ieng Sary quite rightly thought that if they trained their young recruits on cruel games, they would end up as soldiers with a love of killing and consequently war" (p. 30). He believed that young KR fledglings were hardening their hearts by murdering cats, dogs, and other small animals with bayonets and clubs. Torture games were utilized by the KR as a principal training tool. The school of cruelty advocated intimidation and its use on children and encouraged children to practice it on avowed class enemies. Children progressed through the school of cruelty with practice; they graduated when they killed their first enemy of the Party.

Linkages between primary and secondary schooling and CPK ideology

Tyner (2011), in *Geographic education as genocidal policy under the Khmer Rouge*, argued that "the Khmer Rouge explicitly sought to justify their political and economic programs through education" (p. 31). Tyner opined that the Democratic Kampuchea used education to foster a child's political development. The Party made explicit their intentions to introduce Party ideology into primary and secondary schooling. As evidenced by Kiernan (2002), political instruction in primary and secondary schools would begin after the Party procured "expert teachers" who have educated "themselves in the people's movement first" (p. 98). The Party sought subject matter experts (SME) fluent in Party ideology and a general teachable subject, e.g., chemistry. Having such an instructor would allow the Party's ideology to be blended effectively, for example, in a chemistry lesson.

Furthermore, *'The Party's Four-Year Plan to Build Socialism in All Fields, 1977-1980* singularly part three entitled in the *Fields of Culture, Literature, Art, Technology, Science, and Education of the People, Propaganda, and Information'* detailed six subjects to be instructed in primary and secondary schools (Chandler, Kiernan, & Boua, 1988, p. 114).

B. General Subjects
- reading and writing
- arithmetic
- geography (importantly that of the nation)
- history of the revolutionary struggle of the people, the revolutionary struggle for the nation, the revolutionary struggle for democracy, the revolutionary struggle for socialist revolution, and the struggle to build socialism
- natural sciences, physics, and chemistry (as base)
- party politics, consciousness, and organization

The unequivocal evidence presented above leaves little doubt in the researcher's mind that the Khmer Rouge emphasized ideological indoctrination – both revolutionary and political – in primary and secondary schooling more than remaining general subjects, e.g., physics and arithmetic. In recognition of this fact, ideological elements also permeated all other subjects' curriculums and lesson plans. In the third part of *'the Culture, Literacy, Art, Technology, Science, Mass Education, News and Information* document titled *Preliminary Explanation Before Reading the Plan, by the Party Secretary created by the Party Center on August 21, 1976'*, the Party makes explicit the definite linkages between general education subjects and the revolution: "we study in order to serve the goals of the revolution. If we study and learn subject 1, it's to serve the movement directly; studying and learning subject 2 is to serve the revolution directly" (Chandler, Kiernan, & Boua, 1988, p. 159). I believe that Tyner's (2011) research on geography and political indoctrination supports my assertion.

Tyner supposed that the Party employed geography texts and lesson plans with hidden revolutionary and political subtext to nourish students' political development. He believed that the teaching of geography was important for the development of political consciousness. The author affirmed that Democratic Kampuchea's primary and secondary school structure "serve[d] to establish and reinforce specific ideologies of nationalism...these practices may be used to justify and legitimate political processes and practices – including mass violence and genocide" (p. 31). Children were taught who to include and likewise who to exclude in Kampuchea's future designs. Tyner analyzed a surviving second-grade geography text, titled *Political Geography of Democratic Kampuchea*, which emphasized lessons on political geography. The text, published by the Ministry of Education in 1977, numbered 72 pages and was composed of twelve chapters. The first few chapters proffered a panoramic overview of the organizational and geographic makeup of Democratic Kampuchea, e.g., provinces, zones, districts, and regions. Children learned of each region's relevancy to the overall revolution. Lesson plans concluded with similar chapter summary questions: "During the period of over five years of revolutionary war, how did our people in Preah Vihear province participate in the struggle?"

All other educational subjects were underpinned by party ideology. KR documents show that culture, science, and technology curriculums were fashioned to nurture political consciousness. Daily and weekly timetables were organized around curriculums to "serve the concrete movement" and for "political study and consciousness building according to the time set" (Chandler, Kiernan, & Boua, 1988, p. 112). In *'Part Three – Preliminary Explanation Before Reading the Plan, by the Party Secretary created by the Party Center, August 21, 1976'*, a section explicated the "Building [of] Political Consciousness in the Party" (p. 202). The following excerpt below is perhaps the most illuminating summary of what political consciousness entailed:

B. Building Political Consciousness in the Party
We have nourished political consciousness, proletarian patriotism and proletarian internationalism. We have also nourished dialectical materialism as a basis. We have not relied on theory. We have acted clearly. Proletarian patriotic consciousness and proletarian internationalism can transform people's nature into something new. As for the problem of nurturing a Marxist-Leninist viewpoint, we should allow this to seep in according to our chosen methods. We don't yet enjoy complete mastery, however. Any law or decree, for example, has implications which we can't grasp entirely. We must study this matter further (p. 202).

This passage is important because it presents a better understanding of which key dogmas took precedence in the political curriculum designed for youth members. It also mentions that theory is not relied upon in their learning program, therefore making it less an educational matter and more an HRD initiative by virtue of its emphasis on workplace learning. The March 1978 issue of *Revolutionary Flags*, translated from Khmer to English by Kem Sos and Tim Carney, is useful here. The germane article in this publication was titled *Pay Attention to Pushing the Work of Building Party and People's Collective Strength Even Stronger*. In this, the Party divulges their educational program relating to the building of political consciousness of cadres and youth. The document outlined: "Meetings, listening to radio broadcasts, studying short documents, by word of mouth itself, by documents from the Regions or the Sectors. The study can be half day, one day or two to three days depending on the concrete situation" (Jackson, 1989, p. 295). The magazine posited that education should be firm in order to cultivate strong party members. If no "educational work" is provided, up-and-coming members would be unable to distinguish "revolutionary comrades from non-revolutionaries", the base class from the oppressing class, which only through schooling will they understand (Jackson, 1989, p. 295). The edict published by the Party dictated, "We must educate people over and over and yet again" (Jackson, 1989, p. 295). This passage is important for four reasons: (1) It highlights the aim of political teachings; (2) there are clear and acknowledged linkages of the Party indicating practice of political learning in the field and the development of leadership skills; (3) political indoctrination and the importance of placing schooling first, before practice of understanding, i.e., "understanding will come after having been through schooling" (Jackson, p. 295); and (4) it suggests over-learning, a condition of practice. Over-learning has been described by Saks and Haccoun (2008) as trainees being provided with ample practice to learn something "until the behavior becomes automatic...in other words, trainees are provided with continued opportunities for practice even after they have mastered the task" (p. 135).

Hitler Youth 1922 – 1945 in Nazi Germany

The Hitler Youth (HJ, Hitler Jugend) was a paramilitary faction of the Nazi Party from 1922 to 1945. The Jugendbund der NSDAP, the predecessor to the HJ, was incepted on March 8, 1922, after an announcement made by the German Nazi Party in the *Völkischer Beobachter* (the newspaper of the Nationalist Socialist German Workers Party), followed shortly thereafter by its inaugural meeting on May 13 of the same year. The Jugendbund der NSDAP was short-lived and momentarily served the Sturmabteilung (SA) from 1922 to 1923, until banned after Hitler's failed Munich Beer Hall Putsch. The Hitler Youth's solidification was born out of the second Reichsparteitag (National Party Day) on July 4, 1926. The HJ were later fashioned into a state agency on December 1, 1936. Children aged 10 to 18 largely composed the movement's membership; by 1939 an estimated eight million children were under the influence of Nazi ideological insemination. The Hitler Youth movement for boys was comprised of three prominent groups: The Pimpfe (aged 6-10), the Jungvolk (aged 10-14), and the Hitler Youth (aged 14-18). The available literature provided prescriptive insights into the lives of HJ in multitudinous detail. Yet the literature is nearly devoid of sufficient exploration of Pimpfe and Jungvolk; therefore this research will focus primarily on HJ aged 14 to 18. Hitler mandated that girls' and boys' education be segregated, since boys were trained to go out and conquer, while women would stay at home to cook, clean, and raise their husbands' children.

Hitler fostered a radical revamping of the pre-1933 collegiate system, introducing new pedagogical reforms, extending as far as to reduce the time spent in class. He substituted this with more physical training: "the shortcomings of the curriculum and of the number of hours...will be of benefit to the training of the body, of the character, and of will power and determination" (Hitler, 1939, p. 630). The curriculum in children's schools were ponderously endowed with ideological fervor, likewise found in Adolf Hitler schools and Ordensburgen (training centres). To serve the purpose of physical education, 300 military fitness camps (Wehrertuchtigungslager) were conceived as early as 1943. As of June 26, 1935, a *de rigueur* period of six months' labour was imposed on all youth. It served a single focus: for youth to envelop the Nazi doctrine: "manual and intellectual labor was equally honorable: an egalitarian process designed to further Hitler's social revolution" (Hilderbrand, 1984, p. 138). Students were offered physical recreation and activity, admiration by the Nazi state, three reichsmarks daily, a plenteous supply of food and clean uniforms, and the promise of an adventurous lifestyle. All Nazi children were required to complete primary school before they reached the age of ten. Children exhibiting disobedience and defiance to a Nazi upbringing were expelled. Minister Rust expounded that those students who do not produce the desired results or who demonstrate significant weakness will be – and must be – kept from attending secondary school. The underlying objective of Nazi education was neither cultural nor spiritual, nor was it to unshackle the mind; it was, in the words of Ziemer (1941), to train "for a life of Might" (p. 18)…"snatched from the hands of Fate only through the political conquests of a Fuehrer" (p. 18).

Pimpfe and Jungvolk education
Pimpfe (ages 6-10) is a colloquial term in German for a boy prior to undergoing change in voice. Pimpfe were the youngest sub-division of the HJ. Hitler had grandiose expectations that Pimpfe would fuel future Party membership (Ziemer, 1972). Pimpfe were issued a number and allotted a Leistungsbuch, namely an efficiency book or autobiography, used for enumerating a student's progress throughout their coursework. Leistungsbuchs documented the child's corporeal development and marked improvements made in military aptitude, and it recorded their ideological growth. Leistungsbuchs also logged a Pimpfe's reminiscences throughout these four years, leading up to and concluding with the Jungvolk stages of their education, particularly aged 13 (Ziemer, 1972). Pimpfe home, school, and party activities were scrupulously supervised, regimented, monitored, and registered by NSDAP representatives. A Leistungsbuch demonstrated the studiousness with which the NSDAP operated and garnered influence over the lives of Pimpfe boys. For this purpose, the Leistungsbuch partitioned a Pimpfe's life by the following activities:

-Weltanschuauliche Schulung (Ideological schooling).
-Pimpfenprobe (Promotion examination).

-Achievements in athleticism, e.g., boxing, running, swimming, and long distance hiking.
-Military accomplishments: The ability to construct a tent (shelter), draft maps, march, employ directions through astronomical design, and identify trees and plants.
- Shooting practice, e.g. using a stuffed dummy.
-Party accomplishments: One's fervour to acquire additional Nazi instruction and knowledge of Hitler songs, Hitler oaths, and Hitler's biography.
-Auslands Kenntnisse (Foreign Affairs): Identified territories, particularly those lost under the Treaty of Versailles, and knowledge of lost East African colonies (Ziemer, 1972, pp. 60-61).

Pimpfe boys were issued *Pimpfe Im Dienst*, otherwise known as *the Young one in service*, a manual chiefly exampling the Party's expectation of youth obedience. The manual established guidelines for Pimpfe activities and behavioral expectations, and it proffered a preliminary outline dictating their lifestyle from age six to ten. The manual's contents teemed with military maneuvering and marching instructions, complemented by exhibits on developing maps, pictorial illustrations on handling a rifle, gymnastics, and recondite descriptions on how to conduct oneself effectively as a spy (Ziemer, 1972). They familiarized children with parachuting techniques: their practice derived from mock parachute jumps. In the meantime, they were introduced to elementary-level flying instruction and European and North American military geography. Ziemer (1972) suggested that Pimpfe, "[were] imbued with one idea, and one idea only: to make the boy [Pimpfe] think, feel, and act as a true Nazi" (p. 63). Younger Pimpfe marched consecutively for twelve and a half miles maintaining a unison formation; older Pimpfe would march invariably longer distances than younger Pimpfe.

Pimpfe school days concluded at one o'clock, freeing the remainder of the day for Nazi Party activities. Textbooks were not used in Pimpfe classes. The only things permitted were paper, pencils, and the orotund voice of the instructor. Writing and reading lessons were simply denoted as German. In German class, they learned to read and write, practiced oratory, recited German literature, and studied dignified aspects of German culture. Ziemer (1972) recollected a sample lesson from a Pimpfe German class: German poems were read aloud and variedly interpreted by the class. Ziemer observed the class' analysis of a dramatic poem, consisting of eight stanzas. The class inferred that this poem was a metaphor for the eternal struggle in nature between the binary of strong and weak. The strong persevered. The poem opened with a fly that landed on a smaller victim and refused to show mercy: "please, begged the victim, let me go, for I am such a little foe." "No," said the victor, "not at all, for I am big, and you are small!" The fly was later consumed by a spider; the spider was then consumed by a sparrow; the sparrow succumbed to a hawk; and a fox later feasted on the hawk, so the poem continued. In all instances represented in this poetic description of struggle, the victors' mercilessness manifests simply because the victors were stronger and bigger, all the more deserving of their win over their affrighted prey. The teacher identified the moral of the poem: "this struggle is a natural struggle [that] life could not go on without it...That is why the Fuehrer wants his boys to be strong, so they can be the aggressors and the victors, not the victims" (Ziemer, 1972, p. 68).

Typically, Pimpfe geography class included lectures on Germany's well-deserved position in world affairs. Geography teachers premised that not all nations could claim credit for breeding a superior race. Ziemer (1972) observed one teacher deeming Czechoslovakia to be "nothing but a few remnants of a race formerly under German rule, mixed with Slavs, Jews, and Galician's...The Poles were no race" (p. 68). This educator proceeded to speak of America and its racial fallacies: unwanted Europeans engaging sexually with Blacks and Jews. He continued to lecture on America's lynching of Blacks throughout the early twentieth century, rampant unemployment, and America's gross mistreatment of Native Americans. The teacher implied American society was diminishing itself from within:

> There are many weaknesses as a result of this lack of racial purity...their government is corrupt. They have a low type of government, a democracy. What is a democracy? [The students replied]...A democracy is a government by rich Jews...A democracy is a form of government in which people waste much time...A democracy is a government that will be defeated by the Fuhrer (Ziemer, 1972, p. 69).

Participating in war games was of particular interest to Pimpfe boys. Ziemer (1972) described a group of boys chosen as spies, others as SS. Boys selected as SS utilized capturing strategies. One strategy called for binding a captured spy's hands and feet, blindfolding him, and leaving him alone in the woods restrained. SS shrewdly sat the spy on a large anthill. Ants crawled profusely over the boy's legs, nibbling and biting his exposed skin. Left for an extended duration alone in the woods, the boy began experiencing starvation – forced starvation being the true test a boy's iron-clad spirit. The SS returned hours later, in other cases sometimes a day later to retrieve the spy. When Ziemer spoke with the boy's instructor, questioning the barbarity of the exercise, the instructor's stern rejoinder was that German boys were made of iron, not puppy tails, snails, and frogs. As an apposite illustration, he recounted one Saxony-based training camp, keeping hundreds of Pimpfe for a month, accustoming them to the myriad hardships of military life. Pimpfe actively participated within prescribed war games, consumed military food prepared in a military kitchen, and were subjected to a thoroughgoing study of Nazi ideology. At the day's closure, Pimpfe gathered around a campfire and chanted songs about sacrifice, referencing great German battles and heroes. Pimpfe swore the following allegiance to Hitler's vision:

> In the presence of this blood flag which represents our Fuhrer, I swear to devote all my energies, all my strength to the savior of our country, Adolf Hitler...I am willing and ready to give up my life for him, so help me God...One People, one Nation, one Fuehrer (Ziemer, p. 59).

All Pimpfe aged ten underwent a comprehensive examination. The examination guidelines decreed an acceptable grade prior to a Pimpfe's succession to the Jungvolk. If a Pimpfe failed garnering a promotion, the boy was made to feel worthless and at times driven to suicide. Ziemer (1972) recounted one Pimpfe's experience after being denied advancement: the boy's father had a dastardly reputation as a Party member; for this reason the boy's acceptance as a Jungvolk was denied. The boy was later found sprawled out and unconscious on his father's kitchen floor. Ashamed by this failure, the boy had tucked newspaper under the kitchen door, closed the windows, and turned on the gas-stove.

Upon gaining admission into the Jungvolk (ages 10-14), Pimpfe boys attended an initiation ceremony. The young multitudes altogether shouted vehemently their commitment to die serving Hitler. The ceremonies' closure symbolized a Pimpfe's ascendency to Jungvolk. Boys continued to enumerate their physical accomplishments in their leistungsbuch, a practice not abandoned until they transitioned into HJ. Jungvolk were apportioned into one of six hundred units, united together under one Jungbanner. Jungvolk had exacting physical standards, superseding those previously experienced by Pimpfe. Students were administered laborious Spartan 'tests of strength' to assess their level of military capability. They endured lengthened marches and were subjected to painstaking periods of starvation.

Ziemer (1972) gave his readership insights on a Jungvolk science class he observed: an SA man, substituting as the science teacher for the day, instructed the class to go to a small fenced-off garden behind the school. Here, the boys positioned themselves beside tomato plants just a few inches high. The teacher sat with them. He opened with a discussion on the holiness of German soil. He pointed to the soil and proceeded to explain how the terms of the Treaty of Versailles forcefully imposed upon Germany to relinquish German land to Germany's foes:

> [Our] enemies had robbed her; Poland, Czechoslovakia, France, England – had all criminally appropriated holy German soil…[chants of 'Sieg Heil']…and the fuehrer will recover all this holy German soil – yes, and more, much more, tenfold more…We will revenge ourselves properly for the insults perpetrated by our second-rate enemies (p. 106).

Jungvolk boys were shown pictures of male and female heads and bodies representing diversified social and ethnic groups. They learnt that blond, tall, straight, and slender figures were Nordic, Aryan types – characteristics Jungvolk personified. Dark, thick, bent, and small bodies, Jungvolk were delusively told, belonged to undesirable "less worthy races" (Herbst, 1999, p. 44). Herbst (1999) spoke from Jungvolk experience, reminiscing about the physical education he received as a young Prussian boy. On winter or rainy days, Herbst and his cohorts trained within gymnasiums. He ascended ropes and ladders, swung from rings dangled from the ceiling, struggled over single and double bars, jumped and tumbled along obstacle courses, and lined-up for prearranged boxing and wrestling matches. Herbst remarked that when the night fell, the boys emerged from the gymnasium bloodied, weakened, and "reeking of sweat" (p. 44). Summer sessions were militarily-themed. In the countryside, Jungvolk learnt to camouflage themselves with tufts of grass and bunches of twigs. They threw wooden clubs bearing resemblance to hand grenades. They read maps, used compasses, and estimated distances between towns and cities. Jungvolk undertook primitive learning constructing fires and tracking nomadic animals and travelling humans (Herbst, 1999).

Hitler Youth education (Ages 14-18)

Hitler-Jugend (HJ) education became staunchly physical and thus more challenging and time-consuming than previously experienced as Pimpfe and Jungvolk. However, in-class education continued to complement knowledge acquisition of the following subjects: Germanic cultural studies, natural sciences, military geography, party history, chemistry, mathematics, and foreign language development. The learning of Nazi dogmas continued throughout their education, engendering within HJ the requisite knowledge of Party politics and principles. Classes started at eight in the morning and ended shortly after one in the afternoon. On Saturdays, classes lasted roughly forty-five minutes per lecture.

Hitler unraveled in *Mein Kampf* his intentions for didactic program reform prior to usurping a position of power. His educational plan emphasized the preferred breeding of "healthy bodies" over "more knowledge...[and] the training of mental abilities" (pp. 613-614). Hitler relegated mental development to secondary importance, after physical development. The National Socialist collegial motto was to pump out 'doers', as opposed to 'thinkers'. Through his 1939 directives on pedagogy, Hitler replaced "critical intellectual and aesthetic reflection" with a "vigorous, purposeful and combative approach" (Hitler, 1939, p. 614). Hitler planned for the Volkish state

> To start from the presumption that a man, though scientifically little educated but physically healthy, who has a sound, firm character, filled with joyful determination and will power, is of greater value to the national community than an ingenious weakling. A people of scholars, when they are physically degenerated, irresolute and cowardly pacifists, will not conquer heaven, nay it will not even be able to assure its existence on this globe (Hitler, 1939, pp. 613-614).

In *Mein Kampf*, Hitler imparted his expectations of youth under the following vision:

> My education system will be hard. The weak must be hammered away. In my castles a generation of young men will grow up who will be the terror of the world. I want forceful young men, majestic, awesome, and fearless; able to

withstand pain; without weakness or gentleness. The free wild beast should state from their eyes. I want my young men to be strong and beautiful. They should have a physical preparation in all sports. I want them to be athletic. This is the first and foremost. This is how I will get rid of a thousand years of human domestication. This way, I have the pure material of nature in front of me...Not for me intellectual education. Knowledge only spoils youth. I prefer them to learn through play. But they must develop a strong will. They must learn to overcome their fear of death through difficult tasks. This is the stage of heroic youth (Rauschning, 1940, p. 100).

In 1938, Prussian Minister of Education, Bernhard Rust, published NSDAPs seminal work on teacher education, entitled *Education and Instruction, Official Publication of the Reich and Prussian Ministry of Knowledge, Education, and National Culture*. According to Ziemer (1941), "the orders Rust gives his teachers are couched in brutal, dogmatic words, saturated with the Nazi ideal that Nordic Nazi might makes Universal Right" (p. 15). Rust (1938) proposed modifying school rubrics to insert a lexicon of Nazi words. Lehrer, which is the equivalent of a teacher, was introduced in Rust's manual. A lehrer was not in the traditional sense an educator but rather an iron discipliner who abandoned conventional instruction methods and clamoured with his students in a commanding tone to be better Nazis. He demanded unwavering submissiveness from his pupils. Rust instructed lehrers to utilize oratory in class, reminiscent of Hitler's speeches. Unmistakably, these instructors were the precise embodiment of Hitler amid in-class lessons. Ziemer (1941) reported on his own observations of lehrers: "Nazi instructors must be unquestioning interpreters; Nazi students must be disciplined hearers of the word of Hitler" (p. 19).

Hitler Jugend in-class education
Rust (1938) decreed that lehrers were to design lesson plans to favor the following subjects (ordered by importance): For boys, physical education, German language development, biology, science, math, and history; for girls, home economics and eugenics. Rust designated a minimum of five class periods per week for theory of physical education, in accordance with "practical execution every afternoon whenever possible" (Ziemer, 1941, p. 157). Moreover, Rust compelled lehrers to allow four periods per week for Germanic

culture, three periods for history, three periods for mathematics, two periods for geography, and two periods for Nazi music; biology, zoology, botany, and chemistry, among other subjects, were awarded two periods a week; and, as Ziemer noted, "English [was] given four periods each week" (p. 157). Rust implored the exploration of subsidiary subjects in class, so long as the subject content was congruous with Nazi ideology. Nevertheless, Rust considered that a superfluous undertaking of general pedagogical subjects dulled students' senses. Pupils were made to master numbers, hard facts, and rigid rules of conduct. He proposed that class discussions be kept to a minimum. Rust believed that class discussions produced criticism and fault-finding in students. Student criticism, he argued, bolstered students egos, thus contributing to some students' inarticulateness. On the whole, he advised lehrers to avoid producing intellectually superior students. He insisted that the intellect of students be on a par with one another. Rust opined that students who exhibited superior comprehension of a subject cultivated a sense of inferiority in students struggling with said subject. Rust was not resolutely insistent upon perfect class attendance; when students preferred outdoor education over academia, lehrers excused their absences from class. They were dissuaded from berating pupils who attended military parades, drills, or other occasional Party functions requiring the pupil to be absent. Students were pardoned for class absences for no more than ten days (Ziemer, 1972).

Curricula design abandoned the practice of circumscribing lesson plans to allow leniently the introduction of new course material. To proffer an example, history curriculums were continually revised to reflect the teetering relationship with Soviet Russia throughout the Second World War. Prior to August 23, 1939 (the date signifies the signing of the Molotov and Ribbentrop non-aggression treaty), lehrers censured the USSR as a state enemy. From the time the treaty was signed onward until its abrogation on June 22, 1941, in the wake of Operation Barbarossa, the Soviet Union was reflected as a neutral state. Meanwhile, after the ill-fated operation, Nazi history curriculums posed Soviets as antagonists of National Socialism. Rust's (1938) manual briefed geography lehrers to expect ongoing curricula changes to reflect new lands annexed by Germany. He assigned geography lehrers an eight-page booklet orienting lehrers how to best organize these curricula. He insisted that lehrers dichotomize geography classes by the study of space and race. They epitomized the German race as flawless and inspiring race-based strides, surpassing those of other European countries. Students were encouraged to boast of German pride and promote Germany's militaristic achievements while travelling abroad.

Science studies curriculums, such as that for chemistry and biology, were altered significantly to envelop theories on race. Ziemer (1941) recalled chemistry laboratories having been *au courant* in every respect. The pupils, he observed, worked "feverishly, solving chemical problems of a military nature" (p. 60). Students struggled with chemical formulae for explosives and were acquainted with gases employed in air raids. Mature students, Ziemer noted, "were busy with gases and their antidotes" (p. 160). Students spent one semester studying the properties of synthetic foods, however, Ziemer commented that they were not "advanced enough to invent synthetic substances...but were learning the rudiments" (p. 160). Rust (1938) insisted that biology lessons be reflective of NSDAPs racial policies. Rust required lehrers to expound:

> In nature the fight for the survival of the fittest eliminates the weak and those unfit to carry on the race. The study of botany and zoology must be taught that this is the normal process in nature; must be made to realize the folly of theory that there is equality anywhere in nature. He must understand that the civilized man has attempted to create for himself an artificial environment, to escape the eliminating process of nature. But the Nationalist Socialist state, through its racial laws and its decrees governing hereditary health, has again permitted the law of survival to function properly (p. 141).

Rust (1938) prompted lehrers of Deutschkunde, in other words, German cultural studies, to divide the curriculum into four units. First, the nation was a blood unit. Lessons on race were best discerned when lehrers illustrated in class the superiority of the German race over other races. In this learning event, German students were described as superior racial beings, bearing attributes directly descendent from Nordics, to which they were taught only Germans could stake a claim. Second, the nation was a fighting unit, consisting of interdependent sub-divisions defending old and recently acquired lands. Third, he argued that the nation was a working unit. Any occupation, albeit a labourer, peasant, or tradesperson – occupations singularly benefiting the state in some capacity – exclusive of forced labor, warranted recognition and prestige. Fourth, the nation was an ideological unit. Discussions included, among other things, acceptance of Nazi precepts, discerning Nazi lifestyles and rank-holding positions, and giving praise to the multi-headed hydra that was the National Socialist leadership under the NSDAP banner.

Rust (1938) prescribed music timetables for students aged fourteen and upward to study. Lessons intertwined medieval marching songs, modern soldiering songs, and National Socialist songs. Students aged sixteen years memorized and recited military folk song lyrics and Wagner's manifold operas. Seventeen-year-olds listened attentively to speeches rebuking the pestiferous Jewish influence on German music. Upon induction into the Hitler Youth, students were issued a Hitler Youth song book. Many youth committed songs to memory. The following lyrics were excerpted from an extant Hitler Jugend song book:

> The world belongs to leaders,
> They alone command the world.
> And we are marching, marching,
> No one can stop our flag unfurled.
> The old must perish,
> The weak must decay.
> We are young storm troopers, yeah.
> Up, up, march, march,
> Our swastika is our torch,
> For the world belongs to leaders.

Mathematics, namely, succumbed under the weight and wielded influence of Nazism. Nazi elementary and secondary school math textbooks infused with Nazi ideology give credence to the researcher's belief that math courses were likely to have been injected with Nazi dogmas more so than other general subjects. To proffer an example, part one of the *National Socialist math textbook for secondary student use* dedicated 22 of 77 pages to serve ideological purposes. Particularly, these 22 pages were foreshadowed by references to racial, eugenic, or disability policy. Hiden and Farquharson (1983) suggested that "sums were based on the assumption that hereditarily unfit families had more children than healthy ones, and asked pupils to work out what proportion of the whole people would be unfit in a hundred or two hundred years time" (p. 55). Another mathematics text, entitled *Mathematics in the Service of National Political Education*, advanced the following problem: "If a lunatic asylum costs six million Reichsmarks to build, and a worker's apartment on average six thousand marks, how many families could have been housed for the money devoted to the mentally unfit?" (Totten & Parsons, 2009, p. 177). Students were passionate about math class, as evidenced by Ziemer (1941). He recounted a student's predilection for math because he "learn[t] about geometry, which gave him sufficient information on how to use trajectory angles to bomb cities" (p. 153).

Foreign language studies were apportioned into four periods a week. Nazi secondary school guidelines stipulated that the English language should be taught, as NSDAP regarded English speakers as being racially related to Germans, in addition to being the universal language of commerce. Foreign language curricula fluctuated regularly: "at first they had learned Italian, then English, then French, then English again...They thought they were learning English...because they might all have to go to England" (Ziemer, 1972, p. 153).

Pine (2010) underscored the medium of film as a significant contributor of Hitler Youth education. Welch (1983) posited that Nazi show-business and aesthetically pleasing propaganda reduced dissension and fostered a national consensus within schools. To appease the student bodies' growing membership, academic administrators incepted the Jugendfilmstunde, translated to *the Youth Film Hour*, on April 20, 1934. Preceding 1936, the Youth Film Hour took place once a month. Afterward, demand swelled for the program, forcing administrators to present films weekly. Pine (2010) noted, "These screenings supplemented the film education that was given in schools" (p. 106). With the assistance of the Ministry of Propaganda, funding was procured for additional screenings, making it an "integral part of its members activities" (p. 106). The films designated valuable products were commissioned by the Ministry of Propaganda. Nazi German films were overtly Party driven, cultural, and couched in anti-Semitic subtext. Repulsive images of rats emerging from sewers, scattering over street waste, and rifling through the gutters of sidewalks were shown, and Halpern (2002) remarked, "exaggerated pictures of Jews were flashed on to the screen, and the long noses of rats were "superimposed over the. . .facial features of Jews" (p. 48; Procknow, 2014, p. 382). The author opined that "it does not take long before the facial features evoke feelings of disgust, which were learned through the repeated pairing of the repulsive rat scenes and the faces" (Halpern, 2002, p. 49; Procknow, p. 382). From 1942-3, the Film program screened in excess of 45,000 Reich Film Hours, with an attendance slightly greater than 11 million (Welch, 1983).

Rust (1938) insisted that his students embrace self-sacrifice. He continued: "the chief purpose of the school [was] to train human beings to realize that the State is more important than the individual, that individuals must be willing and ready to sacrifice themselves for Nation and the Fuhrer" (as cited in Ziemer, 1941, p. 20). In the same breath, Hitler articulated his theory that Aryans eclipse egoism in favor of community. Hitler believed that Aryan men best embodied "the self-sacrificing will to give one's personal labor and if necessary one's own life for others...[they were] not the greatest in his mental abilities as such but was willing to put his abilities in the service of the community" (Hitler, 1939, p. 604). Hitler detested European Jews. He bemoaned their instinctive pursuit of self-preservation, and he reasoned self-sacrifice as an atypical characteristic of Jews.

School textbooks asserted that the Jewish race was a much inferior race to that of "Negros". They said that all Jews have fat stomachs, untrustworthy looks about them, and are rich with curly hair and crooked legs. The Jews were squarely blamed for the Germans' loss of World War One. The Jews were blamed for the Treaty of Versailles and for the 1923 hyperinflation problem. The Jews brought the downfall of the Roman Empire. Karl Marx, a Jew, was a great criminal. All Jews were Communists, and Russia was dominated by Jews.

HJ physical education
In 1933, Hitler instituted mandatory corporeal education, which he proposed would build a stronger Germany. Hitler increased physical education and exercise in secondary schools from three punishing hours per week to, in 1937, seven hours. Then he prescribed that physical education be two hours per day, amounting to ten hours per week. From 1937 onward, physical education commenced daily. Hitler explicitly outlined under Germany's academic tutelage that cultivating physically fit youth, by way of offering thoroughgoing physical education, was the primary purpose of Nazi schooling. The NSDAP revamped secondary school curriculums to include substantially more sports and physical fitness. However, at the time of Hitler's succession to power, Germany had to overcome some slight staffing obstacles. Kruger's (1999) exploration of Weimar pedagogy concluded that there were few military subjects that were as philosophically divided as workout education. The imposition of the Treaty of Versailles considerably reduced the German army and dissolved Germany's auxiliary forces. Kruger continued that, as a result, Germany faced a lack of sufficiently qualified or certified physical education teachers. Corporeal education was perceived at the time as a viable alternative to military training.

War games were designed to improve students' self-confidence and increase the likeliness of becoming violent. Pupils excused from attending in-class instruction were chaperoned by an accomplished Waffen-SS to a spacious field or willow-wacks. Waffen-SS served as physical education lehrers. Lehrers provisioned students with dummy rifles and toy hand grenades that produced a bright flash and blasting noise when detonated. Youths formed two opposing groups. Ziemer (1941) recalled that "the boys became so tense that they resembled soldiers in front-line trenches...they went prowling around the countryside all night in an effort to discover the location of the opposing force and to take prisoners" (p. 165). Apprehended students were accompanied to a makeshift headquarters and temporarily imprisoned. Prisoners were subjected to the harsh realities of POW imprisonment. Ziemer recounted how a prisoner who was forcibly restrained with his hands bound behind his back, blindfolded, and gagged with adhesive tape, was repeatedly kicked and verbally abused. The lehrer supervising the game remarked to Ziemer, "[the] boys might as well get accustomed to seeing other human beings suffer...I don't expect the other side to grant my boys mercy when they get captured...the idea is not to get caught" (p. 165). The war game concluded after six days when an entire side was held captive. Traditionally, a week would elapse prior to the boys reemerging together from the willow-wacks as a larger group.

Violent struggle was viewed as a precondition to all human nature. Lehrers presented compelling historiographical reasons to students for undergoing advanced physical development. For one thing, war was life: war was the father of all animated beings. The interconnectedness of war and being was baldly pronounced in National Socialist chants. Weinstein (1980) adds "that life is struggle, that nature is an arena of perpetual struggle that only force rules, compelling the victory of the strong over the weak, that force is the first law" (p. 126). Undoubtedly, violence was generally accepted as a form of behavior in the Third Reich, dominating the entire spectrum of student physical education. Violence prevailed as the linchpin underlying this education. Lehrers instructed pupils to desire life and required one to fight; those not wanting to fight were not deserving of life. A pupil's willingness to fight signaled their individual worth. HJ, like their adult-counterparts, customarily demonstrated their right to existence by fully immersing themselves in the combative struggle that were Nazi curriculums in physical education. Multiplied violence and struggle were accentuated in physical education curriculums to mobilize students "to resist the humiliation of defeat and the fostering of a spirit of recovery and renewal in the face of a deprived and unjust reality" (Vasey, 2006, p. 81). These curriculums were cunningly contrived to improve pupils' tolerance to pain. Peiffer (1987) stated that boxing was introduced into secondary school curriculums in 1935, specifically for those in their last three years. Hitler Youth ambitious exercise syllabi were designed to internalize feelings of superiority and self-confidence within Nazi students. Once self-confidence and superiority were induced, pupils could adapt to and readily pursue nature's naturally violent struggles. In Hitler's own words, (1939), "this self-confidence has to be instilled into the young fellow from childhood on...His entire education and development has to be directed at giving him the conviction of being absolutely superior to the [enemy]" (p. 618). On the whole, self-confident soldiers persevered in the battlefield. Hitler concluded that, when pupils exhibited such confidence, it transpired into group confidence and thus for this purpose augmented national self-confidence. Hitler believed that self-confident pupils were identifiable by their relentless pursuit of new knowledge; knowledge and strength converged into Nazi superiority.

Analysis of Hitler Youth and Khmer youth political curriculums

Contrasting political, learning, and environmental differences

Before the commonalities of both political curriculums are explicated, it is perhaps useful to discuss the obvious discrepancies between the two groups first. Foremost importance should be given to the difference in the choice of political ideology instructed. Political indoctrination of HJ was guided by Fascist militaristic precepts, while KR was Communistic and highlighted Leninism, Maoism, and voluntarism. Credence is given to the researcher's claim, as evinced by the Hitler Youth swearing allegiance to the Fuhrer first and to the Party second; whereas, the KR never swore fidelity to Pot or any of his small brotherhood. KR youth served the CPK and pledged loyalty to the mythical semblance of Angkar, elsewise described as the Party. The 'leadership principle' within Fascism affirms HJ, "under which each subordinate owes an absolute obedience to his or her immediate superior" (Sargent, 1993, p. 203). In Nazi Fascism, the Fuhrer reflected the collective sprit of his people; in contrast, the Communist Party of Kampuchea reflected its citizenries' collective will. The Fuhrer, Sargent (1993) holds, "is the only one capable of rightly interpreting the will of the people" (p. 203). Hitler's militaristic apparatus impressed his will on the people. In Communist

Kampuchea, a cult of personality was fabricated around the Party; Pot himself didn't command the unwavering loyalty of his countrymen.

The Hitler Youth held a different perspective on the Party's purpose than did Khmer Rouge youth. The Party played a seemingly analogous role in Democratic Kampuchea as it did in National Socialist Germany: "the Party however in fascism is the vanguard of the nation or the race rather than the proletariat, but the general notion is the same" (Sargent, 1993, p. 204). Sargent (1993) opined that the Party is in either ideology the centerpiece of a 'new order'. Communists hold that the new order is engendered in class distinctions; as an example in National Socialism, its rootedness is in racial disparities.

The conditions of learning differed immeasurably from one group to the other. Hitler Youth were principally instructed in class, while Khmer Rouge was inculcated in fields, stables, under trees, and limitedly in class within a formal education structure. On another note, Hitler mandated that girls' and boys' education be segregated, since boys were trained to go out and conquer, while women would stay at home to cook, clean, and raise their husband's children. Pran (1997) confirmed that Khmer girls were educated along the Party line in attendance with boys. Furthermore, the Khmer Rouge organized schools for disabled youth: "organized centers to look after and educate...the disabled and where they can be involved in light production activities" (p. 112). National Socialist textbooks for secondary student use characterized funding for housing and educating the disabled as a boondoggle and a frivolous waste of state spending. As evinced in the text *Mathematics in the Service of National Political Education,* the following problem was presented: "If a lunatic asylum costs six million Reichsmarks to build, and a worker's apartment on average six thousand marks, how many families could have been housed for the money devoted to the mentally unfit?" (Totten & Parsons, 2009, p. 177).

The idea of a *tabula rasa* begs to be analyzed. Young, unprejudiced Khmer minds "most receptive to the revolution" (Sihanouk, 1980), were moulded to "do away with all vestiges of the past" (Clayton, 1998, p. 3). Pot envisaged Khmer children approaching the revolution with a mental *tabula rasa*. Pot and his elite were cognizant of the fact that their ideology would be easier to impress upon children than adults. The researcher could find no empirical evidence confirming Hitler's policies referring to learners as blank slates. Swanson and Holton (2001) hold that behaviourists agree that "organisms are born as blank states" (pp. 151-2). Makino

(2001) suggested that children and juveniles naturally play an integral part under these circumstances "because they are less rooted in tradition and experience" (p. 60). Pinker (2003) defined "Blank Slate" as an "idea that the human mind has no inherent structure and can be inscribed at will by society or ourselves" (p. 2). However, Pinker argued that the blank slate was a "false vision," designed for those who believe that human nature should be changed. The author believed that, as a result, regimes seeking to alter humanity have introduced totalitarianism. Both Pinker and I hold that Nazi Germany did not adhere to the blank slate concept.

The time and length of indoctrination and hours allotted to political conscious development varied significantly between these two groups. The Germans attended class most days, with political themes teeming in all subjects organized for learners aged 6 through 18, for the period of time between Hitler's elevation to the chancellorship in January 1933 until 1945, the year marking his downfall. For the most part, Democratic Kampuchea primary and secondary schooling in general subjects was neglected. Only political lessons gleaned through public meetings, radios, party speeches, and artistic performances were of educational currency: "since the war we have been very busy. Neither children nor youth have received much education" (Kiernan, 2008, p. 98). In recognition of this evidence, the researcher concludes without chance of doubt, that Hitler Youth were exposed to heavier doses of political indoctrination than Khmer youth.

According to the evidence presented, the Khmer Rouge wrote and published their Party documents and books for ease of reading by a largely illiterate group of Khmer learners. The following quote evidenced in the December 20, 1976, issue of *Revolutionary Flags* affirmed that "the important thing is that [books] are easy to read, so that people can learn to follow the revolutionary path" (p. 201). Contrarily, the Hitler Youth educated learners to deduce meaning from complex documents and to recite verbatim texts written in advanced German. The learning materials created by the CPK were adapted to complement Khmer students' rate of learning, poor reading, and comprehension; dissimilarly, Hitler Youth's apperception and learning style assisted them in the reading of advanced texts.

The import of the Party superseded the worth that the Party placed on the individual in Nazi Germany. Rust (1938), as cited in Ziemer (1941), remarked that "the chief purpose of the school was to train human beings to realize the state is more important than the individual" (p. 20). In light of this, the researcher found that self-sacrifice played a main role in HJ curriculums, not in KR courses. Self-sacrifice was a means of preserving the Party's position: "sacrifice themselves for nation and fuehrer" (p. 10). Staudinger (1992) confirmed that students of the Third Reich "had to learn to die not only for the good and glory of Germany but also for the creation of a new world" (p. 124). In no such record, especially in the extant documents relating to education under the CPK, did the researcher find any dictums encouraging acts of self-sacrifice to Angkar.

Contrasting political curriculums
There were assorted similarities that Khmer Rouge and Hitler Youth political curriculums had in common, thus legitimating the political power and ideology propounded by each Party respectively. At this juncture, the researcher will present the similarities identified in both groups' political indoctrination. The first coinciding similarity was the import both Parties placed on developing the political consciousness of youth. This was the educative event in which both Parties invested the most time. In the October 1976 issue of *Revolutionary Flags*, CPK claimed "from the very beginning the Party determined to take the work of political consciousness as the most important work of all" (p. 1).

Subject matter expertise of Party politics beyond cleverness in a general teachable subject was a requisite for teaching either group. Hitler Youth lehrers were required to be educated in the Party's agenda and principles prior to instructing Hitler Youth; likewise, teachers in Khmer youth classes were held to the same standard. Lehrers in Hitler Youth schools, despite their expertise in general subjects, were required to be foremost accustomed in the ideology of the Party. Nazi instructors were expected to be "unquestioning interpreters" of Nazism (Ziemer, 1941, p. 19), as their students "must be disciplined hearers of the word of Hitler" (p. 19). The Khmer Rouge called for the involvement of expert teachers to instruct on core course content, however, the educational imperatives presented in the surviving Party documents maintained that "they would have to educate themselves among the people's movement first" (Chandler et al., 1988, p. 41). Correspondingly, Khmer teachers, as documented by Chandler, Kiernan, and Boua (1988), "were not selected or trained systematically, although the Plan asserts in passing that reliable ones must grasp the Party's educational line and apply it concretely and continuously" (p. 41).

Another striking similarity of both political curriculums was that they were resolutely anti-family. Political indoctrination would be fruitless if youth retained loyalty to family, thus negating either Parties' influence over children. Teng (1997) recalled that Khmer youth were instructed that "families do not love [you]" (p. 150). Indoctrination tore the family structure asunder from within. Both Khmer (Hinton, 2005) and Hitler Youth (Johnson & Reuband, 2006) were hoodwinked into spying on their parents and family members and report all subversive and suspicious activity to Party leaders. At the same time, youth replaced familial obedience with implicit Party obedience, thus permitting easier inculcation of youth in Party politics. Duty and obedience shifted toward the Party, with CPK speeches suggesting the following in Marston (1994): "Your number one duty is to Angkar…You are the children of Angkar!...Angkar loves you above all else" (p. 110). Likewise, Minister of Education Rust promoted a Spartan understanding of life, committed youth as life-long members, and subjected the disciple to a variety of obstacles to gauge their obedience to a Nazi upbringing. Lukacs (2011) commented that Hitler "plays not the role of a severe father but of a mother, a source of many pleasures and of love" (p. 100). Furthermore, Khmer youth were approved family visitations once a month, whereas Hitler Youth schools were remote and inaccessible to the general populace and family members.

Both curriculums decried competition and individualism. In Kampuchea, the CPK argued that full communism required individualism to be stricken from the collective Cambodian consciousness. To placate students from feeling inferior in educative undertakings, KR education abolished examinations and the conferment of certificates of achievement. Pot believed that grades and certificates nurtured competitiveness and a competitive attitude. Likewise, Rust (1938) opined that class discussions fostered criticism and fault-finding in students. Student criticism, Rust argued, made students ostentatious in their display of learning, which in turn left very few students inarticulate. Rust advised lehrers to avoid creating intellectually superior students. He insisted that students' intellect be on par with one another.

The destruction of political enemies through violence and murder pervaded both curriculums. Perceptions of who the enemy was differed markedly between the two groups. Khmer Rouge abhorred capitalists, Lon Nol Republicans, city people, and imperialists, admonishing each group equally in the evidentiary materials reviewed (Carney, 1977). Hitler's expressed enemies were race-based and Communist. Hitler's eugenics policies evinced a blithe disregard for the lives of Jews, homosexuals, Gypsies, and the disabled. He referred to these groups in speeches and writings as weak and enemies, though to Jews specifically as economic and social oppressors. Class exploitation by capitalists and imperialists aroused anger and resentment in Khmer students. The CPK advised students to subdue their hatred through a thorough smashing of the enemy (Hinton, 2005). In the school of cruelty, children practiced intimidation and violence on avowed class enemies. Politically-themed songs for both youth groups aestheticized violence against enemies. Hitler Youth songs teemed with belligerence: "the weak must decay" (Rust, 1938). Likewise, KR songs spouted messages of hatred for those accused of having wrought death or suffering upon their loved ones.

In the researcher's opinion, the congruous point relating the two curriculums the most was how both parties decried intellectual development in favor of physical education. Hitler maintained that the "training of mental abilities" (Hitler, 1939, p. 613) bred thinkers, not doers. Hitler referred to intellectuals as "ingenious weaklings" and "physically depredated" (Hitler, p. 613). Mental development was relegated to secondary importance, after physical development. Hitler believed that "knowledge only spoil[ed] youth", (Rauschnig, 1940, p. 100) and dulled students' senses (Rust, 1938). Hilderbrand (1984) contended that manual and intellectual labour were equally prestigious in Nazi Germany. Party documents germane to educating Hitler Youth demonstrated that the cultivation of intellectual abilities took a back-seat to corporeal development. If Germany's education system failed to rid students' ascribed social status and class consciousness, serving six to seven months in the Labour service supervised by the Wehrmacht would take care of it (Hitler, 1939). In a vein similar to Rust, Khieu Samphan argued that traditional education borrowed from foreign educational models and textbooks was inadequate for educating Khmer students. Samphan claimed that textbooks and models of education predicated on western theories were "useless and could not serve the needs of our people, nor could it be of any help in building our nation" (Jackson, 1992, p. 74). He noted to his comrades in Phnom Penh, "did you ever see any Cambodian operate a lathe? Very rarely. No Cambodian would touch anything that had to do with machinery" (FBIS April 18 1977, p. 7-8). Samphan's concern was that the educated were not cultured in farming techniques. They saturated cities and towns with unneeded expertise. Vickery (1984) contended that "most local cadres considered higher education as useless and people who had obtained it less reliable than the uneducated" (p. 173). On October 4, 1977,

CPK prescribed that "theory should be learned at the same time it is being applied to actual work. Our people study and at the same time directly serve the production movement" (Jackson, 1989, p. 96). Their goal was to keep schooling close to production: "our goal is to keep schooling close to production work...you should learn while working. The more you work, the more you learn and more competent you become" (Jackson, p. 76). The bulwark of Party documents discussing educational subjects portrayed the teaching of general subjects as inadequate for educating students in natural sciences – the only science needed to fulfill CPK's vision of an agrarian utopia. Samphan averred, "[students] were oblivious to how rice was sown or transplanted" (Jackson, p. 74). Contrastingly, Hitler's educative reforms emphasized the preferred breeding of "healthy bodies" over "more knowledge" (p. 613). Healthy bodies were the proverbial fodder for the militarization of German youth; whereas physical expertise in the fields, sowing and plowing, garnered Khmer youth the required practice to cultivate Kampuchea's agrarian goals.

Another remarkable similarity shared by the two is that both learning groups used a form of journaling to track their political progress. Khmer youth enumerated their political advancement in autobiographies consonant with Pimpfe- and Jungvolk-aged youth using Leistungsbuchs. Autobiographies were compiled by all youths in cooperatives. They espoused pupils' cogitative reflections on their progress in revolutionary and political consciousness. Cadres ascertained, through a rigorous review of autobiographies, the autobiographer's class background (Ly, 2000). Seasoned cadres also completed an autobiography which was "more formal and crucial to one's career" (Hinton, 2005, p. 198). It was an educational mandate for youth to complete a dozen pages or so of a biographical questionnaire every so often. The Party supplied space for the respondent to compile a detailed manifest, chronicling the following: occupations, class, and revolutionary background of the respondent's peers. Questions were ingeniously invented to determine class status, history of membership in other revolutionary agencies, and educational background, as well as to appraise the respondent's current state of political consciousness (Hinton, 2005). Self-scrutinizing political thought would also define respondents. Cadres tasked with monitoring biographies gained introspective insight into how respondents perceived their own character: "How clearly do you know your character? To what level? How well do you know your strengths and weaknesses? How have you changed your non-revolutionary character and weaknesses?" (Hinton, 2005, p. 201). Responses were customarily typified to record the respondent's revolutionary strengths, weaknesses, and intent to direct change in their lives toward compliance with Khmer Rouge values (Hinton, 2005). To ensure one's corresponding survival, the respondent, according to Hinton (2005), had to "carefully balance one's strengths and weaknesses, while asserting the potential of one's revolutionary consciousness" (Hinton, 2005, p. 203). Writing a biography was a dangerous enterprise, requiring participants to use undetectable deception when recording their answers. Comparatively, Leistungsbuchs required Hitler youth to detail their political progress and political lessons of the day, as well as to note improvements made in their ideological growth as National Socialists. In stark contrast to how autobiographies were apportioned into varied sections for Khmer Youth, Leistungsbuchs were made alike, offering students several sections upon which to provide reflections, e.g., ideological schooling and achievements in athleticism. Both methods of articling went hand-in-glove with the evolution of pupils' political consciousness.

Conclusion

As for identifying the linkages between primary and secondary schooling and political indoctrination, little has been accomplished so far to fill this gap in Khmer Rouge and Hitler Youth historiography. Furthermore, the researcher has shown how Party ideology was interwoven into the fabric of Democratic Kampuchea's primary and secondary school system to benefit the Khmer Rouge revolution, likewise for the Hitler Youth and Hitler's Fascist agenda. Both Parties infiltrated primary and secondary school subjects with political indoctrination and subtext to advance their respective political agendas. This present chapter is sufficient as an introductory study comparing political curriculums contrived for youth; however, more academic attention is needed. Genocide research on control-based curriculums still has great strides to make.

CHAPTER FIVE
Literature Review: Sudan's Janjaweed as a Performance System

Introduction

In this chapter, a comprehensive literature review and analysis will be provided on how Sudan's roaring Janjaweed were trained. Furthermore, suggestions will be offered on how the learning organized and provided to the Janjaweed resembles the human resource development's performance system and the performance paradigm theories. In this case, the researcher will demonstrate how the Janjaweed's learning at times is performance-driven, reminiscent of the learning paradigm's argument of the ills associated with performance-based learning. Absent from the body of comparative genocide research, and subsequently the research of human resource development (HRD) academia, is the use of an HRD lens to identify how the Janjaweed, as a performance system, trained and developed into a genocidal group. Can a genocide operate much like an organization that upholds a performance paradigm perspective? How do we identify one government pursuing the HRD paradigm of performance separately from a government pursuing the HRD paradigm of a learner?

I will liken the learning undertaken by the Janjaweed genocidists and compare it to the misconceptions of the performance paradigm, or performance system, as held by those who harbor a learning paradigm perspective of HRD. Advocates of the learning paradigm argue the performance paradigm is unethical, exploitive, and organization-driven. I intend on portraying the Janjaweed as a befitting example of an organization that the abusive-nature learning advocates hold the performance paradigm of HRD to be, primarily that it is organization-driven. Most importantly, I will demonstrate through the performance paradigm lens how the performance system theory applies to the Darfur Genocide.

The limitations of this research are manifold. This work will only focus on one known genocidal group, the Janjaweed. Although other genocidal groups exist(ed) throughout history, this one in particular is the subject of this research. The researcher holds that the overriding limitation is that much of the data accumulated for this research was gleaned from secondary sources. Very few phenomenological experiences were documented of erstwhile Janjaweed or Government of Sudan executives, hence the failure to confirm much of the findings posited in the available literature. Another limitation is there have been no similar studies to compare this present research to. Much of the historical record on the Janjaweed speaks little of the training it received, except a few personal accounts proffered by Aegis Trust, the rest is sourced as subsidiary knowledge. Moreover, there is a paucity of HRD scholarship and academic contribution detailing genocidal governments offering training and development to its citizenry, specifically speaking of the Government of Sudan (GOS) and the Darfur Genocide. Furthermore, no a priori research has applied the HRD's paradigm of performance or performance system theory to genocidal instances in history. Given the sensitivities surrounding the discussion of genocide through an HRD lens and the humanistic principles that HRD is known to espouse, HRD academics and practitioners I surmise will take offense to the use of HRD to make sense of terrible moments in history.

Performance Paradigm and Performance System Theory
Swanson and Holton (2001) suggest that, like other professional disciplines, HRD also consists of "multiple paradigms of practice and research" (p. 127). A paradigm, the authors remark, is defined as "a coherent tradition of scientific research" (as cited in Kuhn, 1996, p. 10)…"thus paradigms represent fundamentally different views of human resource development, including its goals and aims, values, and guidelines for practice" (p. 127). HRD paradigms are typically divided into two dominant views: learning and performance. Bierema (2009) maintains that the field of human resource development "has long engaged in a debate over learning versus performance" (p. 10). This duality, the author contends, has thus created an "artificial either-or relationship" (p. 10), making it more difficult to ascertain how either paradigm could complement one other.

Watkins and Marsick (1995) offer a useful definition of the learning paradigm of HRD (Swanson & Holton, 2001): "HRD is the field of study and practice responsible for the fostering of a long-term, work-related learning capacity at the individual, group, and organizational level of organizations" (p. 2). Proponents of the learning paradigm include Barrie and Pace (1998), Bierema (1997), Dirkx (1997), and Watkins and Marsick (1995). Learning advocates, as noted by Swanson and Holton (2001) "object to characterizing people as "resources" to be utilized to achieve a goal, particularly in an organization" (p. 135). The inherent worth of individuals should be deliberated from this perspective: considering human worth, not merely utilizing human resources as cogs to obtain organizational outcomes. Organizational needs are peripheral: as human needs are of primary import, or at a bare minimum equal (Swanson & Holton, 2001; Bierema, 2000; Dirkx, 1997). Contriving learning to avail the individual and to assist them to realize their fullest potential as humans from this perspective is central to the learning advocates' argument. Once an individual's potential is actualized, so then will the performance outcomes of the organization. The individual development of the learner works hand-in-glove with organizational development to obtain performance outcomes. Most HRD practices have now advanced to performance-based learning or whole systems learning. The key changes when moving from individual learning to a whole systems approach (individual, team, and organization) are the interventions used to foster learning. The primary intervention continues to be learning, but interventions are also focused on building organizational systems to maximize the likelihood that learning will improve broader performance at both the individual and organizational level.

Performance is the dominant discourse and paradigm within the field of human resource development (Holton, 2002). Swanson and Holton (2001) hold that performance can be defined as "accomplishing units of mission-related outcomes or outputs" (p. 137). Performance transpires in patently everything, whether a church, a non-profit or a for-profit; the authors maintain, "under this broad definition, performance is not seen as inherently harmful or non-humanistic" (p. 202). More to the point, a performance system is "any system organized to accomplish a mission or purpose" (p. 137). The purpose of HRD as seen by performance paradigm advocates is to "advance the mission of the performance system that sponsors the HRD efforts by improving the capabilities of individuals working in the system and improving the systems in which they perform their work" (Swanson & Holton, 2001, p. 137). The authors look to replace 'organization' with 'performance system' or with 'performance organization' (Swanson et al., 2001; Holton, 2002). Performance systems serve a mission. Holton (2002) opined that all organizations can be performance systems, however, not all performance systems can be organizations. A community may adapt to the role of a performance system if the community were to adopt a mission. The performance system's mission and goals attained within the system should specify the expected outcomes of the system (Holton, 2002). The author advances "every purposefully organized system operates with a mission, either explicitly or implicitly, and the role of the mission is to reflect the system's relationship with its external environment" (p. 202). The mission can be defined by the performance system organized to achieve some specific purpose. If the system is purposeful, it will have desired outputs; therefore performance theory would be applicable (Holton, 2002). Holton believes "the particular system's definition of its performance relationship with the external environment is fully captured by the mission and goals of the organization" (p. 202). When discerning the performance paradigm's import, Holton (2002) suggests asking whether HRD sponsored by a performance system could thrive if there is no improvement in the performance of the system. Moreover, would it survive if performance does not improve the mission of the organization?

Three prominent views pervade the performance paradigm scholarship, according to Swanson and Holton (2001): Performance is "a natural outcome of human activity", "necessary for economic activity", and "an instrument of oppression" (p. 132). The first view, *performance is a natural occurring human activity*, defines human beings engaging in variegated activities "with performance as a natural and valued outcome" (p. 132), and when the outcome is accomplished it satisfies an essential human need. The authors opined that to embrace performance is to embrace improving the human experience. Improvements in both performance and human capability are viewed as exceptionally complementary. The second view, *performance as necessary for economic activity*, holds performance as essential to enhancing individual and societal domains by cultivating increased economic gains. The authors claim that "this view sees performance as neither inherently good nor bad but rather as a means to other ends" (p. 132). Performance here is viewed as: Mandatory for people to earn a living, to make indelible contributions to their community, and to foster a better society. The third view and perhaps the most germane view for the purpose of this research is *performance as an instrument of organizational oppression*. This perspective advances performance as ultimately controlling and, in the process, dehumanizing. Organizations are coercive and demand relatively permanent behavioral change in lieu of compensation. Performance threatens human potential and, in sum, abuses the performer. The authors contend that this perspective of performance is seemingly most advanced by thoroughgoing critics of performance-based HRD, and, therefore, will be the perspective covered in this research.

Swanson and Holton (2001) claim that "when properly and clearly framed, the performance paradigm is not what the learning paradigm advocates present it to be" (p. 131). The authors continue to suggest that there is less of a chasm amid these paradigms than erroneously upheld by learning paradigm advocates. As a matter of fact, the authors assert that many of the criticisms levied at the performance paradigm are actually myths. Holton has made strident attempts to clear up the misunderstandings and to "lessen the gap between learning and performance" (Bierema, 2009, p. 10). Bierema (2009) maintains that those who lambaste the dominant performance paradigm, such as Barrie and Pace (1998; 1999), Bierema (1997), and Dirkx (1997) have been publishing research which she cites "[as] contain[ing] rather gross errors and misunderstandings of the performance paradigm" (Holton, 2002, p. 2000). In recognition of these authors as sources for critique, it's imperative to explicate what these "misunderstandings" and "gross errors" are, thus necessitating a more detailed discussion of the performance paradigm. In Holton's (2002) opinionated view the paradigm actually deserves critique, "since its advocates have failed to define the construct" (Bierema, 2009, p. 10).

Swanson and Holton (2001) argue that "for HRD to value people only with regard to their contribution to performance outcomes is offensive because it invalidates them as human beings" (p. 135). Generally, the authors opine, it can culminate in work spaces that devalue the inherent currency of people and may lead to abuse of employees. Learning and development, the authors contend, "should be a means to enhance people and their humanness, not to accomplish performance goals" (p. 135). Barrie and Pace (1999) view the performance paradigm as negating humans' "fundamental and inherent agency and self-determination, not the learning perspective" (p. 295). The performance paradigm perspective of human resource development is attributed to conditioning and leveraging individual behavior "through methods that allow for very little if any willingness and voluntariness on the part of the performers" (Holding, 1981, p. 130). Holding (1981) contends that performers are not encouraged, or perhaps are restricted by the performance organization, to develop "willingness of consciousness" as rational agents (p. 130). Holding maintains that such individuals "function in a change process purely as 'means' and not 'ends'" (p. 130). In a similar vein, Peterson and Pravo (1999) have likened the performance paradigm to behaviorism and conditioning. Barrie and Pace (1998) also agree that performance improvements are rendered through conditioning and behavioral control. Dirkx (1997) is of the same mind that performance is enhanced by inculcating passive workers with knowledge and skills required to improve the performance organization. Although Swanson and Holton (2001) hold that the performance paradigm cultivates the growth of learners as much as the learning paradigm, they, however, note that the "key difference is that the performance paradigm expects that learning and growth will benefit the performance system in which it is embedded" (p. 145). Individual growth and learning for the sole benefit of improving an employee with no avail to the organization, is unacceptable to organizational sponsored HRD.

Bierema (1997) has equated the performance paradigm with the mechanistic model of work (Swanson & Holton, 2001). She comments that "the machine mentality in the workplace, coupled with obsessive focus on performance, had created a crisis in individual development" (p. 23). The mechanistic approach to valuing development is the manner in which it accords value to productivity. Peterson and Provo (1999) also refer to the mechanistic or machine model of work when referring to the performance perspective. Swanson and Holton (2001) contend that learning advocates bemoan "emphasizing performance outcomes in HRD, and targeting HRD interventions to improve performance, results in an overly mechanistic approach to HRD and organizational life. As a result, people in organizations are limited and many fail to reach their full potential" (p. 137). Moreover, the authors remonstrate against this approach to HRD, believing that it deters human capabilities from achieving magnificent accomplishments, resulting in the performer feeling alienated from the sponsoring organization "ultimately hurting the organization" (p. 137).

The authors persist that all deleterious effects of training are derived from the performance perspective. The presumption underpinning this perspective is that performance is antithetical to human development. The viewpoint held by Laird, Holton, and Naquin (2003) is that this presumption "seems to be most closely aligned with critical theorists who wish to challenge organizational power structures that seek to control performance outcomes" (p. 11). By the same token, Dirkx (1997) argues that HRD is influenced "by an ideology of scientific management and reflects a view of education where the power and control over what is learned, how, and why is located in the leadership, corporate structure, and HRD staff" (p. 42). He further comments on the view of market-driven education, where learning benefits the bottom-line, "learning itself is denied in particular ways, largely by the perceived needs of the sponsoring corporation and the work individuals are required to perform" (p. 43).

The Sudanese Janjaweed

The Darfur conflict began in February, 26, 2003. The Janjaweed, predominantly Arab, accoutered with AK-47s and other armaments, ravaged non-Arab communities throughout Darfur. They were militiamen known to continuously conflict with Darfurian-African farmers darker in complexion. 'Janjaweed' is an Arabic colloquialism, which has variably been defined as 'a man with a gun on a horse' or 'a genie on a horse'. Their attacks were calculated to incite fear, with fierce strength and consistency. Whomever they didn't kill, the fear alone instigated a mass-exodus of thousands into the surrounding arid desert. The Janjaweed behaved like indomitable and selfish souls. They plundered the scarce possessions of affected non-Arab communities, leaving homes destitute, engulfed in flames, and in rubble. The Janjaweed doubtlessly had an insatiable appetite for wealth and land. They were chiefly composed of diminutive Arab nomadic tribes, for example, the Northern Rizeigat. The Northern Rizeigat tribe was composed of Ireqat, Mahamid, Beni Hussein, and Mahariya sub-clans (HRW, 2005 December). For years, the Janjaweed's deplorable havoc had gone unchecked by the Government of Sudan (GOS).

A defining moment for the counterinsurgency occurred on April 25, 2003, when a combined force of the Sudan Liberation Army/Movement (SLA or SLM) and the Justice for Equality Movement (JEM) drove into Al-Fashir with one SPG-9 rocket launcher, one *Dushka* (DShK) machine gun, and one 120-mm anti-aircraft gun, illegally expropriated from the Sudanese army. They destroyed every plane confined within the national airport's military zone, including: two Antonovs (cargo planes used to drop crude-oil, shrapnel-loaded bombs), and five helicopter gunships. They entered the airport with thirteen vehicles, and left with eighteen. The Government of Sudan privately determined to crush the rebels and anyone who sympathized and sided with them (Flint, 2009). Subsequently, after the GOS avowed declaration of war against all rebel factions involved, the GOS' military apparatus began incessantly recruiting militia and Janjaweed, putatively in the tens of thousands (Reeves, 2007). Ahmad Harun, the Interior Minister and distinguished Commander of the Darfur Security Desk supervised the activities of in situ and state-wide Sudanese Army, Sudanese Police, and relevant intelligence agencies. The aforementioned groups counseled Harun on all information pertaining to "staffing, funding, and arming of the Militia/Janjaweed in the context of counterinsurgency" (Reeves, 2007, p. 3). The GOS dispensed Harun to increase Janjaweed enrollment. He initially intended to assimilate the Janjaweed under the auspices of the Sudanese Armed Forces (SAF) "with full knowledge that they, often in the course of joint attacks with forces of the Sudanese Army, would commit crimes against humanity and war crimes against the civilian population of Darfur" (Reeves, 2007, p. 3). Reeves, a leading academic on the Darfur genocide and a Professor at Smith College in Massachusetts, contributes to this assessment further:

> The Sudanese Armed Forces and Militia/Janjaweed did not target any rebel presence within these particular villages. Rather, they attacked these villages based on the rationale that the tens of thousands of civilian residents in and near these villages were [presumed] supporters of the rebel forces. This strategy became the justification for the mass murder, summary execution, and mass rape of civilians who were known not to be participants in any armed conflict. Application of the strategy also called for, and achieved, the forced displacement of entire villages and communities (p. 3).

Reeves had provided a most glaring look at the rapaciousness of the Janjaweed. His work appositely captured the devastation they wrought, leaving little to no survivors and few muted witnesses. The *International Criminal Court* (ICC) prosecutor suggested evidence that alluded that 80-90 percent of all non-Arab villages had been displaced by Janjaweed attacks and that they had been responsible for disbanding more than two million Darfurians. The ICC reliably estimated the death toll at 200,000 – 500,000 (Reeves, 2007).

Article 35 of the Constitution of Sudan, referring to endorsed conscription, stipulates: "Every citizen shall defend the country and respond to the call for national defense and national service" (as cited in the Coalition to Stop the Use of Child Soldiers, 2004, p. 1). Conscripts served for a period of 24-months, 18-months for high school graduates, and 12-months for post-secondary graduates bearing some recognizable scholarly attainment e.g., diploma or degree from a college or university. The *People's Armed Forces Act* (1986) pointedly stated that all able-bodied, physically fit men, who could shoulder weapons and provisions were sought after. The age for compulsory enrollment in the SAF was 17. Voluntary enlistment remains to have no established minimum age. Meanwhile, paramilitary forces only accepted volunteers over the age of 16.

The GOS presaged an inevitably long-drawn-out battle with JEM and SLA rebels. The SAF was limited in military strength. To assuage the army of its military inadequacies, the GOS determined "to recruit, train, and equip Arab proxy militias called 'Janjaweed' to help suppress what was purportedly perceived as a Black African Rebellion in Darfur" (Totten & Parsons, 2009, p. 457). The GOS proposed amalgamating Arab tribes under their sphere of influence. A Darfurian refugee testified that, "Janjaweed always outnumber[ed] government soldiers, but arrived with them and left with them...It is not clear which force is the commanding force...It is clear that the Janjaweed [were] not restrained, in any way" (Human Rights Watch HRW, 2004 May, p. 9). The hierarchical structure of the Janjaweed intimately resembled that of the SAF. The only negligible difference between the military uniforms sported by Janjaweed regimentals and those of the SAF was the badge with an armed horseman on the breast pocket of the Janjaweed's shirts (Flint, 2009). Nevertheless, they drove "the same Land Cruisers as the army and [were] accompanied by armed bodyguards...They carry the same Thuraya satellite phones as senior army officers" (Flint, 2009, p. 45).

In 2007, a local Masalit Sheikh confided to an HRW representative that the GOS preferred the Arab Janjaweed over the SAF and the auxiliary *Peoples Defense Force* (PDF). The government entrusted the Janjaweed, more than the SAF, to suppress Tutsi rebellions in Fur, Masalit, and Zaghawa. According to Flint (2009) they "looked beyond the army to a nomadic fighting force that seemed ready-made for its purposes" (p. 75). Human Rights Watch (HRW) suggested high-ranking civil servants were pivotal in the recruitment of Janjaweed. An HRW representative acquired a document, dated November 22, 2003, disclosing the extent to which a state governor in Southern Darfur earmarked 300 horsemen for combat in Khartoum. Ahmed, a former Sudanese senior officer, then employed by the Darfur finance division from 1999-2008, vouched to Aegis Trust (2006), "[Janjaweed] were used without formal recruitment, without soldier numbers, without military techniques, without being members of the army" (p. 1). Aegis Trust continued to question Ahmed: "How did you [the defector] get involved in the Janjaweed?". His mild rejoinder simply was "the militia was started on orders from the Government. There [were] certain people who recruit[ed] people to the Janjaweed" (p. 1).

Elbagir (2008) traversed hundreds of kilometers over Darfur's wild landscape to interview Janjaweed members and those of the diametrically opposed JEM. Elbagir queried Jaffna al Bakheet, an erstwhile Janjaweed officer, concerning his recruitment. Jaffna remarked in a laconic response exactly who recruited him, "The Government of Sudan". Recruitment was selective and hinged on the fledgling's ethnicity. When the 2003 conflict ignited, government recruiters circulated recruitment posters, namely in Arab communities, soliciting support. Proselytizers targeted Arab groups harboring grievances against the varied ethnic groups that comprised the rebels. At times, posters propagated false promises of lavish rewards in exchange for taking up arms against JEM and SLA rebels. They endeavored to draw as many youth to the Janjaweed as possible, "there was a rush to join...But [the recruiter would] say these rewards, [were] being looked after by the government and investments in Arab villages, never came" (Elbagir, 2008, para. 3).

The Government of Sudan approached Sheikh Musa Hilal, former leader of the Um Jalal clan in Mahamid, to head the Janjaweed recruitment effort in Northern Darfur (HRW, 2005, December). Since June 2003, abashed community members believed Hilal "ha[d] [became] emblematic of the role of the militia forces in the attacks on civilians and the impunity conferred upon them by the Sudanese government" (p. 10). Zalingel, a neutral nomadic leader residing in Western Darfur, informed HRW (2004, October 18):

> The worst atrocities [were] committed by the Um Jalal of Musa Hilal because historically they have tensions with the Fur and Zaghawa. They're all camel herders, not cattle herders, and they have no respect for farmers, they have a superiority complex and they need their camels. When the war started, the Sudanese government asked Musa Hilal to be the leader of the Janjaweed (p. 10).

Police stations were brazenly attacked by the SLA in both Bindisi and Mukhar localities. This resulted in the upper-echelons from the GOS being summoned to meet in Wadi Saleh. Government officials continued to meet with Bindisi and Mukhar commissioners to discuss logistical arrangements for recruiting community members in the Janjaweed. The end of the Wadi Saleh meetings signaled the moment that Janjaweed enlistment began to skyrocket (HRW, 2005, December). GOS concerns continued to grow amid rumors of increased membership in the rebel opposition; thereby necessitating the recruitment of 20,000 Janjaweed shortly thereafter (Oswald, Durham, & Bates, 2010). A Messiria elder recalled the reason his tribe aligned with the GOS: "[they] were afraid that unless [they] stood together [they] would be finished" (Flint, 2009, p. 29).

Non-Arabs seeking enrollment in the Janjaweed were unequivocally rejected. Any Arab keenly determined to join, reprobate criminals included, were without doubt accepted. The GOS intended to "actively recruit criminals for the Janjaweed" (Levy, 2009, p. 25). Stalwart rebels in turn amplified their attacks with guerrilla tactics previously enshrouded in the South-North Sudanese War. In response, the government arbitrarily recruited any Arab who claimed familiarization with the rugged Darfur terrain.

Incentives for recruitment
Janjaweed were motivated by the appeal of expropriating land from non-Arab foes. The government proffered a reasonable wage to novices. Janjaweed were supplied with war accoutrements and the express permission to ride roughshod over the rights of others, thereby legitimizing the Janjaweed's invasion of villages, raping of inhabitants, murdering the resistance, and, in the end, irrevocably oppressing the downtrodden lives of those affected for decades to come. Accounts from Darfur affirm the GOS:

> Compensate[d] Janjaweed officers and militia members [by giving them] homes, cars, and satellite phones [which are all] part of the compensation for the officers…They are also paid monthly stipends or salaries…four different persons agreed on the exact amounts - £300,000 Sudanese Pounds a month (U.S. $ 117 as of mid-2003) for a man with a horse or camel, and £200,000 a month (U.S. $ 79) for a man without – roughly twice as much as a soldier of similar rank (Flint, 2009, p. 46).

By and large, Janjaweed were generously remunerated. Money procured by the selling of booty from recent village incursions was awarded to the Janjaweed. This vicious cycle further incentivized the Janjaweed's rape and plunder to an unspeakable degree (Koerner, 2005). Cox and Dutton (2009) documented that Ahmed Harun, forenamed earlier, organized sacks of money to be distributed to Omdas, also known as tribal leaders, and to Sheikhs, to pay them for their participation in the conflict. The sale of property expropriated from villages no longer sufficed. In late 2005, the Janjaweed began demanding salaries. The GOS entrusted salaries to Omdas, who in turn, redistributed monies to the appropriate tribesmen. HRW (2004,

May) postulated that Janjaweed were issued stipends superseding salaries paid to the SAF. They were recompensed $100 to $400 U.S per month for services rendered. In line with Cox and Dutton, another Janjaweed defector in 2006 was questioned about the incentives from the government. He rejoined, "they [gave me] a camel worth 2m Sudanese pounds...They [told me] this camel is for you, and you will be on a monthly salary of 500,000 Sudanese pounds" (p. 1). Aside from wealth, the government promised Janjaweed marked access to administrative power within Sudan. Omdas were permitted propriety over annexed lands and property of non-Arabs, thus increasing their chiefdoms and economic-political prestige. When the government's money supply dissipated, so did most Omdas' support. In the meanwhile, the government set out to replace exacting members of the Janjaweed with men of the Abbala tribe. Abbala men were outwardly uneducated and poor, possessing all the hallmark characteristics that GOS recruiters looked for. Abbala tribesmen swelled the Janjaweed ranks shortly after. Abbala men also demanded money, not ideology. Moreover, the government pledged to provide for the families of slain Janjaweed who perished amidst the chaos of war. Janjaweed were also allured by oil and sugar incentive packages (HRW, 2004, May).

Janjaweed Training Centers

Steidle and Wallace (2007) noted that the preeminent Janjaweed training facility was located in El Gardut. An examination of the sources, as deduced by Sherwell (2004), concedes that Janjaweed were trained at remote and isolated locations scattered throughout Sudan. Training encampments were erected in the open. Trainees slept under trees in full view, all the while officers cooked, carelessly exposing their positions with charcoal clouds hovering over camp (Elbagir, 2008). As an example, sections of El Geneina, a few miles from the city's center, were fashioned into training compounds for the Janjaweed (HRW, 2004, April). Sherwell further noted "two camps in the hills near Kass, but the poor security situation meant that The Telegraph [UK newspaper] at the time in 2004 was unable to confirm the locations" (p. 2). Steidle and Wallace (2007) reported that "old al-Qaeda camps in the Nuba Mountains were now used as GOS military training facilities; rumor had it that al-Qaeda still had active training camps in the pipeline area as well as Darfur" (p. 34). The GOS also converted a derelict animal research center near Ghazawal Jawzet into a training facility equipped with an obstacle course.

Misteriha, South-West of Kebkabiva, housed Northern Darfur's largest training compound. Misteriha operated conjointly from 2003 onward as Musa Hilal's personal residence and as a base for coordinating the Janjaweed's movements (HRW, 2004, October). Hilal's Chief Lieutenant, Abdul Wahid, functioned as his liaison between the SAF and the Janjaweed that were recruited from, and trained in, Misteriha. The nom de guerre committed to the Misteriha Janjaweed was "mobile, light, quick, and horrible forces", a name befitting of this tempered camel paramilitary (HRW, 2005, December, para. 8). One defector was asked by Aegis Trust (2006) who trained him. His retort was "the government provides a number of people who train us...the weapons [were] provided by the Government" (p. 1). The defector recollected that his training transpired "in a camp west of El Kebkabiva called Misteriha" (p. 1). As training continued to inculcate the Janjaweed for ethnic cleansing, Steidle and Wallace (2007) commented "the GOS realized it is becoming increasingly expensive to pay the nomads to attack" (p. 207). By 2004, two separate training centers emerged within Misteriha. The first, governed by the Sudanese Reserve Police, accommodated 200 to 250 draftees with three months of weapons training. The second camp was SAF supervised and had a larger Islamic educative element introduced. Sudanese army inductees were composite of the majority population trained here. It is likely that the first camp saw the continued training of Hilal's Janjaweed. Trainees demonstrating leadership qualities were transferred to Khartoum for advanced military education. Few exceptional trainees were sent abroad to Syria.

Janjaweed Training
Many authors have critiqued the homespun training curriculum designed for the Janjaweed. As an example, Sherwell (2004) posited that when the conflict escalated in 2003 the Janjaweed were "ill-trained Arab nomad fighters set loose on the majority of the Darfur population by the government, (and) are now receiving formal military instruction represent[ing] an alarming new development" (p. 1). In the next section I will, as comprehensively as possible, detail all aspects of Janjaweed training as I have inferred from an overview of the available literature.

Orientation preceded training. Little by little, inductees were provided with preparatory information on what the job entailed. Cadres tasked fledglings to shave one another's heads with a dull, unsanitary rustic hand-blade. HRW (1996, May) posited that "degrading treatment and insults followed this opening ritual" (p. 273). Recruits arranged in formation as a hardened cadre steadily ambled back and forth in front, sizing these greenhorns up. He informed the group that any semblance of self-esteem and / or reverent pride was to be buried and forgotten. Educated enlistees were instructed to dig a mediocre-sized pit in the dirt, place their scholarly attainments within and set them ablaze.

An erstwhile rebel remarked to Steidle and Wallace: (2007) "Originally, the GOS...simply paid the Janjaweed to raid and attack...Over time, they also decided to provide further training – to improve the nomad's military effectiveness" (p. 207). Both PDF and SAF instructors spent entire afternoons running the Janjaweed through arduous military training routines. Forty five days of training were given to most Janjaweed, others endured two months. Trainees were busily immersed in overexerting physical drills throughout the day. Rest was only allotted when it coincided with prayer and mealtime. Trainees reveled in the physicality of training: marching and jogging through rugged terrain, and reciting songs transfused with Islamic themes glorifying martyrs of the Islamic brotherhood (HRW, 1996, May). Trainees paraded themselves down the village walk-ways parroting religious chants, arrayed in full military gear. An anonymous defector asked by Aegis Trust (2006) how he was trained, rejoined:

> It's not a long course of training. Just to train you how to use the weapon. It's not like in the military. They give you sufficient training. They train you to recognize targets and to use certain weapons against those targets. They give you a certain type of weapon to use against those targets. We were told about the villages. You cannot find people without villages. So we were trained to target those villages (para. 5).

Military training averaged one month in length for an estimated 150-200 Janjaweed per session. Sessions honed in on rendering soldiers dexterous in hand-to-hand combat. Three hundred Janjaweed evincing implicit leadership properties were hand-selected by Western Darfur's senior officers for relocation north of Omdurman, to acquire advanced intelligence and infantry training, provided by a joint contingent of Russian and Sudanese officers. Steidle and Wallace (2007) observed:

A new class of Janjaweed trainees that ha[ve] just graduated from the training facility in El Gardut...intelligence suggests that many of these graduates have trained to be specialists such as snipers or reconnaissance experts...Some militia will move on-to special forces schools north of Khartoum, in the desert just south of the Egyptian border...this is unbelievable, these guys are obviously well trained and getting some major support (p. 186).

I have provided a sample of a Janjaweed training timetable below, derived from HRW (1996, May):

Daily Training Schedule
4. am–Rise to pray; followed by field marching.
9. am–Breakfast; then field training.
1. pm–Lunch; standing at attention under the Sudanese sun.
3-4. pm–Rest.
4. pm–Field training, continued marching.
6. pm–Praying during sunset.
7. pm –Dinner.
8-9. pm–Stand attentively until 2-3 am, deprived of sleep.

Lecturers cunningly concocted lesson plans for Janjaweed, to further deepen their views on the Arab-non-Arab fissure in Sudan. In-class instruction looked down upon Sudanese rebels and accomplices as unholy outlaws; their ultimate defeat only obtainable by Jihad, the Holy War. In the evening they sat through Islamic lectures on Muslim culture and traditions. The meager cultural education that the Janjaweed received emphasized exegetical analysis of Islamic scripture. According to HRW (1996, May) "mandatory training, was infused as it was with Islamic religious fervor, create[d] an atmosphere of coercion on all participants to convert to Islam" (p. 11). Members of the *National Islamic Front* (NIC) customarily attended Islamic lectures as guests, proffering religious support to instructors. The NIC showcased Islamic videos to novices. In the end, all PDF, SAF, and even Janjaweed, who were provided with scant cultural education, measured up as full-fledged Mujahedeen.

The PDF membership was well-educated, fluent in Arabic, and familiarized well with the Quran. Having undergone Islamic-themed training, the PDF in turn served the Janjaweed as ideology instructors. PDF training objectives differed immensely from that of Janjaweed training. In 1995, President Omar al-Bashir broadcast on a Republic of Sudan radio program that the religious aims of PDF development were, "to provide spiritual and religious lessons to recruits to help create a prudent Muslim society" (Sherwell, 2004, p. 1). PDF received education in the spirit of Jihad, ripely imitating mujahedeen warriors destined for posthumous glory. Conscripts into the PDF included abducted Africans, some of whom were Judeo-Christian. The government forced abductees to relinquish previously held religious convictions in favor of Islam, contravening Article 18 of the *UN International Covenant on Civil and Political Rights* (HRW, 1996, May).

Literature that documents Janjaweed training has discussed very few outcomes of the cultural education they received. I have located one empirical source (Elbagir, 2008) that describes the influence that their religious training had on their performance. In battle, the Janjaweed strung Koran-versed amulets, blessed by local Sheikhs, from their machine guns. They believed the amulets could deter bullets and prevent spearheads from piercing their blessed skin. Jok Madut Jok (2007) offers his conjecture on why Janjaweed forays on non-Arab tribes were so virulent:

> Where Islam could function as a tool for the training of a soldier to shed his remorse for his victims, as is the case for soldiers who [were] sent to the south, the Muslim soldier is imbued with the belief he does not have to adhere to any boundaries because the enemy is not a co-religionist (p. 17).

Adult participants were permitted to seek out subsidiary employment in neighboring towns, while their dependents stayed behind to be educated in elementary Arabic and made to memorize Quran scripture. Instructors easily engendered a deep loyalty to Islam in the minds of susceptible children.

In the same manner as PDF and GOS forces were limitedly assimilated as Janjaweed, trained and experienced Janjaweed circa 2004-2005 were, to a greater extent, reciprocally integrated into the PDF and GOS. To assuage complaints made by international watchdogs peering in on the conflict from afar, the GOS covertly hid their resolute support of proxy militias. Steidle and Wallace (2007) procured a document detailing the depth to which Janjaweed were integrated into GOS and PDF groups. The document, addressed to the Commander of the Western Military Area, the Commander of

Training and Operations Department, the Commander of Intelligence and Security Department, and the Director of Security and Military Intelligence and National Security, was intercepted by Steidle during a field operation in Northern Darfur. The document reported, "After graduation of 45,000 [Janjaweed], they were added and merged into the police, military, and security organs and are now in position" (p. 187). Subsequently, the level of military knowledge acquired by Janjaweed members during their tenure, determined their legitimate role in the government within one of three occupations:

(1) Sudanese Border Guards: Issued military identification and remunerated monthly salaries. They received the most training of these three occupations.

(2) Peoples Defense Force: Supplied with uniforms, ammunition, guns, and food; however, not issued salaries. Few were paid piece-rate per operation completed, often a nominal sum of 100,000 Sudanese pounds.

(3) Mustanfareen (reserves): Recruited by force, or abduction; allotted uniforms and dispatched weapons, no salary. Recalcitrant reserves risked being placed in jail or being fined (Flint, 2009).

Janjaweed as a Performance System

Performance systems serve a mission. At this juncture, having organized the corpus of literature through an HRD lens, there is no denying that the empirical evidence tends to establish the unassailable culpability of the Government of Sudan in the organization of the Janjaweed. The performance system theory holds a performance system as "any system organized to accomplish a mission or purpose" (Swanson & Holton, 2001, p. 137). The performance system requires the sponsorship of a host organization, alternatively called a host performance system. The host organization in this case, the Government of Sudan, expressed the mission to annihilate non-Arabs through the use of a group distinct from the Sudanese Armed Forces, the Janjaweed.

As explicated by Flint (2009) the GOS "looked beyond the army to a nomadic fighting force that seemed ready-made for its purposes" (p. 75). We know decidedly that the Janjaweed was organized accordingly to serve the purpose of extirpating non-Arabs. Hypothetically, the Janjaweed, on the whole, became a performance system itself, with its own mission, or purpose, to kill non-Arabs for the host performance system, again the Government of Sudan (Aegis Trust, 2006; Human Rights Watch, 2003, November 22; Steidle & Wallace, 2007).

The purpose of HRD, as held by the performance paradigm, is to "advance the mission of the performance system that sponsors the HRD efforts by improving the capabilities of individuals working in the system and improving the systems in which they perform their work" (Swanson & Holton, 2001, p. 137). The host performance system sponsored the HRD efforts that culminated in performance improvements of the Janjaweed. The purpose of HRD in this case, was the host performance system providing HRD to the sponsored performance system to augment their performance in achieving their express mission of killing non-Arabs. Steidle and Wallace (2007) held "originally, the GOS...simply paid the Janjaweed to raid and attack...Over time, they also decided to provide further training – to improve the nomad's military effectiveness" (p. 207).

The expected outcomes of the host performance system can be extrapolated from their mission e.g., the use of the Janjaweed to eradicate non-Arabs. The purpose of HRD interventions here was to advance the mission i.e., the Janjaweed's performance as a system to kill, to avail the host performance system. The Janjaweed, as an infant system, could not have existed without the host or parent system, namely the Government of Sudan. All things considered, it may appear to be a matter of semantics. The Government of Sudan is the host system and the Janjaweed is the host system's mission. The Janjaweed's mission was to see that the overall mission of the host system was achieved.

Holton (2002) opined that all organizations can be performance systems; however, not all performance systems can be organizations. The Janjaweed was not necessarily an organization. Its existence or purpose would be rendered null and of no consequence if it were not for the nurturing of the host organization. The Janjaweed became its own performance system once it adopted a mission. If learning interventions for the performance system failed to improve the overall performance of the system in which the HRD was designed, then the HRD effort failed. The Janjaweed became a formidable force due to the training its members received. If the sub-performance system advanced the mission of the host system by attaining the goal of drastically reducing Darfur's non-Arab population, the host system can be deemed as having successfully created a well-trained performance system to serve such a purpose.

Even performance advocates concur that steps taken toward organizational performance may bring about abusive and unethical implications (Swanson & Holton, 2001). Unfortunately, critics of performance-based HRD have shoehorned all emerging views of performance under the *'instrument of organizational oppression'* perspective. When the host system instituted HRD measures to improve the performance of the Janjaweed, it in turned improved the position of the host organization. This organization-driven approach, learning paradigm advocates maintain, represents oppressive consequences. The host organization does not simply oppress those operating within one of its auxiliary systems, but also individuals and communities outside the host performance system's ambit of operations. Here, I suggest that Janjaweed learning induced by a genocidal curriculum, in turn culminated in the abuse of its external environment, even affecting those outside the purview of their targeted killing. To this end, how does one authenticate the abusive nature of curricula on learners, if an assessment is not undergone to measure the performance of the knowledge learned? How can one determine the abusive substance of curricula if the knowledge imparted is not observed whilst being performed? Since the Janjaweed performed in a sphere extraneous to its own e.g., non-Arab communities, the nature of organizational oppression cannot be inferred unless the calamitous effects on those whom the learning of genocidal practices most affected are assessed e.g., Darfurians, non-Arab and black.

The performance paradigm perspective of human resource development is attributed as controlling behavior and conditioning individuals. In a similar vein, Peterson and Pravo (1999) have likened the performance paradigm with behaviorism and conditioning. Barrie and Pace (1998) also contend that performance improvements are realized through conditioning and behavioral control. It is not of the opinion of the researcher that Janjaweed members, prior to training, were of a genocidal mind. Woodward (2000) believes "soldiers are not born but made...They are fashioned through their training in specific ways, for specific ends" (p. 640). Members of the sponsored performance system were conditioned to exact violence against the expressed enemy of the host performance system. Holding (1981) is of the opinion that performers are discouraged, or perhaps restricted, by the performance organization to develop "willingness of consciousness" as rational agents (p. 130). Detracting from Janjaweed's rational thought was their ardent pursuit of rewards and an escape from abject poverty (Elbagir, 2008; Aegis Trust, 2006). As a sub-performance system, Janjaweed were motivated differently from those performing in the host system to undergo performance enhancement. The derelict position of Janjaweed inductees was exploited by GOS recruiters. In exchange for entering Janjaweed service, recruits drawn from the poorest regions of Darfur were proffered land, money, farming equipment, and, in lesser known cases, prestige. Enlisting in the Janjaweed meant survival. The historical record demonstrates that many registered, not in the name of ideology, or deeply-grounded hate toward non-Arabs, but to accumulate the wealth that propagandist recruitment posters promised. To reap the rewards of wholesale slaughter, Janjaweed need first be inculcated in the GOS agenda. Learning and development, Swanson and Holton (2001) contend, "Should be a means to enhance people and their humanness, not to accomplish performance goals" (p. 135). When the host system, through the use of a well-trained sub-performance system, obtained its performance goals, Janjaweed members were then remunerated. The Janjaweed partook in the genocidal plan to gain wealth. Once promises of wealth subsided, the Janjaweed experienced high turnover, signaling the recruits' true motivation for participating in training (Steidle & Wallace, 2007). This perspective advanced performance as ultimately controlling and, in the process, dehumanizing. The host system was coercive and demanded behavioral change of its performers e.g., the Janjaweed / sub-performance system, in lieu of compensation. All in all, performance subjugated the potential of the Janjaweed to be humane and rational and consequently affected the most those injured by its trained actions.

Conclusion

In this section, "the multiple perspectives of performance...can be identified within the learning versus performance debate and argue that neither performance or learning can be considered inherently "good" or "bad" and that human resource development can embrace both as humanistic" (Swanson & Holton, 2001, p. 132). Swanson and Holton (2001) hold that performance driven practitioners can adopt a humanistic approach to human resource development, so long as their approach results in positive performance outcomes. Performance advocates claim that ignoring performance "in favor of individual control may ultimately be bad for the individual if the organization is not able to survive or prosper" (Swanson & Holton, 2001, p. 138). Principally focusing on individual development is likely to culminate in feeble attempts in human resource development. Swanson and Holton (2001) suggest that HRD professionals abandon the argument that either learning or performance can be oppressive and abusive, likewise, this researcher agrees.

References

Adelman, H., & Suhrke, A. (2000). *The path of a genocide: The Rwanda crisis from Uganda to Zaire.* Piscataway, New Jersey: Transaction Publishers.

Aegis Trust. (2006, October 17). Janjaweed defector first interviewed by Aegis Trust. Retrieved from http://www.aegistrust.org/Sudan/-Darfur/janjaweed-defector-first-interviewed-by-aegis-trust.html

Alagaraja, M., & Dooley, L. M. (2003). Origins and historical influences on human resource development: A global perspective. *Human Resource Development Review, 2* (82), 82-96.

Alverez, A. (2009). *Genocidal crimes.* Kentucky, U.S: Routledge.

Alverez, A. (2006). Militias and genocide. *War crimes, genocide, & crimes against humanity, 2,* 1-33. Retrieved from http://www.aa.psu.edu/journals/warcrimes/articles/V2/v2a1.pdf

Amanpour, C. (1997). *Transitions online: Exclusive CNN Documentary on Arkan. Part 1 – Arkan Wanted.* Retrieved January 12, 2014. http://www.tol.org/client/article/17801-exclusive-cnn-documetary-on-arkan.html?print

Anonymous. (2004, January 14). Witness provides corroboration, but little else: Day 271. Coalition for international justice trial reports archive. *Institute for war and peace reporting.* http://iwpr.net/report-news/witness-providescorroboration-little-else

Antischolio. (1999). *Srebrenica.* Athens: Carthago.

Armatta, J. (2010). *Twilight of impunity: The war crimes trial of Slobodan Milosevic.* Durham, North Carolina: Duke University Press.

Arnold, J. R., & Wiener, R. (2012). *Civil Defence in Cold War. The Essential Reference Guide.* Santa Barbara, California: ABC-Clio

Aswathappa, K. (2007). *Human resources and personnel management* (4th ed.). New Delhi, India: Tata McGraw-Hill Education.

Australian Government Refugee Review Tribunal. (2010, March 5). Country advice Serbia. Retrieved May, 5, 2013, from: http://www.ecoi.net/file_upload/1930_1295364964_srb3615 4.pdf

Ayres, D. (2000). *Anatomy of a crisis: Education, development, and the state in Cambodia, 1953-1998*. Honolulu, HI: University of Hawaii Press.

Ayres, D. (1999). The Khmer Rouge and education: Beyond the discourse of destruction, *History of education: Journal of the History of Education Society, 28*(2), 205-218.

Bagosora, T., Kabiligi, G., Ntabakuza, A., & Nsengiyumva, A. (2008, December 18). ICTR-98-41-T. http://www.unictr.org/Portals/0/Case%5CEnglish%5CNsengi yumva%5C081218.pdf

Bagosora, T., Kabiligi, G., Ntabakuza, A., Nsengiyumva, A. (2005, February 2). ICTR-98-41-T. ictrarchive09.library.cornell.edu/ENGLISH/cases/.../020205. html

Bandura, A., Ross, D., & Ross, S. A. (1963). Vicarious reinforcement and imitative learning. *Journal of Abnormal and Social Psychology, 67*, 601–607.

Barrie, J., & Pace, R. W. (1999). Learning for performance: Just the end of the beginning – a rejoinder to Kuchinke. *Human resource development quarterly, 10*(3), 293-296.

Barrie, J., & Pace, R. W. (1998). Learning for organizational effectiveness. Philosophy of education and human resource development. *Human resource development quarterly, 9*(1), 39-54.

Barron, P., & Paul, A. (1977). *Peace with horror*. London: Hodder & Stoughton.

Baumann, R. F., Gawrych, G. W., & Kretchik, W. E. (1993). *Armed peacekeepers in Bosnia*. Retrieved April, 01, 2013, from the Combat Studies Institute Press website: http://usacac.army.mil/cac2/cgsc/carl/download/csipubs/bau mann_bosnia.pdf

Becker, H. S. (1986). *Writing for social scientists: How to start and finish your thesis, book, or article.* Chicago, IL: University of Chicago Press.

Bellamy, A. J. (2012). *Massacres and morality: Mass atrocities in an age of civilian immunity.* Oxford, UK: Oxford University Press.

Bell-Fialkoff, A. (1996). *Ethnic cleansing.* New York, NY: St. Martin's Press.

Bierema, L. L. (1997). The development of the individual leads to more productive workplaces. In R. J. Torraco (Ed.), *Academy of Human Resource Development* (pp. 652-659). Baton Rouge, LA: Academy of Human Resource Development.

Bierema, L. L. (2000). Moving beyond performance paradigms in human resource development. In A. L. Wilson & E. R. Hayes (Eds.), *Handbook of Adult and Continuing Education* (pp. 278-293). San Francisco: Jossey-Bass.

Bierema, L. L. (2009). Human performance theory and practice. In V. C Wang & K. P King (Eds.), *Fundamentals of Human performance and training* (pp. 1-23). Charlotte, NC: Information age publishing.

Bikindi, S. (2008, December 2). ICTR-01-72-T. http://www.ictrcaselaw.org/docs/20081202-jgt-0172-01-en.pdf

Bikindi, S. (2001, July 4). ICTR-72-I. http://genderjurisprudence.org/documents/ictr/ICTR_Judgments,_Orders_&_Indictments/Bikindi_ICTR-01-72/Indictment/2001-06-27,_Bikindi-Indictment.pdf

Bizimungu, A. (2004, July 15). ICTR-00-56-I. http://www.ictrcaselaw.org/docs/doc54947.pdf

Bizimungu, A., Ndindiliyimana, A., Nzuwonemeye, F., & Sagahutu, S. (2002, November 14). www.unictr.org/.../Case%5CEnglish%5CMpiranya%5CmilitaryII.pdf

Block, R. (1993, November 18). Killers. *New York Review*, pp. 9-10.

Bolden, C. D. (2008). *Understanding conflict and violence through the application of behavior analysis* (Doctoral Dissertation). Available from Proquest. (UMI No. 3319719).

Brown, M. E. (2001). *Nationalism and ethnic conflict*. Cambridge, MA: MIT Press.

Burg, S., & Shoup, P. (1999). *The war in Bosnia-Herzegovina: Ethnic conflict and international interventions*. Armonk, N.Y: E. Sharpe.

Burgler, R. A. (1990). *The eyes of the pineapple: Revolutionary intellectuals and terror in Democratic Kampuchea*. Saarbrucken, Germany: Verlag Breitenbach.

Callahan, J. L. (2010). Reconstructing, constructing and deconstructing the field: The importance of historical manuscripts in HRDR. *Human Resource Development Review, 9,* 311-313.

Carney, T. (1977). *Communist party power in Kampuchea (Cambodia): Documents and discussion*. Ithaca: Cornell University Southeast Asia Program.

Chalk, F. B. (1990). *The history and sociology of genocide: Analyses and case studies*. New Haven, CT: Yale University Press.

Chandler, D. P., Kiernan, B., & Boua, C. (1988). *Pol Pot plans the future: Confidential leadership documents from Democratic Kampuchea, 1976-1977*. New Haven, CT: Yale University Southeast Asia Studies.

Chandler, D. P. (1996). *Facing the Cambodian past, selected essays, 1971-1994*. Chiang Mai, Thailand: Silkworm Books.

Chen, D. (2012, October 18). Detailed discussion of Party communications and defendant's relationships with Pol Pot. Retrieved February 11, 2014, from the Cambodia Tribunal Monitor website: http://www.cambodiatribunal.org/blog/2012/10/detailed-discussion-party-communications-and-defendants%E2%80%99-relationships-pol-pot

Child Soldiers International. (2001). *Child Soldiers Global Report 2001 – Cambodia, 2001*. Accessed August 9, 2014. http://www.refworld.org/docid/4988060bc.html

Chuong, S. (1997). Memories of victims under the Khmer Rouge regime on the 17th of April 1975. *Documentation Center of Cambodia.* Retrieved from http://www.d.dccam.org/Survivors/26.htm

Cigar, N., & Williams, P. (1997). War crimes and individual responsibility: A prima facie case for the indictment of Slobodan Milosevic. Retrieved May 20, 2011, from The Balkan Institute, New England Center for International Law and Policy website: http://balkanwitness.glypx.com/balkan1.htm#execsummary

Clayton, T. (2005). Re-orientations in moral education in Cambodia since 1975. *Journal of Moral Education, 34*(4), 505-517.

Clayton, T. (1998). Building the new Cambodia: Educational destruction and construction under the Khmer Rouge, 1975-1979. *History of Education Quarterly, 38*(1), 1-16.

Clymer, K. J. (2004). *The United States and Cambodia, 1969-2000: A troubled relationship.* Abingdon, UK: Psychology Press.

Coalition to stop the use of child soldiers. (2004). *Child soldiers global report.* London, UK: Coalition to stop the use of child soldiers. Retrieved from www.child-soldiers.org/document/get?id=966

Comer, R., & Gould, E. (2010). *Psychology around us.* San Francisco, CA: John Wiley & Sons.

Connell, R. W. (1970). Propaganda and Education: Political Training in the Schools. *Australian Journal of Education, (14)*2, 155-167.

Cookson, P. S. (1998). *Program planning for the training and continuing education of adults: North American perspectives.* Malabar, FLA: Krieger Publishing.

Cox, B. J., Estrada, S. D., Lynham, S. A., & Motii, N. (2005). Defining human resource development in Morocco: An exploratory inquiry. *Human Resource Development International, 8*(4), 435-447.

Cox, P., & Dutton, F. (2009). Darfur destroyed: Sudan's perpetrators break silence. Retrieved April 23, 2013, from the Aegis Trust Films website: http://www.aegistrust.org/Films/darfur-destroyed-sudans-perpetrators-speak-out.html

Dallaire, R. (2003). *Shake hands with the devil: The failure of humanity in Rwanda*. Toronto, Canada: Random House Canada.

Des Forges, A. (1999). Leave none to tell the story: Genocide in Rwanda. Retrieved February 8, 2011, from the Human Rights Watch website: http://www.hrw.org/reports/1999/rwanda/Geno1-3-11.htm

Des Forges, A. (1996). Call to genocide: Radio in Rwanda, 1994. In A. Thompson (Ed.), *The media and the Rwandan Genocide* (pp. 41-55). Ann Arbor, MI: Pluto Press.

Dirkx, J. M. (1997). Human resource development as adult education: Fostering the educative workplace. In R. Rowden (Ed.), *Workplace learning: Debating five critical questions of theory and practice* (pp. 41–47). San Francisco: Jossey-Bass.

Dorn, A. W., & Matloff, J. (2000). Preventing the bloodbath: Could the UN have predicted and prevented the Rwandan Genocide. *The Journal of Conflict Studies, 20*(1), 1-44.

Druian, G., & Butler, J. A. (2001). Effective schooling practices and at-risk youth: What the research shows. Retrieved March 10, 2012, from the Northwest Regional Educational Laboratory website:http://www.michigan.gov/documents/Community_Resource_Articles_85520_7.pdf

Elbagir, N. (2008, June 3). Meet the Janjaweed. *Foreign correspondent by ABC News*. Retrieved from http://www.abc.net.au/foreign/content/oldcontent/s2464863.htm

Eleftherotypia. (1993, July 8).

Encyclopedia of violence, peace and conflict (1999). Waltham, MA: Academic press.

Erlanger, S. (1996, June 10). The dayton accords: A status report. *New York Times*. Retrieved from http://www.nytimes.com/specials/bosnia/context/dayton.html

European Center for the Development of Vocational Training (CEDEFOP). (2008). Terminology of European education and training policy: A selection of 100 key terms. *Office for Official Publications of the European Communities, Luxembourg*. Retrieved on October 29, 2012. http://www.cedefop.europa.eu/EN/Files/4064_en.pdf

Flint, J. (2009). *Above "beyond 'Janjaweed': Understanding the militias of Darfur*: Small Arms Survey. Geneva: Graduate Institute of International and Development Studies. Retrieved from: http://www.smallarmssurveysudan.org/pdfs/HSBASW P-17-Beyond-Janjaweed.pdf

Foer, F. (2011). *How football explains the world*. New York, NY: Random House.

Foreign Broadcast Information Service (FBIS). (1977, May 5). Springfield, Va., U.S: Department of Commerce. IV (Asia and Pacific).

Foreign Broadcast Information Service (FBIS). (1977, April 18). Springfield, Va., U.S: Department of Commerce. IV (Asia and Pacific).

Gahima, G. (2013). *Transitional justice in Rwanda: Accountability for atrocity*. London, UK: Routledge.

Garrick, J. (1998). *Informal learning in the workplace: Unmasking human resources development*. London, UK: Routledge.

Gatete, J. B. (2011, March 31). Case No. ICTR-2000-61-T. www.unictr.org/.../Case%5CEnglish%5CGatete%5Cjudgement%5C110331. pdf

Gow, J. (2003). *The Serbian project and its adversaries: A strategy of war crimes*. Montreal, Canada: McGill-Queens Press.

Gourevitch, P. (1998). *We wish to inform you that tomorrow we will be killed with our families: Stories from Rwanda*. New York: Farrar Straus, and Giroux.

Grossman, D. A. (1995). *On killing: The psychological cost of learning to kill in war and society.* New York, NY: Little, Brown, and Company.

Grunfeld, F., & Huijboom, A. (2007). *The failure to prevent genocide in Rwanda: The role of bystanders.* Boston, U.S: Martinus Nijhoff publishers.

Hadzic, G. (2004, May 21). The prosecutor of the tribunal against Goran Hadzic. Case No. IT-04-75-I. http://www.icty.org/x/cases/hadzic/ind/en/had-ii040716e.htm

Halpern, D. F. (2002). *Thought and knowledge: An introduction to critical thinking.* London, UK: Routledge.

Heidenrich, J. G. (2001). *How to prevent genocide: A guide for policymakers, scholars, and the concerned citizen.* Westport, CT: Greenwood Publishing Group.

Herbert, D. (2003). *Religion, ethics and civil society: Rethinking public religion in the modern world.* Farnham, UK: Ashgate Publishing.

Herbst, J. (1999). *Requiem for a German past: A boyhood among the Nazis.* Madison, Wisconsin: The University of Wisconsin Press.

Hiden, J., & Farquharson, J. (1983). *Explaining Hitler's Germany: Historians and the Third Reich.* New Jersey, U.S: Barnes & Noble Books.

Hilderbrand, K. (1984). *The Third Reich.* London, UK: George Allen & Unwin.

Hinton, A. (2005). *Why did they kill? Cambodia in the shadow of genocide.* Ewing, NJ: University of California Press.

Hirondelle News. (2005, January 13). ICTR/Military II – French Soldiers Trained Interahamwe Militia in 1992. Retrieved October 13, 2012 from, http://allafrica.com/stories/200501130680.html

Hitler, A. (1939). *Mein Kampf.* New York, NY: Reynal and Hitchcock.

Hodzic, R. (2012, May 17). Bosnia: The haunting legacy of Ratko Mladic. *Aljazeera.* Retrieved from http://www.aljazeera.com/indepth/opinion/2012/05/2012517 855566451.html

Holding, D. H. (1981). *Human skills.* Hoboken, New Jersey: Wiley.

Holton, E. F. III. (2002) Theoretical assumptions underlying the performance paradigm of human resource development. *Human Resource Development International, 5*(2), 199-215.

Human Rights Watch. (2005, December). *Entrenching impunity. Government responsibility for international crimes in Darfur, 17*(17). Retrieved from http://www.hrw.org/sites/default/files/reports/darfur1205web wcover.pdf

Human Rights Watch. (2004, October 18). Interview with Zalingei, West Darfur. Retrieved from http://www.hrw.org/sites/default/files/features/darfur/fiveyea rson/report4.html

Human Rights Watch. (2004, May 1). *Darfur Destroyed, 16*(6). Retrieved from http://www.hrw.org/sites/default/files/reports/sudan0504full. pdf

Human Rights Watch. (1996, May 1). Behind the red line: Political repression in Sudan. Retrieved from http://www.unhcr.org/refworld/docid/3ae6a8450.html

Hutu Hate Propaganda. (2009). Retrieved from educ.jmu.edu/~vannorwc/assets/...150/.../hutu%20propagand a.pdf

Iordanova, D. (2001). *Cinema of flames: Balkan film, culture and the media.* UK: British Film Institute.

Irwin, R. (2012, March 26). Sesalj defiant in closing arguments. TRI issue 735. Retrieved November 2, 2013 from the Institute for war peace and reporting website: http://iwpr.net/report-news/seselj-defiant-closing-arguments

Jackson, K. D. (1989). *Cambodia 1975-1978: Rendezvous with death.* Princeton, NJ: Princeton University Press.

Johnson, E. (1999). *A Nazi Terror. The gestapo, jews, and ordinary germans*. New York, NY: Basic Books.

Johnson, E. A., & Reuband, K. H. (2006). *What we knew: Terror, mass murder, and everyday life in Nazi Germany: An Oral history*. New York, NY: Basic Books.

Jok, M, J. (2007). *Sudan: Race, religion, and violence*. Oxford, UK: One world publications.

Kajelijeli, J. (2003, December 1). ICTR-98-44A-T. http://www1.umn.edu/humanrts/instree/ICTR/KAJELIJELI_ ICTR-98-44A/KAJELIJELI_ICTR-98-44A-T.pdf

Kajelijeli, J. (2001, January 1). ICTR-98-44A-T. http://sim.law.uu.nl/sim/caselaw/tribunalen.nsf/4ba30447706 bba25c12571b5004ee3f7/669d1c3002c8d29cc12571fe004fa 2c9?OpenDocument

Kamuhanda, J. D. (2003, January 22). ICTR-99-54A-T. http://www.ictrcaselaw.org/docs/doc41191.pdf

Kandic, N. (1995, March 24). "Nas tuzilac u Hagu" [Our Prosecutor in the Hague]. *Intervju*. Retrieved from http://balkanwitness.glypx.com/balkan4.htm

Kanyabashi, J. (2009, January 14). ICTR-96-15-T. http://www.unictr.org/Portals/0/Case%5CEnglish%5CSikub wabo%5C090114a.pdf

Kanyabashi, J. (2008, February 15). ICTR-96-15-T. http://www.unictr.org/Portals/0/Case%5CEnglish%5CSikub wabo%5C080215.pdf

Karemera, E., & Ngirumpatse, M. (2012, February 2). ICTR-98-44-T. http://www.unictr.org/Portals/0/Case%5CEnglish%5CKarem era%5CJudgement%5C120202%20-%20JUDGEMENT.pdf

Karemera, E., Ngirumpatse, M., & Nzirorera, J. (2006, June 16). ICTR-98-44-T. http://www.unictr.org/Portals/0/Case%5CEnglish%5CNziror era%5Cdecision%5C160606.pdf

Karemera, E., Ngirumpatse, M., & Nzirorera, J. (2005, August 24). ICTR-98-44-T. www.unictr.org/.../Case%5CEnglish%5CKaremera%5Cindic tment%5C050824.pdf

Karera, F. (2007, December 7). ICTR-01-74-T. http://www1.umn.edu/humanrts/instree/ICTR/KARERA_IC TR-01-74/KARERA_ICTR-01-74-T.pdf

Kiernan, B. (2008). *Blood and soil: A world history of genocide and extermination from Sparta to Darfur.* New Haven, CT: Yale University Press.

Kiernan, B. (2002). *The Pol Pot Regime: Race, power, and genocide in Cambodia under the Khmer Rouge, 1975-79.* (2nd ed.). New Haven, CT: Yale University Press.

Kim, N. (2012). Societal development through Human Resource Development: Contexts and key changes. *Advances in Developing Human Resources, 14*(3), 239-250.

Klip, A., & Sluiter, G. (2001). *The International Criminal Tribunal for the Former Yugoslavia, 1997-1999.* New York, NY: Transnational Publishers.

Koerner, B. I. (2005, July 19). Who are the Janjaweed? A Guide to the Sudanese Militiamen. *Slate Magazine.* Retrieved from http://www.slate.com/articles/news_and_politics/explainer/2 004/07/who_are_the_janjaweed.html

Kruger, A. (1999). Breeding, rearing and preparing the aryan body: Creating supermen the nazi way. In J.A. Mangan (Ed.), *Shaping the superman: Fascist body as political icon-aryan fascism* (pp. 42-68). London, UK: Frank Cass.

Kuhn. T. (1996). *The structure of scientific revolutions* (3rd ed.). Chicago, IL: University of Chicago Press.

Laird, L., Holton, E. F., & Naquin, S. S. (2003). *Approaches to training and development* (3rd ed.). Cambridge, MA: Basic Books.

Lebor, A. (2012). *Milosevic: A biography.* London, UK: Bloomsbury publishing.

Lee, M. (2002). Defining the research question: On seizing the moment as the research question emerges. In J. McGoldricks, J. Stewart & S. Watson, S (Eds.), *Understanding Human Resource Development: A research-based approach* (pp. 18-40). London, UK: Routledge.

Letica, S. (1996). The Genesis of the current Balkan War. In S. G. Mestrovic (Ed.), *Genocide after emotion* (pp. 91-112). London, UK: Rutledge.

Levy, J. (2009). *Genocide in Darfur.* New York: The Rosen Publishing Group, Inc.

LudiSrbijanac. (2008, January 26). Arkanovi Tigrovi [Video File]. Retrieved from http://www.youtube.com/watch?v=uFhMQ-K0z9M

Lukacs, J. (2011). *The Hitler of history.* New York, NY: Random House, LLC.

Ly, Y. (2000). *Heaven becomes hell: A survivors story of life under the Khmer Rouge.* New Haven, Conn.: Yale University Southeast Asia Studies.

Mace, S. L., Venneberg, D. L., & Amell, J. W. (2012). Human trafficking: Integrating human resource development toward a solution. *Advances in Developing Human Resources, 14*(3), 333-344.

Mackic, E. (2012, May 16). Mladic's Trial: Main strategic goal was ethnic cleansing. Retrieved November 11, 2012 from the Balkan transitional justice website: http://www.balkaninsight.com/en/article/mladic-dropping-by-and-killing-someone

Magnarella, P. (2003, August 30). *Explaining Rwanda's 1994 genocide.* Retrieved December 21, 2011 from the Human Rights and Human Welfare website: http://www.du.edu/korbel/hrhw/volumes/2002/2-1/magnarella2-1.pdf

Makino, U. (2001). Final solutions, crimes against mankind: On the genesis and criticism of the concept of genocide. *Journal of Genocide Research, 3*(1), 49-73.

Malvern, L. (2006). Conspiracy to murder: The Rwandan genocide. Brooklyn, New York: Verso.

Mann, M. (2005). *The dark side of democracy: Explaining ethnic cleansing.* Cambridge, UK: Cambridge University Press.

Manz, C. C., & Sims, H. P., Jr. (1982). Modeling influences on employee behavior. *Personnel Journal, 61*(1), 45-51.

Marjanovich, B. S. (1997, April 20). *Organization of paramilitary formations*. Center for collecting documentation and processing data on the liberation war Opaticka. Retrieved from http://www.tomathon.com/RF/RN7.html

Marston, J. (1994). Metaphors of the Khmer Rouge. In M. M. Ebihara, C. A. Morland & J. Ledgerwood (Eds.), *Cambodian Culture since 1975: Homeland and exile* (pp. 105-118). Ithaca, NY: Cornell University Press.

Martic, M. (2007, June 12). The prosecutor of the tribunal against Martic. IT-95-11-T. http://www.icty.org/x/cases/martic/tjug/en/070612.pdf

Martin, G. (2006). *Understanding terrorism: Challenges, perspectives, and issues*. Thousand Oaks, CA: Sage publications.

Maxwell, J. (2008). Designing a qualitative study. In L. Bickman, & D. J. Rog (Eds.), *The handbook of applied social research methods* (pp. 214-253). Thousand Oaks, CA: Sage Publications.

McDonald, G. K., & Swaak-Goldman, O. (2000). *Substantive and procedural aspects of international criminal law, the experience of international and national courts: Volume II, documents and cases*. Hague: Netherlands: Kluwer Law International.

McGoldrick, J., & Stewart, J. (1996). The HRM-HRD nexus. In J. McGoldricks & J. Stewart (Eds.), *Human resources development perspectives, strategies and practice* (pp. 9-27). London, UK: Pitman publishing.

McLagan, P. A., & Suhadolnik, D. (1989). *Models for HRD practice: The research report*. Alexandria, VA: American Society for Training and Development.

McLean, G. N. (2004). National human resource development: What in the world is it? *Advances in Developing Human Resources, 6*(3), 269-275.

Mezirow, J. (1991). *Transformative dimensions of adult learning*. San Francisco: Jossey-Bass.

Michas, T. (2002). *Unholy alliance: Greece and Milosevic's Serbia.* Texas, US: Texas A&M University.

Ministry of Education. (1984, June 1). Peoples Republic of Kampuchea, Education in the People's Republic of Kampuchea, Phnom Penh.

Montreal Institute for Genocide and Human Rights Studies. (2014). *Rwanda radio transcripts.* Retrieved from http://migs.concordia.ca/links/RwandaRadioTranscripts.htm

Moore, J. (2009, April 24). No small mercy: How a Rwandan genocide survivor made peace with the man who almost killed he. *University for Peace: United Nations.* http://www.monitor.upeace.org/documents/Peace_and_Confl ict_Monitor_Special_Edition__Genocide_in_Rwanda_v2.pdf

Morris, P., & Sweeting, A. (1991). Education and politics: The case of Hong Kong from an historical perspective. *Review of Education, 17*(3), 249-267.

Mpambara, J. (2007, August 9). ICTR-2001-65-I. http://www.ictrcaselaw.org/docs/doc25320.pdf

Mubangutsi, U. (1995, August). Interahamwe, the source of Hutu refugees. In African Rights (Eds.), *Rwanda: Death, despair and defiance.* London, UK.

Mueller, J. (2001). The banality of ethnic war. In M. E. Brown, O. R. Cote, S. M. Lynn-Jones, & S. E. Miller (Eds.), *Nationalism and Ethnic Conflict* (pp. 97-125). Cambridge, MA: The MIT Press.

Mueller, J. (2000, July 26). The banality of "ethnic war": Yugoslavia and Rwanda. Retrieved January 12, 2014 from the Ohio State University website: http://www.politicalscience.osu.edu/faculty/jmueller/apsa200 0.pdf

Muhimana, M. (2004, April 11). ICTR-95-1B. http://www.ictrcaselaw.org/docs/doc37323.pdf

Munyakazi, Y. (2010, July 5). ICTR-97-36A-T. http://www.refworld.org/pdfid/4c722d350.pdf

Nabb, L. W., & Armstrong, B. (2005). *An adult education critique of HRD of training for atrocities in German occupied Europe*. Chicago, IL: Discovery Association Publishing House.

Nadler, L. (1994). *Designing training programs: The critical events model* (2nd ed.). Houston, US: Gulf.

Nadler, L., & Nadler, Z. (1989). *Developing Human Resources*. San Francisco, CA: Jossey-Bass Inc., Publishers.

Nadler, L. (1982). *Designing training programs: The critical events model*. Menlo Park, NJ: Addison-Wesley.

Nahimana, F., Barayagwiza, J.B., & Ngeze, H. (2005, January 12). ICTR-99-52-T. http://sim.law.uu.nl/sim/caselaw/tribunalen.nsf/eea9364f418 8dcc0c12571b500379d39/a7b1a96649d442cbc12571fe004fa 50e/$FILE/NAHIMANA,%20NGEZE,%20BARAYAGWIZ A-4.pdf

Nahimana, F., Barayagwiza, J. B., & Ngeze, H. (2003, December 3). ICTR-99-52-T. http://www.concernedhistorians.org/le/64.pdf

National dropout prevention center network. [N.D]. Economic impacts of dropouts Clemson University. Retrieved March 1, 2014 from http://www.dropoutprevention.org/statistics/quick-facts/economic-impacts-dropouts

Nchamihigo, S. (2008, November 12). ICTR-01-63-T. www.refworld.org/pdfid/49216e9b2.pdf

Ndindiliyimana, A., Bizimungu, A., Nzuwonemeye, F., & Sagahutu, I. (2007, September 11). ICTR-00-56-T. http://www.ictrcaselaw.org/docs/20070911-dco-0056-01-en.pdf

Ndindiliyimana, A., Bizimungu, A., Nzuwonemeye, F., & Sagahutu, I. (2005, December 2). ICTR-00-56-T. http://ictrarchive09.library.cornell.edu/ENGLISH/cases/Ndin diliyimana/decisions/021205.html

Nevid, J. S. (2012). *Psychology: Concepts and applications*. (4th ed.). Belmont, CA: Wadsworth-Cengage Learning.

Ngirabatware, A. (2012, December 20). ICTR-99-54-T. http://www.unictr.org/Portals/0/Case%5CEnglish%5CNgirabatware%5CJudgement%20d%20Sentence%5CNgirabatware%20121220.pdf

Ngor, H. (1987). *A Cambodian odyssey.* New York: Warner Books.

NIN. (1991, December 13). Interview with Arkan "Vec imam kucu na Dedinju" [I Already Have a House on Dedinje Hill]. Retrieved from http://balkanwitness.glypx.com/balkan4.htm

Ntagerura, A., & Bagambiki, E., & Imanishimwe, S. (2005, February 25). ICTR-99-46-A. www.unictr.org/Portals/0/Case/English/Imanishimwe/.../judgment-en.pdf

Ntagerura, A., Bagambiki, E., & Imanishimwe, S. (2004, February 25). ICTR-99-46-T. http://opil.ouplaw.com/view/10.1093/law:icl/408ictr04.case.1/law-icl-408ictr04?rskey=cmKxmU&result=3&prd=OPIL

Ntagerura, A., Bagambiki, E., & Imanishimwe, S. (2006, July 7). ICTR-99-46-T. www.refworld.org/docid/48abd51dd.html

Nyirubugara, O. (2008, February). Rwanda: The genocide ideology then and now. *Comments on Ugur Ungor's 'Justifier l'injustifiable: Ideologie en genocide in Rwanda' in Vrede en Veiligheid* 33, 2004-3; pp. 342-358. Retrieved from http://www.olny.nl/RWANDA/Lu_Pour_Vous/Olivier_Nyirubugara_Genocide_Ideology.html

Ol, E. S. (1991). The situation of higher and technical education in the state of Cambodia since January 7th, 1979. Paper presented at the Cambodian workshop on reconstruction and Development, Penang, Malaysia.

Oppenheim, J., & Van der Wolf, W. (1997). *Global war crimes tribunal collection, 3.* Global law association.

Oswald, B., Durham, H., & Bates, A. (2010). *Documents on the law of UN peace operations.* London, UK: Oxford University Press.

Otuzniak. (2009, April 15). Arkan's Tiger Training [Video File]. Retrieved from http://www.youtube.com/watch?v=9dqr0hOv_Eo

Partos, G. (2003, March 26). Serbia's 'elite' enemy within. *BBC News*. Retrieved from http://news.bbc.co.uk/2/hi/europe/2888943.stm

Pavlovic, R. (1994, March 30). Why Arkan's Tigers pulled in their claws. *Politika*. Retrieved from http://balkanwitness.glypx.com/balkan4.htm

Peiffer, L. (1987). *Turnunterricht im Dritten Reich. Erziehung fur den Krieg?* Cologne, Germany: Köln Pahl-Rugenstein.

Peterson, S. L., & Provo, J. (1999). A case study of academic program integration in the United States: Andragogical, philosophical, theoretical and practical perspectives. *International Journal of Lifelong Learning Education, 19*(2), pp. 103-114.

Picq, L. (1989). *Beyond the horizon: Five years with the Khmer Rouge*. New York, NY: St. Martins Press.

Pine, L. (2010). *Education in Nazi Germany*. Oxford, England: Berg.

Pinker, S. (2003). *The blank slate: The modern denial of human nature*. New York, NY: Penguin Books.

Postiglione, G. A., & Tan, J. (2007). *Going to school in East Asia*. Westport, CT: Greenwood publishing group.

Pran, D. (1997). *Children of Cambodia's killing fields. Memoirs by survivors*. New Haven, CT: Yale University Press.

Procknow, G. (2014). Human resource development in Democratic Kampuchea, 1975-1979. *Human Resource Development Review, 13*(3), 369-388.

Prunier, G. (1995). *Rwanda crisis: History of a genocide*. New York, NY: Columbia University Press.

Quinn, K. M. (1976). Political change in wartime: The Khmer krahom revolution in southern Cambodia, 1970-1974. *U.S Naval War College Review, Spring*, 3-31.

Radović, B. (2006). They wanted them, and he did not: About the context, organization and form of the forcible conscription of refugees in Serbia in 1995. In G. Opačić, V. Jović, B. Radović, & G. Knežević (Eds.), *Redress in action: Consequences of forcible mobilization of refugees in 1995* (pp. 11-42). Belgrade, Serbia: International Aid Network.

Radović, B. (1995). *They wanted them and he did not: About the context, organization and form of the forcible conscription of refugees in Serbia in 1995.* Retrieved from http://www.ian.org.rs/publikacije/erdut/book/04%20THEY%20WANTED%20THEM,%20AND%20HE%20DID%20NOT.pdf

Ramet, S. P. (2005). *Serbia since 1989: Politics and society under Milosevic and after*. Seattle, WA: University of Washington Press.

Rauschning, H. (1990). Gesprache mit Hitler (1940). In H. Kanz (Ed.), *Der nationalsozialismus als padagogisches Problem. Deutsche Erziehungsgeschichte, 1933-1945* Frankfurt, Germany.

Reeves, E. (2007, February 28). The ICC 'application' concerning international crimes in Darfur. *Sudan Tribune*. Retrieved from http://www.sudantribune.com/The-ICC-Application-Concerning,20496

Revolutionary Flags. (1978, March). Cambodia. Translated by Sos, K., & Carney, T.

Revolutionary Flags. (1977, July). Cambodia.

Revolutionary Young Men and Women. (1977, May). Cambodia.

Revolutionary Young Men and Women. (1976, October). Cambodia.

Ristic, M. (2012, October 2). Belgrade DJ investigated for war crimes. Retrieved October 12, 2013 from the Balkan Transitional Justice website: http://www.balkaninsight.com/en/article/belgrade-dj-investigated-for-war-crimes

Ristic, M. (2005, November 12). Villager from Erdut testifies at Hadzic's trial. Retrieved October 12, 2013 from the Balkan Transitional Justice website: http://www.balkaninsight.com/en/article/villager-from-erdut-testifies-at-hadzic-s-trial

Robinson, N. (2010, April 17). Dragan Vasiljjkovic linked to Serb war criminals. *The Australian.* Retrieved from http://www.theaustralian.com.au/news/nation/dragan-linked-to-serb-war-criminals/story-e6frg6nf-1225854723773

Ross, R. R. (1990). *Cambodia: A country study.* Library of Congress, Federal research division. Retrieved from http://lcweb2.loc.gov/frd/cs/khtoc.html

Royaume de Cambodge. (1967). Ministre du Plan, Annuaire Statistique du Cambodge, Phnom Penh.

Rust, B. (1938). *Education and Instruction, Official Publication of the Reich and Prussian Ministry of Knowledge, Education, and National Culture.* Germany.

Rummel, R. J. (1997). *Death by government.* Piscataway, NJ: Transaction publishers.

Rwamakuba, A. (2006, September 20). ICTR-98-44C-T. ictrarchive09.library.cornell.edu/.../Rwamakuba/.../rwamakuba-indictment-e. pdf

Saks, A. M, & Haccoun, R. R. (2008). *Managing performance through training and development.* (4th ed.). Toronto, ON: Nelson series in Human resource management.

Šarić, V. (2012, January 20). Former paramilitary denies Serbia state support. Retrieved April 1, 2013 from the Institute for war and peace reporting website: http://iwpr.net/report-news/former-paramilitary-denies-serbian-state-support

Sarin, I. (1973). Nine months with the marquis. In M. T. Carney (Ed.), *Communist party power in Kampuchea (Cambodia): Documents and discussion, volumes 106-110* (pp. 38-41). Ithaca, NY: Cornell University Press

Sargent, L. T. (1993). *Contemporary political ideologies: A comparative analysis.* Belmont, CA: Wadsworth Publishing Company.

Sells, M. A. (1998). *The bridge betrayed: Religion and genocide in Bosnia.* Ewing, NJ: University of California Press.

Sense Tribunal. (2012, May 11). Kitchen with a view of Arkan's Tigers. Retrieved May 1, 2013 from the Sense Agency website: http://www.senseagency.com/icty.29.html?news_id=14340

Setako, E. (2010, 25 February). ICTR-04-81-T. http://www.refworld.org/pdfid/4b8f89c52.pdf

Sheared, V., & Sissel, P. A. (2001). *Making space: Merging theory and practice in adult education.* Westport, CT: Greenwood Publishing Group.

Sherwell, P. (2004, August 15). Janjaweed vow to fight any intervention by 'infidels. *UK Telegraph.* Retrieved from http://www.telegraph.co.uk/news/worldnews/africaandindianocean/sudan/1469472/Janjaweed-vow-to-fight-any-intervention-by-infidels.html

Sihanouk, N. (1980). *War and hope: The case for Cambodia.* New York, NY: Random House.

Simba, A. (2005, December 13). ICTR-01-76-T. http://www1.umn.edu/humanrts/instree/ICTR/SIMBA_ICTR-01-76/SIMBA_ICTR-01-76-T.pdf

Simba, A. (2004, May 6). ICTR-01-76-T. http://www.unictr.org/Portals/0/Case%5CEnglish%5CSimba%5CIndictment%5Csimba.pdf

Simons, M. (2003, April 24). Mystery witness faces Milosevic. *New York Times.* Retrieved from http://www.nytimes.com/2003/04/24/world/mystery-witness-faces-milosevic.html

Smith, D. L. (2009). *The most dangerous animal: Human nature and the origins of war.* New York, NY: Macmillan.

Smeulers, A., & Grunfeld, F. (2011). *International crimes and other gross human rights violations: A multi-and interdisciplinary textbooks.* Leiden, Netherlands: Martinus Nijhoff publishers.

Spiric, Z., Knezevic, G., Jovic, V., & Opacic, G. (2004). (Eds.). *Torture in war: Consequences and rehabilitation of victims: Yugoslav experience*. IAN center for the rehabilitation of torture victims. Retrieved from http://www.ian.org.rs/publikacije/tortura/booktortura.htm

Stanišić, J., & Simatović, F. (2013, February 15). The prosecutor of the tribunal against Stanišić and Simatovic. IT-03-69-T. http://icty.org/x/cases/stanisic_simatovic/custom5/en/130215.pdf

Stanišić, J., & Simatović, F. (2013, February 28). The prosecutor of the tribunal against Stanišić and Simatovic. IT-03-69-T. http://icty.org/x/cases/stanisic_simatovic/custom5/en/130228.pdf

Stanišić, J., & Simatović, F. (2013, February 21). The prosecutor of the tribunal against Stanišić and Simatovic. IT-03-69-T. icty.org/x/cases/stanisic_simatovic/custom5/en/130211.pdf

Stanišić, J., & Simatovic, F. (2012, January 24). The prosecutor of the tribunal against Stanišić and Simatović. IT-03-69-T. http://www.icty.org/x/cases/stanisic_simatovic/trans/en/120124ED.htm

Stanišić, J., & Simatović, F. (2012, January 19). The prosecutor of the tribunal against Stanišić and Simatović. IT-03-69-T. http://www.icty.org/x/cases/stanisic_simatovic/trans/en/120119ED.htm

Stanišić, J., & Simatović, F. (2012, January 18). The prosecutor of the tribunal against Stanišić and Simatović. IT-03-69-T. http://www.icty.org/x/cases/stanisic_simatovic/trans/en/120118ED.htm

Stanišić, J., & Simatovic, F. (2012, January 17). The prosecutor of the tribunal against Stanišić and Simatović. IT-03-69-T. http://www.icty.org/x/cases/stanisic_simatovic/trans/en/120117ED.htm

Stanišić, J., & Simatović, F. (2011, December 14). The prosecutor of the tribunal against Stanišić and Simatović . IT-03-69-T. http://www.icty.org/x/cases/stanisic_simatovic/trans/en/111214ED.htm

Stanišić, J., & Simatović, F. (2010, June 29). The prosecutor of the tribunal against Stanišić and Simatović. IT-03-69-T. http://www.ictytranscripts.org/trials/stanisic_simatovic/1006 29ED.htm

Stanišić, J., & Simatović, F. (2009, June 30). The prosecutor of the tribunal against Stanišić and Simatović. IT-03-69-T. http://www.icty.org/x/cases/stanisic_simatovic/trans/en/0906 30ED.htm

Staudinger, H. (1992). *Inner Nazi: A critical analysis of Mein Kampf.* Baton Rouge, LA: Louisiana State University Press.

Steidle, B., & Wallace, G. S. (2007). *The devil came on horseback: Bearing witness to the genocide in Darfur.* New York, NY: Public Affairs.

Stewart, C. S. (2007). *Hunting the tiger: The fast life and violent death of the Balkans most dangerous man.* New York: St. Martin's Press.

Su, Y. (2011). *Collective killings in rural China during the cultural revolution.* New York, NY: Cambridge University Press.

Svarm, F. (Producer & Director). (N.D.) The Unit: The untold story of the Red Berets. *VREME magazine and B92.* Available from http://www.b92.net/specijal/jedinica-eng/1_epizoda.php

Swanson, R. A., & Holton, E. F. (2001). *Foundations of Human Resource Development.* San Francisco, CA: Berrett-Koehler Publishers.

Teng, S. K. (1997). The end of childhood. In D. Pran (Ed.), *Children of Cambodia's Killing Fields* (pp. 155-160). New Haven, CT: Yale University Press.

Testimony of Dragan Vasiljkovic. (2003, February 19). International Criminal Tribunal for the Former Yugoslavia. http://www.icty.org/x/cases/slobodan_milosevic/trans/en/030 219ED.htm

Testimony of Jovan Dimitrijevic. (2012, January 17). International Criminal Tribunal for the Former Yugoslavia. IT-03-69-T. http://www.icty.org/x/cases/stanisic_simatovic/trans/en/1201 17ED.htm

References 197

Testimony of Milan Babic. (2006, February 17). International Criminal Tribunal for the Former Yugoslavia. IT-95-11-T. http://www.ictytranscripts.org/trials/martic/060217IT.htm

Testimony of Nenad Zafirovic. (2004, January 13). International Criminal Tribunal for the Former Yugoslavia. IT-02-54. http://www.ictytranscripts.org/trials/slobodan_milosevic/040113ED.htm

Testimony of Rade Raseta. (2006, May 2). International Criminal Tribunal for the Former Yugoslavia. http://www.icty.org/x/cases/martic/trans/en/060502ED.htm

Testimony of Radislav Stalevic. (2010, April 22). International Criminal Tribunal for the Former Yugoslavia. Case No. IT-05-87/1 –T. http://www.icty.org/x/cases/djordjevic/trans/en/100422IT.htm

Testimony of Witness B-129. (2003, April 17). International Criminal Tribunal for the Former Yugoslavia. http://www.icty.org/x/cases/slobodan_milosevic/trans/en/030417ED.htm

Testimony of Witness B-129. (2003, April 16). International Criminal Tribunal for the Former Yugoslavia.

Testimony of Witness B-161. (2003, May 22). International Criminal Tribunal for the Former Yugoslavia. http://www.icty.org/x/cases/slobodan_milosevic/trans/en/030522ED.htm

Testimony of B-1738. (2003, March 17). International Criminal Tribunal for the Former Yugoslavia. No. IT-02-54-T. http://www.slobodan-milosevic.org/documents/trial/2003-03-17.html

Testimony of Witness C-047. (2003, June 4). International Criminal Tribunal for the Former Yugoslavia. http://www.icty.org/x/cases/slobodan_milosevic/trans/en/030604ED.htm

Testimony of Witness JF-039. (2013, January 29). International Criminal Tribunal for the Former Yugoslavia. IT-03-69-T. http://www.icty.org/x/cases/stanisic_simatovic/trans/en/130129ED.htm

The Commission on Security and Cooperation in Europe. (1996, May 28). *The war crimes trials for the former Yugoslavia: Prospects and problems: Briefing of the Commission on Security and Cooperation in Europe, (4)*. Retrieved from http://www.csce.gov/index.cfm?FuseAction=ContentRecords.ViewDetail&ContentRecord_id=131&ContentType=H,B&ContentRecordType=B&UserGroup_id=48&region_id=48&year=0&month=0&Subaction=Hearings&IsTextOnly=True&CFID=30206518&CFTOKEN=22492095

The New Times. (N. D). Managing fault lines in the Rwandan conflict. Retrieved from http://www.newtimes.co.rw/news/views/article_print.php?14281&a=29896&icon=Print

Thompson, W. C. (2013). *Nordic, central, and south-eastern Europe 2013*. Lanham, Maryland: Rowman & Littlefield.

Totten, S. (2011). *An oral and documentary history of the Darfur genocide*. Santa Barbara, California: ABC-CLIO LLC.

Totten, S., & Parsons, W. (2009). *Century of genocide: Critical essays and eyewitness accounts*. London, UK: Taylor and Francis.

Totten, S., & Bartrop, P., & Markusen, E. (2008). *Dictionary of genocide*. Westport, CT: Greenwood Press.

Tyner, J. A. (2008). *The killing of Cambodia: Geography, genocide and the unmaking of space*. London, UK: Ashgate Publishing.

U.S. Department of State. (1994, January 31). *Croatian Human Rights Practices, 1993*. Retrieved from http://dosfan.lib.uic.edu/ERC/democracy/1993_hrp_report/93hrp_report_eur/Croatia.html

United States Department of Defense. (1943). Handbook on the German Military. U.S.

Valentino, B. A. (2004). *Final solutions: Mass killing and genocide in the 20th century*. Ithaca, NY: Cornell University Press.
Vasey, C. M. (2006). *Nazi Ideology*. Lanham, Maryland: Hamilton Books.
Vasic, M. (1996). The Yugoslav army and the post-Yugoslav Armies. In D. A Dkyer & I, Vejvoda (Eds.), *Yugoslavia and After: A study in fragmentation, despair and rebirth* (pp. 116-137). London, UK: Longman.
Verwimp, P. (2004, June 22). Development ideology, the peasantry and Genocide: Rwanda represented in Habyarimana's speeches. Retrieved from http://www.yale.edu/gsp/publications/Rwanda.pdf
Verwimp, P. (2004). Peasant ideology and genocide in Rwanda under Habyarimana. In S. Cook (Ed.), *Genocide in Cambodia and Rwanda: New perspectives* (pp. 1-24). Piscataway, New Jersey: Transaction Publishers.
Vickery, M. (1984). *Cambodia, 1975-1982*. Cambridge, MA: South End Press.
Vostrukhov, E. (1992, November 25). *"Umeret' v Yugoslaviy" [To Die in Yugoslavia], Izvestiya*. Moscow, Russia. Retrieved from http://balkanwitness.glypx.com/balkan4.htm
Walque, D. D. (2007). The socio-demographic legacy of the Khmer rouge period in Cambodia. *Population studies: A Journal of Demography. 60*(2), 223-231.
Watkins, K. E., & Marsick, V. J. (1995). *The case for learning*. In proceedings of the academy of human resource development research conference. Baton Rouge, LA: The Academy of Human Resource Development.
Weinstein, F. (1980). *The dynamics of Nazism: Leadership, ideology, and the holocaust*. Waltham, MA: Academic Press.
Welch, D. (1983). *Nazi propaganda: The power and limitations*. London, UK: Croom Helm.
Whitaker, D. (1973). *Area handbook for the Khmer Republic*. Washington. U.S: Supt. of Docs., U.S. Govt. Print.

Williams, S. W. (2001). The effectiveness of subject matter experts as technical trainers. *Human Resource Development Quarterly, 12*(1), 91-97.

Wilson, J. P. (2012). *International Human Resources Development: Learning, education and training for individuals and organizations* (3rd ed.). London, UK: Kogan Page Publishers.

Woodward, R. (2000). Warrior heroes and little green men: Soldiers, military training, and the construction of rural masculinities. *Rural Sociology, 65*(4). 640-657.

Yanagizawa-Drott, D. (2012, August). Propaganda and conflict: Theory and evidence from the Rwandan Genocide. *Harvard University*. Retrieved from http://www.hks.harvard.edu/fs/dyanagi/Research/RwandaDYD.pdf

Ziemer, G. (1972). *Education for death: The making of the Nazi.* New York, NY: Octagon Books / Farrar, Straus, and Giroux.

Ziemer, G. (1941). *Education for death: The making of the Nazi.* London: Oxford University.

Zigiranyirazo, P. (2008, December 18). ICTR-01-73-T. http://www.unictr.org/Portals/0/Case%5CEnglish%5CZigiranyirazo%5CJudgement%5C081218e.pdf

INDEX

101st Training Center, 10, 64
Abbala Tribe, 162
Adolf Hitler Schools, 129
Aegis Trust, 152, 159, 163, 164, 167, 169, 171, 174
Akagera National Park, 74
Alliance of Democratic Khmer Youth, 117
Al-Qaeda, 162
Alvarez, Alex, 33, 171
Amulets, 166
Angkar, 121, 122, 142, 145, 146
Anti-bureaucratic Revolution, 28
Anti-Semitic, 139
Arab, 157, 158, 159
Arab Villages, 160
Arabic, 157, 165, 166
Arkan, ii, 2, 10, 21, 23, 24, 25, 33, 34, 36, 37, 38, 39, 40, 41, 42, 43, 44, 45, 47, 48, 49, 50, 51, 52, 55, 56, 57, 58, 59, 60, 61, 62, 63, 64, 65, 66, 68, 171, 183, 184, 186
Arkan's Tigers, ii, 2, 10, 21, 23, 24, 33, 34, 36, 37, 38, 41, 42, 43, 44, 49, 50, 52, 53, 54, 55, 56, 57, 65, 184, 186
Armenian Genocide, 21
Arusha Accords, 75, 93, 97
Aryan, 133, 140, 179
Asia, 18, 123, 173, 176, 180, 184
Australian Government Refugee Review Tribunal, 42, 171
Autobiographies, 148
Autogenocide, 4, 11

Ayres, David, 2, 7, 12, 13, 14, 19, 116, 118, 171
Babić, Milan, 26, 62, 64
Bagosora, Theoneste, 71, 75, 77, 78, 80, 81, 82, 84, 85, 86, 91, 100, 105, 107, 108, 110, 172
Bahima, 75
Bandura, Albert, 16, 51, 172
Bangamwabo, Francois-Xavier, 86
Base People, 3, 4, 8, 11, 20
Bashir, Omar al, 165
Behavior Modelling, 15, 16, 22, 24, 120
Behaviorism, 17, 18, 155, 169
Belgrade, 30, 33, 40, 56, 185
Bierema, Laura, 152, 155, 156, 172
Bigogwe, 93, 94, 97, 102, 103, 108
Bikindi, Simon, 88, 91, 93, 94, 97, 106, 110, 172, 173
Bizimungu, Augustin, 82, 91, 96, 106, 108, 110, 173, 183
Black African, 159
Blank States, 144
Bolshevism, 28
Bosnia-Herzegovina, 26, 173
Bosniaks, 27, 30
Bosnians, 23, 40
Bosnian-Serbs, 25, 39
Bourgeoisie, 3, 12
Bourgmestres, 72, 82, 87, 92, 94, 95, 107, 111, 113
Boxing, 130, 133, 142
Bruska, 62
Brutality, 41, 55, 124
Bulatović, Momir, 27, 34
Caddick-Adams, 77, 110
Cadres, 6, 148, 163

Callahan, Jamie, 1, 21, 72, 173, 208
Cambodia, 3, 14, 23, 116, 118, 119, 120, 123, 124, 171, 173, 174, 177, 178, 179, 184, 185, 186, 187, 189, 190, 191, 208
Cambodian Genocide, i, 3, 115
Chemistry, 125, 134, 136, 137
Chetnik, 34
Cigar, Norman, 28, 29, 30, 32, 37, 39, 40, 41, 51, 174
Civilian Defense, ii, 71, 72, 73, 76, 77, 78, 80, 81, 83, 84, 85, 86, 92, 98, 101, 106, 107, 109, 110, 111, 112, 113, 114
Class-enemies, 4, 11
Classical Conditioning, 17, 18
Clayton, Thomas, 2, 6, 7, 8, 10, 13, 19, 116, 143, 174
Collective Killings, 114
Colonels, 61
Communal Police, 83, 84, 111
Communism, 28
Communist Party of Kampuchea (CPK), i, 1, 4, 6, 7, 9, 14, 18, 19, 22, 115, 119, 120, 121, 123, 125, 142, 144, 145, 146, 147
Communists, 3, 29, 117, 119, 143
Compensation, 31, 66, 154, 161, 170
Conscripts, 158, 166
Convention on the Prevention and Punishment of the Crime of Genocide, 4
Convicts, 25, 34, 42

Cookson, Peter, 35, 37, 39, 41, 44, 46, 47, 48, 50, 51, 52, 53, 55, 64, 174
Ćosić, Dobrica, 27
Councilors, 79, 82, 92, 94, 111
Crimes Against Humanity, ii, 5, 20, 23, 52, 115, 158
Critical Events Model (CEM), ii, 23, 24, 25, 35, 37, 44, 47, 48, 51, 55, 56, 59, 61, 64, 65, 67, 68
Criticism Sessions, 19
Croatia, 10, 25, 26, 27, 30, 32, 37, 38, 40, 45, 56, 62, 63, 64, 190
Croatian Catholics, 46
Croatian War of Independence, 26
Croatians, 23, 29
Cross-fertilization, 21, 67
Cyangugu, 79, 92, 96, 102, 104, 105, 108
Danube, 42, 50, 56
Darfur, 151, 152, 157, 159, 160, 161, 163, 164, 167, 168, 170, 171, 174, 175, 177, 179, 180, 185, 188, 190
Darfurians, 158
Dehumanization, 43, 44, 48, 51, 52, 55, 68
Delije, 33, 49
Democratic Kampuchea, i, 1, 3, 9, 23, 85, 115, 117, 125, 126, 143, 144, 149, 173, 184
Demons, 101
Demonstrations, 15, 16, 22, 24, 53
Des Forges, Alison, 73, 76, 77, 79, 82, 84, 86, 89, 91, 93,

98, 100, 102, 103, 108, 110, 113, 175
Desensitize, 16, 59
Development, i, ii, i, 1, 5, 19, 71, 72, 76, 91, 111, 115, 116, 171, 173, 175, 177, 179, 181, 184, 188, 191, 208
Diaspora, 75
Dimitrijevic, Jovan, 57, 58, 60, 66, 189
Dirkx, John, 152, 155, 156, 175
Discipline, i, 36, 42, 46, 47, 49, 51, 55, 56, 66, 79, 102
Drill and Practice, 52
Drina, 38
East Timor, 21
Education, i, ii, iii, 1, 2, 3, 5, 6, 7, 8, 9, 11, 12, 13, 14, 15, 19, 20, 21, 23, 35, 43, 49, 55, 67, 73, 76, 96, 99, 102, 112, 114, 115, 116, 117, 118, 119, 121, 123, 125, 126, 127, 128, 129, 133, 134, 135, 139, 140, 141, 143, 144, 145, 146, 147, 156, 163, 165, 166, 171, 172, 174, 175, 182, 184, 191
El Geneina, 162
Elbagir, Nima, 160, 162, 169, 175
England, 133, 139, 174, 184
Erdut, 10, 24, 25, 36, 41, 42, 43, 44, 45, 46, 48, 50, 51, 53, 54, 55, 56, 57, 58, 59, 60, 61, 62, 64, 65, 66, 68, 69, 185
Essential, 48, 49
Ethnic Cleansing, 10, 23, 25, 32, 33, 34, 35, 37, 38, 39, 40, 41, 43, 45, 46, 49, 57, 59, 63, 65, 68, 163, 180
Europe, 2, 31, 32, 34, 75, 182, 190
Evaluation and Feedback, 35
Experiential Learning, 52, 54
Experiments, 52
Exploitation, 6, 121, 124, 146
False Flag, 74
Farmland, 12
Field Marching, 165
Firearms, 58, 61, 66, 79, 83, 84, 85, 86, 92, 93, 104, 105, 109
Firing Range, 54
Flint, Julie, 157, 159, 161, 167, 175
Football, 33, 84, 88, 105, 108, 176
Foreign Broadcast Information Service (FBIS), 119
Formative Evaluation, 35
Four Year Plan, 122
Francophone Africa, 74
Fuhrer, 131, 132, 140, 142
Gagić, Gvozden, 45, 59, 60, 61
Gang, 33
Gendarmes, 78, 79, 81, 83, 84, 94, 97, 110
Genocide, i, ii, 2, 4, 11, 18, 21, 23, 32, 37, 38, 40, 43, 67, 72, 73, 74, 76, 78, 85, 87, 89, 91, 96, 97, 98, 100, 101, 104, 106, 109, 111, 113, 114, 123, 126, 151, 152, 158, 166, 173, 176, 177, 179, 180, 181, 183, 184, 188, 190
Geography, 116, 125, 126, 130, 134, 136

German, 2, 11, 17, 128, 129, 130, 131, 132, 133, 135, 137, 138, 139, 140, 144, 148, 177, 182, 190
Gihundre, 88
Gikongoro, 79, 83, 84, 94
Gisenyi, 84, 96, 97, 102, 103, 108
Golubić, 62, 63, 64
Government of Sudan (GOS), iii, 151, 159, 160, 161, 162
Greece, 30, 31, 35, 181
Greek Volunteer Guard (GVG), 31
Grenades, 40, 57, 58, 85, 92, 104, 105, 109, 134, 141
Guerrilla, 75
Gymnastics, 130
Gypsies, 115
Habyarimana, Juvenal, 73, 74, 75, 76, 77, 85, 86, 91, 92, 93, 95, 96, 98, 100, 102, 108, 112, 113, 191
Hadžić, Goran, 26, 37, 38, 40
Hands-on Experience, 10, 119
Hegemonic Advantage, 2, 21, 74
Hinton, Alexander, 2, 6, 7, 8, 15, 19, 121, 123, 124, 146, 147, 148, 177
History, i, ii, iii, 17, 21, 23, 67, 106, 112, 125, 134, 135, 136, 148, 151, 173, 178, 179, 180, 190
Hitler, Adolph, i, ii, 2, 18, 115, 116, 117, 128, 129, 130, 132, 133, 134, 135, 138, 139, 140, 142, 143, 144, 145, 146, 147, 149, 177, 180, 185
Hitler Youth, i, ii, 2, 18, 115, 116, 117, 128, 134, 138, 139, 142, 143, 144, 145, 146, 147, 149
Hodzic, Refik, 38, 177
Holocaust, 2, 98
Holton, Elwood, 16, 17, 25, 143, 152, 153, 154, 155, 156, 167, 168, 170, 177, 179, 188
Homogeneity, 28, 29, 33
Homosexuals, 115, 146
Hooligan, 33, 41, 44
Human Resource Development (HRD), i, ii, iii, 1, 2, 5, 6, 7, 8, 9, 10, 11, 12, 13, 14, 15, 16, 17, 18, 19, 20, 21, 22, 23, 25, 35, 37, 45, 47, 59, 67, 71, 72, 73, 93, 106, 107, 108, 109, 110, 111, 113, 114, 115, 116, 127, 151, 152, 153, 154, 155, 156, 167, 168, 169, 170, 176, 181, 182, 208
Human Rights Watch, 159, 167, 175, 177
Humiliation, 11, 142
Hutu, 71, 73, 74, 75, 76, 77, 78, 79, 80, 82, 85, 86, 88, 89, 90, 91, 95, 97, 98, 99, 100, 101, 102, 106, 112, 113, 114, 177, 182
Hutu Power, 88, 97, 98, 100, 101
Ideological Indoctrination, iii, 44, 120
Ideological Training, 62
Ideology, 4, 44, 76, 85, 97, 98, 99, 100, 101, 111, 113, 115, 117, 120, 125, 126, 132, 136, 138, 142, 143, 145, 156, 162, 165, 170, 183, 191

Imanishimwe, Samuel, 82, 92, 102, 107, 109, 110, 183
Imperialists, 4, 121, 124, 146
Independence-mastery, 123
Individualism, 121, 122, 146
Instruction, 6, 12, 49, 51, 52, 53, 59, 69, 83, 84, 86, 94, 104, 110, 119, 125, 130, 135, 141, 163, 165
Instructional Resources, 48, 55
Instructional Strategies, 52
Instructors, 59, 84, 95, 103, 124, 166
Interactive, 52, 69
Interahamwe, ii, 71, 72, 73, 76, 78, 83, 84, 86, 87, 88, 89, 90, 91, 92, 93, 94, 95, 96, 97, 98, 100, 101, 102, 103, 104, 105, 106, 107, 108, 109, 110, 111, 177, 182
Interim Government, 73, 78, 107
International Criminal Court (ICC), 39, 158
International Criminal Tribunal for Former Yugoslavia (ICTY), 24, 47, 58, 66
International Criminal Tribunal for Rwanda (ICTR), 1, 72, 74, 78, 79, 81, 85, 87, 88, 95, 97, 99, 172, 173, 176, 177, 178, 179, 182, 183, 186, 187, 192
Islamic, 163, 164, 165
Jackson, Karl, 8, 9, 12, 15, 124, 127, 147, 178
Janjaweed, i, iii, 2, 21, 151, 157, 158, 159, 160, 161, 162, 163, 164, 165, 166, 167, 168, 169, 171, 175, 176, 179, 186, 187
Jews, 11, 17, 18, 115, 131, 139, 140, 146, 178
Jihad, 165, 166
Jungbanner, 133
Justice for Equality Movement (JEM), 157
Kadijević, Veljko, 26
Kajelijeli, Juvenal, 80, 86, 87, 88, 91, 92, 93, 94, 95, 96, 97, 101, 104, 105, 106, 108, 109, 110, 111, 178
Kalashnikovs, 62, 105
Kambanda, Jean, 71, 72, 77, 78, 80, 81, 84
Kangura, 90, 98
Kanyabashi, Joseph, 79, 80, 81, 106, 107, 178
Karadžić, Radovan, 27, 29, 31, 32, 37, 38, 40
Karorero, Joseph, 95, 104
Khartoum, 159, 163, 165
Khmer Rouge, i, ii, 1, 3, 6, 23, 85, 115, 116, 117, 118, 119, 120, 121, 123, 124, 125, 143, 144, 145, 146, 148, 149, 171, 174, 179, 180
Kibuye Meeting, 77
Kiernan, Ben, 1, 3, 7, 9, 18, 115, 123, 125, 126, 144, 145, 173, 179
Kigali, 74, 79, 80, 82, 84, 85, 86, 89, 94, 95, 96, 100, 102, 103, 108
Kinesthetic Learning, 53
Kinyarwandan, 98
Knowles, Malcolm, 50
Kosovo, 25, 28, 29
Kruger, Arnd, 140, 179
Land Cruisers, 159
Lecture, 52, 131, 134

Legion (Legija), 48, 60, 61
Lehrer, 135
Leistungsbuch, 129
Lenin, Vladimir, 124
Leninism, 124, 142
Letica, Slaven, 27, 28, 29, 30, 179
M-70, 58
Machetes, 85, 91, 104, 105, 109
Malvern, Linda, 75, 76, 80, 87, 90, 93, 96, 102, 103, 105, 108, 110
Mao Zedong, 118
Maoism, 142
Martic, Milan, 62, 180, 181
Marx, Karl, 124, 140
Masalit Sheikh, 159
Mathematics, 134, 136, 138
Mathematics in the Service of National Political Education, 138, 143
Meetings of the Consuls of Ministers, 81
Mein Kampf, 115, 134, 177
Metaphors, 18
Military Preparations, 28, 76
Military Training, 12, 42, 43, 49, 56, 79, 83, 85, 86, 87, 88, 91, 93, 94, 95, 102, 103, 109, 112, 118, 141, 162, 164, 191
Milošević, Slobodan, 24, 27, 28, 29, 30, 31, 32, 33, 34, 37, 38, 47, 57, 64
Misteriha, 163
Molotov and Ribbentrop Non-aggression Treaty, 136
Montenegro, 25, 27, 28, 29
Montreal Institute for Genocide, 90, 181
Mount Tara, 57

Mujahedeen, 31
Mukamira, 83, 93, 94, 95, 102, 103, 108
Mukingo, 80, 82, 86, 87, 92, 93, 95, 101, 104, 108
MUP, 46, 59, 60
Muslims, 27, 29, 30, 31, 32, 34, 37, 38, 43, 44, 46, 49, 63
Mustanfareen, 167
Nabb, Lee, and Armstrong, Keith, 2, 23, 35, 37, 39, 43, 44, 52, 55, 65
Nadler, Leonard, ii, 23, 35, 36, 39, 41, 44, 47, 48, 50, 52, 64, 68, 182
Nadler and Nadler, ii, 35, 45, 47
Nahimana, Ferdinand, 73, 76, 78, 80, 81, 86, 98, 103, 106, 107, 112, 182
National Human Resource Development (NHRD), 11, 112, 113, 114
National Islamic Front (NIC), 165
National Republican Movement for Democracy and Development (MRND), 71, 73, 75, 76, 78, 86, 87, 88, 89, 91, 92, 94, 95, 97, 98, 100, 101, 102, 103, 105, 107, 110, 111, 113, 114
National Socialism, 28, 136, 143
National Socialist, 134, 138, 141, 143
National Socialist German Workers' Party (NSDAP), 128, 129, 138, 139, 140
Natural Struggle, 131

Index 207

Nazi, 2, 11, 17, 21, 115, 128, 129, 130, 132, 134, 135, 136, 138, 139, 140, 141, 142, 144, 145, 146, 147, 178, 179, 184, 188, 190, 191, 192
Nazi Germany, 2, 11, 21, 115, 128, 144, 147, 178, 184
Nchamihigo, Simeon, 88, 89, 92, 96, 110, 183
Ndindiliyimana, Augustin, 77, 82, 91, 92, 96, 97, 102, 103, 106, 108, 110, 173, 183
Negros, 140
New People, 3, 4, 8, 10, 11, 13, 18, 20
Ngirumpatse, Mathieu, 72, 75, 77, 78, 80, 81, 82, 85, 86, 87, 88, 89, 92, 94, 97, 98, 100, 102, 103, 107, 108, 109, 111, 113, 178, 179
Non-Arab, 157, 161, 165, 166, 168, 169
Nordic, 133, 135, 190
Northern Riziegat, 157
Nsabimana, Callixte, 79, 82
Ntabakuze, 75
Obedience, 102, 121, 130, 142, 146
Objectives, 10, 21, 44, 46, 47, 48, 49, 80, 87, 111, 120, 165
Omdas, 161
Operation Barbarossa, 136
Ordensburgen, 129
Orgasmic Learning Theory, 50
Original 28, 62
Orthodox, 31, 34, 36, 46, 49
Osas, 57
Osijek, 45, 56, 66
Paradigms, 1, 21, 152, 155

Paramilitaries, 21, 25, 26, 31, 32, 37, 38, 61, 64, 91, 163
Party Ideology, 85, 125, 149
Party Politics, 125, 134
Paux Operation, 57
PDF, 164
Pedagogy, 134, 140
Peer-partner, 53
Pelević, Borislav, 45, 48, 58, 59, 60, 61, 65
Peoples Defense Force (PDF), 159
Performance, iii, 10, 11, 20, 22, 35, 36, 39, 41, 45, 46, 65, 67, 84, 89, 107, 110, 151, 152, 153, 154, 155, 156, 166, 167, 168, 169, 170, 172, 177, 186
Performance Organization, 153, 155, 169
Performance Paradigm, iii, 151, 153, 154, 155, 156, 168, 169, 177
Performance System, iii, 151, 153, 156, 167, 168, 169
Peripheral Content, 49
Phnom Penh, 3, 85, 116, 124, 147, 181, 186
Pimpfe, 116, 128, 129, 130, 131, 132, 134, 148
Pol Pot, i, 1, 3, 6, 12, 15, 16, 18, 85, 115, 117, 124, 173, 179
Poland, 133
Political Consciousness, 2, 3, 7, 8, 15, 19, 120, 124, 126, 127, 145, 148
Political Education, 3, 4, 5, 6, 7, 8, 10, 11, 15, 19, 117
Political Indoctrination, i, ii, 111, 116, 117, 120, 121, 125, 128, 144, 145, 149

208 Procknow

Political Learning, 5, 6, 7, 19, 20, 115, 117, 120, 127
Political Training, 4, 5, 6, 7, 8, 14, 19, 20, 117
Populism, 28
Prefects, 72, 79, 95, 107, 113, 114
Presidential Guard, 75, 90, 94, 95, 110
Prison Inmates, 32, 53
Procknow, Gregory, i, ii, i, iii, i, 23, 24, 67, 117, 139, 184, 208
Proletarian, 74, 127
Propaganda, 4, 17, 18, 28, 29, 30, 44, 85, 90, 97, 99, 100, 114, 120, 123, 124, 139, 191
Puki, Colonel, 48, 61
Quinn, Kenneth, 120, 184
Quran, 165, 166
Radio Television des Milles Collines (RTLM), 90, 91
Rape, 158, 161
Raskovic, Jovan, 29
Ražnatović, Željko 10, 33
Rebels, 157, 158, 161, 164
Red Berets, 62, 64, 188
Red Star, 33
Reeves, Eric, 157, 158, 185
Rehearsal, 55
Religious Ideology, 49, 101
Republic of Macedonia, 25
Republicans, 4, 146
Republika Srpska, ii, 10, 25, 27, 31, 37, 38, 39
Revolutionary Flags, 1, 15, 19, 115, 120, 127, 144, 145, 185
Revolutionary Struggle, 125
Revolutionary Young Men and Women, 115, 120, 122, 185
Rewards, 66, 101, 120, 160, 169
Role Plays, 52
Rwandan Patriotic Front (RPF), 74, 75, 76, 77, 80, 81, 91, 98, 101, 104, 109, 110
Ruhengeri, 76, 80, 82, 84, 92, 95, 96, 102, 104, 108
Rukondo, 83
Rural Identities, 12
Rurality, 12
Russia, 136, 140, 191
Rust, Bernard, 115, 129, 135, 136, 137, 138, 140, 144, 146, 147, 186
Rutaganda, Georges, 87
Rwanda, i, ii, 71, 72, 73, 74, 75, 76, 77, 81, 83, 85, 87, 88, 89, 90, 96, 98, 99, 100, 101, 102, 106, 112, 114, 171, 174, 175, 176, 180, 181, 182, 183, 184, 191
Rwandan Armed Forces, 74, 75, 80, 85, 95, 96, 110
Rwandan Civil War, 74, 75, 89
Samphan, 123, 147
SAO Eastern Slavonia, Baranja and Western Syrmia (SAO SB WS), 26
Sarajevo, 38
Sary, Ieng, 15, 16, 124
School of Cruelty, 121, 124, 147
Schools, 12, 73, 117, 118, 119, 120, 123, 125, 129, 139, 140, 143, 145, 146, 165
Schutzstaffel (SS), 21

Sciences, 123, 125, 134, 148
Scorpions, 32
Scouting, 63
Scythes, 110
Self-criticism, 19
Self-reliance, 121, 123
Sequencing, 50
Serb Autonomous Region of Slavonia, Baranja and Western Srem (SO SBZS), 56
Serbia, 2, 21, 25, 26, 27, 28, 29, 30, 31, 32, 33, 34, 35, 36, 37, 38, 46, 52, 57, 59, 171, 181, 184, 185, 186
Serbian Academy of Arts and Sciences, 28
Serbian Autonomous Oblast of Krajina (SAO Krajina)., 26
Serbian Autonomous Oblast of Western Slavonia (SAO Western Slavonia), 26
Serbian Krajina, 25, 26, 43, 56
Serbian National Council (SNC), 26
Serbian Volunteer Guard (SDG), i, ii, 10, 11, 23, 24, 25, 31, 32, 33, 34, 35, 36, 37, 38, 39, 40, 41, 42, 43, 44, 45, 46, 48, 49, 50, 51, 52, 53, 54, 55, 56, 57, 58, 59, 60, 61, 64, 65, 66, 67, 68
Shadrack, Sendugu, 88
Shagsha Tea, 83, 84
Sheikhs, 161, 166
Shovels, 110
Sihanouk, Norodom, 15, 16, 118, 119, 120, 123, 124, 143, 187

Index 209

Simatović, Frenko, 24, 43, 45, 47, 56, 57, 58, 59, 60, 61, 62, 63, 64, 65, 66, 187, 188
Simba, Aloys, 79, 83, 84, 94, 96, 107, 108, 110, 187
Simulations, 15, 16, 22, 24, 39, 52, 54
Sites of Indoctrination, 43, 100
Sites of Learning, 22
Slovenia, 25, 45, 57
Social Learning Theory, 24, 51
Socialist Federal Republic of Yugoslavia (SFRY), 25, 27
Soviet Union, 26, 112, 136
Spartan, 132, 133, 146
Spears, 85, 86, 109
Special Anti-Terrorist Unit (SAJ), 45, 59
Specify Job Performance, 39
Srebrenica, 31, 32, 171
Standard Total View (STV), 13
Stanišić, Jovica, 24, 43, 45, 47, 56, 57, 58, 59, 60, 61, 62, 63, 64, 65, 66, 187, 188
Steidle, Brian, 162, 163, 164, 166, 167, 168, 188
Stewart, Christopher, 9, 11, 25, 33, 34, 36, 37, 40, 41, 42, 43, 49, 50, 51, 65, 66, 179, 181, 188
Street Thugs, 25, 33, 42
Sturmabeilung, 128
Subject Matter Expert (SME), 14, 125
Subject Matter Specialist, 47
Sudan, i, iii, 2, 21, 151, 157, 160, 162, 165, 166, 167, 168, 171, 174, 177, 178, 185

Sudanese Armed Forces (SAF), 158, 159, 162, 163, 164, 165
Sudanese Pounds, 161, 162, 167
Sudanese Reserve Police, 163
Summative Evaluation, 35
Superiority, 160
Swanson, Richard, 16, 17, 25, 143, 152, 153, 154, 155, 156, 167, 168, 170, 188
Swords, 85, 109
Tabula Rasa, 120, 143
Tactile Learning, 53
Tanzania, 74, 75
Target Practice, 63, 64
Task Analysis, 39
Territorial Defense (TO), 57, 58, 62
Textbooks, 116, 119, 138, 143, 147, 187
The Church of Regret, 34
The People's Armed Forces Act (1986), 158
The Serbian Memorandum, 28
The Telegraph, 162
The Ten Commandments, 98
Third Reich, i
Tito, 28, 29
Torture Dummies, 51, 59
Torture Games, 15, 124
Totten, Samuel, 11, 77, 139, 143, 159, 190
Training Camps, 163
Train-the-trainers, 62, 68, 111
Treaty of Versailles, 130, 133, 140
Tuol Sleng, 116
Turkey, 35
Tutsi, iii, 71, 74, 75, 76, 77, 78, 79, 80, 81, 82, 85, 86, 87, 88, 90, 91, 95, 97, 98, 99, 100, 101, 103, 106, 107, 109, 110, 111, 112, 113, 114, 159
Tyner, James, 18, 125, 126, 190
U.N, 31
Uganda, 74, 77, 171
Ugandan Bush War, 74
Ulemek, Milorad, 60, 61
Umaganda, 112, 113, 114
UN International Covenant on Civil and Political Rights, 166
UN Refugee Agency (UNHCR), 118
USSR, 136
Ustache, 40
Ustashahood, 63
Vasiljković, Dragan, 47, 61, 62, 63, 64, 185, 189
Verwimp, Philip, 73, 85, 97, 98, 100, 111, 113, 191
Vickery, Michael, 9, 13, 14, 119, 120, 147, 191
Vietnamese, 4
Violence, 2, 3, 15, 16, 20, 29, 32, 33, 43, 51, 52, 55, 67, 91, 98, 120, 124, 126, 141, 146, 169, 173, 175, 178
Virunga Force, 80
Vojvodina, 25, 28
Völkischer Beobachter, 128
Voluntarism, 124, 142
Voluntary Enlistment, 159
Voyvodina, 40
Wadi Saleh, 160
Wagner, 138
Wallace, Gretchen, 162, 163, 164, 166, 167, 168, 170, 188
Woodward, Rachel, 12, 169, 191

World War II, 25
Yellow Wasps, 32
Youth Film Hour, 139
Yugoslav Peoples Army
   (JNA), 25, 26, 27, 30, 31,
   32, 34, 36, 39, 40, 42, 44,
   48, 51, 56, 57, 61
Yugoslavian League of
   Communists, 26
Yungvolk, 116
Zaire, 74, 75, 76, 80, 81, 171
Ziemer, Gregor, 115, 129, 130,
   131, 132, 133, 135, 136,
   137, 139, 140, 141, 144,
   145, 191, 192
Zoljas, 57, 58, 60

Acknowledgements

This project would never have been possible without the help of a number of people and institutions. Enormous thanks to the Documentation Center of Cambodia for all of the great support and resources provided throughout this book's process. And of course, there are only few books that are published without the support of family and loved ones. To my grandparents both Bernie and Fran Goleski, now deceased. I dedicate this book to the love of my life Katherine.

...

Parts of Chapter four were previously published in different form, in the following place: Greg Procknow, Searching for the Truth, Fourth Quarter: November 1, 2010, Documentation Center of Cambodia, p.7-14. And parts of Chapter one are set for print publication in, *Human Resource Development Review, 13*(3), in the last quarter of 2014.

www.ingramcontent.com/pod-product-compliance
Lightning Source LLC
LaVergne TN
LVHW091542060526
838200LV00036B/673